# Confucius'
# Courtyard

**Xing Ruan** 阮昕 was born in Kunming, China in 1965. He studied architecture, and currently is Guangqi Chair Professor and Dean at the School of Design, Shanghai Jiao Tong University, China. He was Professor of Architecture at Sydney's University of New South Wales (2004–20). His previous books include: *Fusheng Jianzhu* [Floating Life and Architecture 浮生·建筑], 2020; *Allegorical Architecture*, 2006; *New China Architecture*, 2006; *Hand and Mind*, 2018; *Topophilia and Topophobia*, 2007. He is co-editor, with Ronald Knapp, of the book series *Spatial Habitus: Making and Meaning in Asia's Architecture*.

# Confucius' Courtyard

## Architecture, Philosophy and the Good Life in China

*Xing Ruan*

阮昕

BLOOMSBURY VISUAL ARTS
LONDON • NEW YORK • OXFORD • NEW DELHI • SYDNEY

BLOOMSBURY VISUAL ARTS
Bloomsbury Publishing Plc
50 Bedford Square, London, WC1B 3DP, UK
1385 Broadway, New York, NY 10018, USA
29 Earlsfort Terrace, Dublin 2, Ireland

BLOOMSBURY, BLOOMSBURY VISUAL ARTS and the Diana logo are trademarks of
Bloomsbury Publishing Plc

First published in Great Britain 2022

Cover design by Eleanor Rose | Cover images: 'An Eastern Han brick relief unearthed
in Chengdu, Sichuan province. Source: Drawn by Xing Ruan after Liu Dunzhen 刘敦桢,
Zhongguo gudai jianzhushi 中国古代建筑史 (Beijing: Zhongguo jianzhu gongye
chubanshe 中国建筑工业出版社, 1978), 51'; Old paper © Getty Images

A catalogue record for this book is available from the British Library.

Library of Congress Cataloging-in-Publication Data
Names: Ruan, Xing, 1965– author.
Title: Confucius' courtyard : architecture, philosophy and the good life in China / Xing Ruan.
Identifiers: LCCN 2021011461 (print) | LCCN 2021011462 (ebook) |
ISBN 9781350217621 (hardback) | ISBN 9781350217614 (paperback) |
ISBN 9781350217638 (pdf) | ISBN 9781350217645 (epub) | ISBN 9781350217652
Subjects: LCSH: Architecture and society–China. | Courtyard houses–China. |
China–Civilization–Philosophy.
Classification: LCC NA2543.S6 R83 2021 (print) | LCC NA2543.S6 (ebook) |
DDC 720.1/03—dc23
LC record available at https://lccn.loc.gov/2021011461
LC ebook record available at https://lccn.loc.gov/2021011462

| ISBN: | HB: | 978-1-3502-1762-1 |
| | PB: | 978-1-3502-1761-4 |
| | ePDF: | 978-1-3502-1763-8 |
| | eBook: | 978-1-3502-1764-5 |

Typeset by RefineCatch Limited, Bungay, Suffolk
Printed and bound in India

To find out more about our authors and books visit
www.bloomsbury.com and sign up for our newsletters.

*For Dongmin*

# Contents

*List of Illustrations* x

*Acknowledgements* xxii

*Prologue* xxv

**Part One Heaven**
A Panacea from the Courtyard 1

**1** What Makes the Chinese House 3

The conceptual *parti* 5
Confucius' courtyard 10
From object to void 21

**2** Heaven and What Is Below 27

The Chinese *tian* 27
The King's City 37
The built world and the literary world 43

**Part Two Heaven and Earth**
Equilibrium in the Courtyard 51

**3** The Divergent Tower 53

The emergence of the individual and metaphysics 56
Immortality and freedom imagined 62

**4**   Secluded World and Floating Life  75

The middling hermit  77
The artful transition  91

**5**   A Deceiving Symbol  101

The travelling merchant and the oddity of their
   courtyard  104
Women in Chinese marriage and household  113
Behind good taste and refinement  116

**6**   Literary Enchantment and the Garden House  129

Li Yü's world  131
Internalized garden and the 'horizon' beyond  138
Courtyard and decorum  153

**7**   The Golden Mean Finely Tuned  157

The anatomy of a Beijing quadrangle  159
Life and ambience in the Hutong  164
The city as a large quadrangle  175
Distinctive character versus uniformity  179

**8**   Living like 'the Chinese'  193

The 'guest' Chinese and their Chinese courtyards  194
Chinese form and exotic meaning  204

**Part Three Earth**
The Emancipation of Desire and the Loss of
Courtyard  217

**9**   The Irresistible Metropolis  219

Modern city born of refugee crisis  223
From diminishing courtyard to porous house  232

**10** The Assault of Modernity  245

Quadrangle without the Confucian world  249
The lingering courtyard  257
Nothingness, horizon and discreet pleasure  262

Epilogue: The Four or the Five  279

*Notes*  283
*Index*  307

# *Illustrations*

**I.1 a.** Bird's eye view of the Li House in Xi Baitazi Lane in Suzhou;                                                                 xxviii

**b.** Figure (blackened as buildings) and ground (left white as courtyard voids) plan of Gu House in Tieping Lane in Suzhou, showing a fraction of the city fabric knitted together by continuous courtyard matrix. Source: Drawn by Xing Ruan after and based on the survey drawings in Chen Congzhou 陈从周, *Suzhou jiu zhuzhai* 苏州旧住宅 (Shanghai: Shanghai Joint Publishing 上海三联出版社, 2003), 178 and 169.             xxix

**I.2** Floor area comparison of courtyard and free-standing building placed on a 10-square grid. Source: Drawn by Xing Ruan.                                                            xxxviii

**I.3** Floor area and height comparison of court and pavilion (tower) forms placed on a 4-square grid. Source: Drawn by Xing Ruan after Leslie Martin and Lionel March. 'Speculations' in *Urban Space and Structures*, ed. Leslie Martin and Lionel March (Cambridge: Cambridge University Press, 1972), 20.                        xxxix

**1.1** 'One bright and two darks' courtyard pattern illustrated by a single courtyard example. Source: Drawn by Xing Ruan.                                                            5

1.2   Western Zhou courtyard *parti* by the Qing scholar
      Zhang Huiyan. Source: Drawn by Xing Ruan after
      Zhang Huiyan's *Liyi Tujuan* 礼仪图卷. The Chinese
      annotations in the plan have been eliminated.                          7

1.3   Bird's eye perspective with cutaway roof showing
      internal configuration, and longitudinal section of the
      Western Zhou courtyard house found at the Fengchu
      site. Source: Drawn by Xing Ruan according to the
      speculative reconstruction by Fu Xinian. *Fu Xinian
      jianzhushi lunwenji* 傅熹年建筑史论文集 (Beijing:
      Wenwu chubanshe 文物出版社, 1998), 39.                                    8

1.4   Plans of the Western Zhou courtyard and the Ming-
      Qing Beijing quadrangle juxtaposed. Source: Drawn by
      Xing Ruan.                                                             9

1.5   Reconstruction of Banpo houses F1 and F3, showing
      the configuration of the 'front hall and back room'
      pattern of internalized rooms. Source: Drawn by Xing
      Ruan based partially on Liu Dunzhen 刘敦桢,
      *Zhongguo gudai jianzhushi* 中国古代建筑史 (Beijing:
      Zhongguo jianzhu gongye chubanshe 中国建筑工业
      出版社, 1978), 24.                                                       22

1.6   A cluster of Dong house plans in Ma'an village,
      Sanjiang region in Guangxi province, showing free-
      standing buildings with 'front hall and back room'
      pattern. Source: Surveyed and drawn by Dongmin
      Zhao and Xing Ruan.                                                    23

2.1   The coffers in the dome of the Pantheon, shrinking in
      size towards the oculus. Source: Photo by Xing Ruan.                   32

2.2 a.  The atrium in the House of Menander, Pompeii;                        34
     b.  Section through the House of Pansa (now identified as
         *insula* Arriana Polliana, property of Cnaius Alleius

Nigidius Maius, with upper floor rental apartments
wrapping around the *domus* of atrium and peristyle),
Pompeii, showing the verticality of the Roman
courtyard. Source: Drawn by Xing Ruan based on a
photograph of Spiro Kostof, *A History of Architecture:
Setting and Rituals* (New York: Oxford University
Press, 1995), 199; and after Banister Fletcher, *A
History of Architecture on the Comparative Method*
(Butterworths, 1987), 230.                                              35

2.3   A reconstruction of the Yuan dynasty courtyard
      complex of Houying Fang 后英房, showing the
      expansive voids framed by the courtyard. Source:
      Drawn by Xing Ruan after Li Yunhe李允鉌 *Huaxia yi
      jiang* 华夏意匠 (Tianjin: Tianjin daxue chubanshe,
      2005), 87.                                                        35

2.4   Diagrams of King's City from *Sanli tu* 三礼图 by Nie
      Chongyi 聂崇义 (left) and *Kaogong ji tu*考工记图 by
      Dai Zhen 戴震 (right), showing schematic
      interpretations of *Kaogong ji*. Source: Drawn by Xing
      Ruan after He Yeju 贺业炬, *Kaogong ji yingguo zhidu
      yanjiu* 考工记营国制度研究 (Beijing: Zhongguo
      jianzhu gongye chubanshe 中国建筑工业出版社,
      1985), 24.                                                       41

2.5   Diagrams of King's City as advised by *Kaogong ji* (left),
      and the Tang Chang'an (right), showing similarities
      and discrepancies. Sources: Drawn by Xing Ruan.                  42

3.1   Examples of unearthed clay house models (*mingqi*) of
      the Han dynasty, with one showing a tower atop the
      courtyard house (excavated in Wuwei county, Gansu
      province). Source: Drawn by Xing Ruan based on

sketches and photos in Pan Guxi 潘谷西, *Zhongguo gudai jianzhushi* 中国古代建筑史 (Beijing: Zhongguo jianzhu gongye chubanshe, 2001), 81, and Fu Xinian 傅熹年, *Chinese Architecture*, ed. Nancy Steinhardt, trans. Alexandra Harrer (New Haven and London: Yale University Press; Beijing: New World Press, 2002), 37.     55

3.2   An Eastern Han brick relief unearthed in Chengdu, Sichuan province. The History Museum of China. Source: Drawn by Xing Ruan.     66

3.3   Elevations of an Eastern Han *mingqi*, with a tower in the courtyard complex. Source: Drawn by Xing Ruan after Xu Qiaohua 徐桥华, Zhang Zedong 张泽栋 and Cai Xianqi 蔡先启, 'Hubei yunmeng lailidun yihaomu qinli jianbao' 湖北云梦瘌痢墩一号墓清理简报, *Archaeology* 考古, No. 7, (1984): 609.     68

3.4   A Western Han *mingqi* courtyard model (from Tomb No. 1 at Yuzhuang in Huaiyang, Henan province), showing a towering building atop the hall as well as a corner tower. Museum of Henan Province. Source: Drawn by Xing Ruan based on a photo in Guo Qinghua, *The Mingqi Pottery Buildings of Han Dynasty China, 206 BC-AD 220: Architectural Representations and Represented Architecture* (Sussex Academic Press, 2010), cover.     69

3.5   The section and plan of the Zengchong drum tower in the Congjiang region, Guizhou province, showing the tower centred around a fire pit on the ground without any upper floors. First built in 1672 CE (early Qing dynasty), this drum tower is considered one of the

oldest surviving examples in the whole Dong region.
Source: Drawn by Xing Ruan. For a full discussion of
Dong drum tower, see Chapter 3 in Xing Ruan,
*Allegorical Architecture* (Honolulu: University of
Hawai'i Press, 2006).                                                                73

4.1    Two examples of Tang dynasty Buddhist murals in
       Mogao Caves in Dunhung, showing dotted trees in the
       main courtyard before the *tang*, as well as its elevated
       position and openness to the lower court. Source:
       Drawn by Xing Ruan based on Fu Xinian 傅熹年, *Fu
       Xinian jianzushi lunwenji* 傅熹年建筑史论文集
       (Beijing: Wenwu chubanshe 文物出版社, 1998),
       466, and Liu Dunzhen 刘敦桢, *Zhongguo gudai
       jianzhushi* 中国古代建筑史 (Beijing: Zhongguo
       jianzhu gongye chubanshe 中国建筑工业出版社,
       1978), 126.                                                                     83

4.2    A courtyard house in Spring Outing (*Youchun tu* 游春
       图) by Zhan Ziqian 展子虔, showing courtyards
       artfully nested in the idyllic mountainous landscape.
       Source: Drawn by Xing Ruan based on the original
       painting.                                                                       84

4.3    The Portrait of a Superior Shi (*Gaoshi tu* 高士图) by
       the late Five Dynasties painter Wei Xian. Source:
       Drawn by Xing Ruan based on the original painting.               85

4.4    The first scene in Night Revels of Han Xizai (*Han xizai
       yeyan tu* 韩熙载夜宴图) – Han Xizai and his guests
       listen to the *pipa*. Source: Drawn by Xing Ruan based
       on the original painting.                                                      90

4.5    The centre-left section of Qingming Festival on the
       River (*Qingming shanghe tu* 清明上河图), showing the
       hints of enclosed courtyards behind the layer of shops

fronting the street. Source: Drawn by Xing Ruan based
on the original painting.                                                94

4.6     Details of one version of Lady Wenji's Return to the
        Han (*Wenji gui han tu* 文姬归汉图), showing a
        free-standing screen behind the first gate of the
        courtyard. Source: Drawn by Xing Ruan based on the
        original painting.                                              97

4.7     Palace Banquet (the original Chinese title *Qiqiao tu*
        乞巧图) by an unidentified painter during either the
        Five Dynasties (907–960 CE), or the later Northern
        Song (960–1127 CE). Source: Drawn by Xing Ruan
        based on the original painting.                                 99

5.1     A Roman atrium-like void in Hongcun, Yi county of
        Huizhou. Source: Drawn by Xing Ruan.                          105

5.2 a.  The village centre of Hongcun, Yi county of Huizhou;          106
    b.  Fieldwork sketch of building elevations surrounding
        the crescent-shaped pond in the village centre of
        Hongcun, 1988. Source: Drawn by Xing Ruan.                    107

5.3 a.  The ground plan of a single void house in Huizhou,
        with dotted line showing the size of the void in the
        roof;                                                         108
    b.  A cutaway bird's eye view of a three-void Huizhou
        house. Source: Drawn by Xing Ruan.                           109

5.4     Diagrams showing the four types of Huizhou
        courtyard. Source: Drawn by Xing Ruan.                       109

5.5 a.  Diagram of the upper floor of a Huizhou courtyard,
        showing the homogenous divisions of rooms
        surrounding a large ancestry hall (with ground floor
        hall for daily activities half of its size);                 110
    b.  Diagram of Farnsworth House – a weekend retreat for
        a medical doctor, by Mies van der Rohe, designed and

built between 1945 and 1951. Source: Drawn by
Xing Ruan.                                                                         111

**5.6**    East elevation of house Jiushi Tongtang in the village of
Zhanqi in Huizhou. Source: Drawn by Xing Ruan after
*Zhanqi* 瞻淇 (Nanjing: Dongnan daxue chubanshe 东
南大学出版社, 1996), 49.                                        120

**5.7 a.**    A Ming table top and leg joint detail;                      120

**b.**    Horseshoe-shaped back armchair. Source: Drawn by
Xing Ruan after Wang Shixiang 王世襄, *Mingshi jiaju
yanjiu* 明式家具研究 (Hong Kong: Joint Publishing
三联书店, 1989), Volume I: 122; Volume II: 50.          121

**5.8**    Partial section of Dunhe ancestral temple in the
village of Zhanqi in Huizhou, showing the use of
'crescent moon beam'. Source: Drawn by Xing Ruan
after *Zhanqi* 瞻淇 (Nanjing: Dongnan daxue
chubanshe 东南大学出版社, 1996), 121.                      122

**6.1**    Ground floor plan of house and garden, Bi residence,
Suzhou. Source: Drawn by Xing Ruan based on
Chen Congzhou 陈从周, *Suzhou jiu zhuzhai*
苏州旧住宅 (Shanghai: Shanghai Joint Publishing,
2003), 187.                                                                    142

**7.1**    Bird's eye view of a three-courtyard Beijing quadrangle
and the plan diagram. Source: Drawn by Xing Ruan
based on Liu Dunzhen 刘敦桢 *Zhongguo gudai
jianzhushi* 中国古代建筑史 (Beijing: Zhongguo
jianzhu gongye chubanshe 中国建筑工业出版社,
1978), 319.                                                                    160

**7.2**    A *zhaobi* screen in the Beijing quadrangle. Source:
Drawn by Xing Ruan.                                                   161

**7.3**    The open gallery veranda in the Beijing quadrangle.
Source: Drawn by Xing Ruan.                                      163

**7.4**    The figure and ground plan of a fragment of urban
fabric in Beijing knitted by courtyards of various sizes.
Source: Drawn by Xing Ruan based on Werner Blaser,
*Courtyard Houses in China: Tradition and Present*
(Birkhäuser Basel, 1979), 12.    165

**7.5**    Diagram of the Ming and Qing Beijing, showing three
courtyards – forbidden city (imperial palace), imperial
city and inner city, and one within the other. Source:
Drawn by Xing Ruan.    177

**7.6 a.**    Diagram of the plan of Prince Fu's residence, showing
three parallel courtyards and the existing structures in
shade;    182

**b.**    The same courtyard complex as it appeared in
*Jingcheng quantu* 京城全图 (The Complete Map of the
Capital) of the Qianlong period (1750), showing
remarkable details of building layouts in diagrammatic
elevations. Source: Drawn by Xing Ruan based on
Jia Jun 贾珺, *Beijing Siheyuan* 北京四合院 (Beijing:
Tsinghua University Press 清华大学出版社, 2009),
131–2.    183

**8.1**    The cutaway bird's eye view of Chengqi Lou 承启楼 in
Yongding county, Fujian province. Source: Drawn by
Xing Ruan based on Liu Dunzhen 刘敦桢 *Zhongguo
gudai jianzhushi* 中国古代建筑史 (Beijing: Zhongguo
jianzhu gongye chubanshe 中国建筑工业出版社,
1978), 329.    195

**8.2**    Diagrams of four plan types of the Hakka house,
showing diverse forms based on one consistent
courtyard pattern. Source: Drawn by Xing Ruan.    200

**8.3**    Ground floor of Zhencheng Lou in Yongding county.
Legend: 1. Courtyard/Voids; 2. Void with a well; 3. Hall;

4. Ancestral hall; 5. Reception hall; 6. Bath; 7. Kitchen;
8. Barn, mill and storage; 9. Main entry; 10. Side door.
Source: Drawn by Xing Ruan based on Liu Dunzhen
刘敦桢 *Zhongguo zhuzhai gaishuo* 中国住宅概说
(Beijing: Zhongguo jianzhu gongye chubanshe 中国建
筑工业出版社, 1957), 125.                                       200

8.4      Plan diagram of a half-circle house, showing an
         unfortified complex with multiple entry points and
         with ancestral hall in the centre before a crescent pond.
         Source: Drawn by Xing Ruan.                               204

8.5 a.   The cross section and the upper level plan of a 'three
         rooms and one screen' Bai courtyard;                      208

    b.   The upper level plan of a 'quadrangle of five courts'
         Bai courtyard. Legend: 1. Courtyard/void; 2. *Zhaobi*
         (screen). Source: Drawn by Xing Ruan based on
         Yunnan Sheng Sheji Yuan 云南省设计院, *Yunnan
         minju* 云南民居 (Beijing: Zhongguo jianzhu gongye
         chubanshe, 1986), 32.                                     209

8.6      A section perspective of the town of Lijiang, showing
         the street canal channelled into a courtyard house for
         water supply. Source: Drawn by Xing Ruan based on
         Yunnan Sheng Sheji Yuan 云南省设计院, *Yunnan
         minju* 云南民居(Beijing: Zhongguo jianzhu gongye
         chubanshe, 1986), 87.                                     211

8.7      A cutaway bird's eye view of No. 87 in Xinhua Street,
         Lijiang, showing multiple courtyards arranged to suit
         the contour of a sloping site. Source: Drawn by Xing
         Ruan based on Zhu Liangwen 朱良文, *Lijiang naxizu
         minju* 丽江纳西族民居 (Yunnan kexue chubanshe
         云南科学出版社, 1988), 68.                                  214

**9.1 a.**   Schematic Chinese map of Shanghai in the early Yuan
dynasty (late thirteenth century);    220

**b.**   Schematic Chinese map of Shanghai in the Ming
dynasty (early seventeenth century) when the city was
walled. Source: Drawn by Xing Ruan after the original
maps included in Alan Balfour and Zheng Shiling, *World
City: Shanghai* (Academy Press, 2002), 30 and 34.    221

**9.2**   The schematic map of foreign settlements in Shanghai
in 1853. Legend: 1. Hongkou; 2. American Settlement;
3. Suzhou Creek; 4. Huangpu River; 5. Race Course;
6. British Settlement; 7. French Settlement; 8. The
Walled Shanghai Town. Source: Drawn by Xing Ruan
based on G. Lanning and S. Couling, *The History of
Shanghai* (Shanghai: For the Shanghai Municipal
Council by Kelly & Walsh, 1921).    225

**9.3 a.**   The cross section of an old style *shiku men* house;    232

**b.**   The figure and ground plan diagram of Mianyangli –
an old style *shiku men* housing complex. Source: Drawn
by Xing Ruan based on Lü Junhua, Peter Rowe and
Zhang Jie, *Modern Urban Housing in China* (Prestel
Pub., 2001), 43 and 44.    233

**9.4**   A comparison of (**a**) the ground and the first floors of a
courtyard house in the Yangtze region and (**b**) that of a
five-bay old style *shiku men* house in Xingren Li *lilong*
complex. Note also that, contrary to any traditional
Chinese courtyard, the *shiku men* house is open via
windows to both the front street and the back lane.
Legend: 1. 'Skywell' Court; 2. Reception Hall; 3.
Secondary Chamber; 4. Subsidiary Room; 5. Subsidiary
Chamber; 6. Kitchen; 7. Miscellaneous Chamber; 8.

Rear 'Skywell' Court. Source: Drawn by Xing Ruan
based on Lü Junhua, Peter Rowe and Zhang Jie, *Modern
Urban Housing in China* (Prestel Pub., 2001), 42.          235

**9.5 a.**  Plans and cross section of two three-level new style
*shiku men* houses, each of which are one and two bays
respectively; Legend: 1. 'Skywell' void; 2. Reception
Hall; 3. Subsidiary Room; 4. Kitchen; 5. Bedroom;
6. Bathroom (with modern sanitary ware).                  237

**b.**  The figure and ground plan diagram of Meilanfang – a
new style *shiku men* housing complex. Source: Drawn
by Xing Ruan based on Lü Junhua, Peter Rowe and
Zhang Jie, *Modern Urban Housing in China* (Prestel
Pub., 2001), 66.                                          238

**10.1**  Liang Sicheng's proposal to turn Beijing's city wall into
a city-ring-park in the sky. Source: Redrawn by Xing
Ruan after Liang Sicheng's original drawing.              247

**10.2**  The figure and ground diagrams of a Beijing
quadrangle, from left to right respectively, in the 1950s,
1970s and 1980s, showing the gradual transformation
of a single-family courtyard house to a 'big
miscellaneous courtyard' with multiple occupants.
Source: Drawn by Xing Ruan based on Wu Liangyong,
*Rehabilitating the Old City of Beijing* (University of
Washington Press, 1999), 59.                              250

**10.3**  The ground floor plan of Ju'er Hutong Phase 1, with the
passageways shaded. Source: Drawn by Xing Ruan
based on Wu Liangyong's original plan.                    253

**10.4**  Plan of Xi'an University of Communication, showing a
walled *danwei* compound. Source: Drawn by Xing
Ruan after Ye Zugui and Ye Zhoudu's original plan.        260

**10.5**   Utzon's sketch of the Sydney Opera House concept, showing the prominent Chinese roof above a raised platform that is likened to a cloud floating over the ocean horizon. Source: Redrawn by Xing Ruan after Utzon's original sketch. This widely referenced sketch first appeared in Jørn Utzon, 'Platforms and Plateaus,' *Zodiac*, No. 10 (1962): 113–40.    267

**10.6**   Utzon's sketch modified by the author to conform to the reality of courtyard enclosure. Source: Drawn by Xing Ruan.    267

**10.7 a.** Plan of Utzon's holiday villa Can Lis. Legend: 1. Courtyard (as rooms open to the sky); 2. Dining room; 3. Kitchen; 4. Study; 5. Entry; 6. Verandah; 7. Living room; 8. Bedroom. Source: Drawn by Xing Ruan based on Utzon's original plan;    270

    **b.** The featured courtyard in Can Lis with openings in the encircling wall enclosure. Source: Drawn by Xing Ruan.    271

**10.8**   Plan and longitudinal section of House for Dr Bartholomeusz, with Bawa's secret escape passageway shaded in the plan. Source: Drawn by Xing Ruan after Bawa's original plan.    274

# Acknowledgements

This book is the result of an overgrown chapter in another long overdue book of mine, tentatively titled *The House and the Floating Life*. For more than a decade, enthusiastic students enrolled in my course, named 'A History of Housing – pattern and meaning' at Sydney's University of New South Wales (UNSW), have supplied me with the persuasion to complete both books, which at times seemed (and still seem, I must admit) impossible. With this book before the reader, my fixation on this topic is partially relieved.

As with my other writings, it is not possible here to provide a complete list of authors and scholars to whom I am indebted. A few memorable moments in the long process of the book's making, nevertheless, shall be recounted. Some five years ago, Joseph Rykwert, who was well into his magnificent nonagenarian years, took Dongmin and me to dine at the Savile. After having glanced at the draft form of the contents (which I forthrightly presented to him), Joseph said: 'I would like to read the book!' Knowing his usual elegant economy of words, I instantly switched to the enjoyment of the meal and the more delicious Rykwertian dining anecdotes that followed. The conversation with Joseph on this topic nonetheless has continued in the Epilogue of this book.

I have always relied on Ronald Knapp as my solid sounding board; this time, apart from his meticulous scrutiny throughout the early drafts, Ron immensely enlightened me by pointing out the difference in *pinyin* between Shaanxi and Shanxi provinces. I am absolutely appalled at myself for not having kept in contact with Yi-Fu Tuan for years. When I last consulted Yi-Fu on writing about the good life and the house, I also complained of my lack of time. Yi-Fu suggested that I should simply publish a record of the making of my own house. This remains an appealing idea, and I have continued to consult his work in this book, including an email discussion we had concerning the Beijing quadrangle. Jean-Louis Cohen and Austin Williams happily read my synopsis and manuscript, and offered great wisdom on both the subject matter and the mysteries of the publishing world.

I forced upon John Blair the role of being my first reader: his robust common sense coming from building science and his keen editorial eye have saved me from numerous stumbles with narration and language. I could never have imagined that this book about *attaining the good life by staying put in the house* would come out during a global pandemic. James Thompson is the only publisher whom I have met on screen more than once. Several hotel quarantine stays in Sydney and Shanghai, incidentally, enabled me to put finishing touches to the book, so James is convinced that he has not met anyone who has spent more time in hotel quarantine than I. The book has benefited from his enthusiasm and care. Wang Hao, with his serenity, was readily available to offer all the necessary technical support during the preparation of the manuscript.

The writing of this book was based at two academic homes: UNSW and Shanghai Jiao Tong University. I am grateful for an academic sabbatical from UNSW, a book grant from the Humanities Book Series Award Scheme of Shanghai Jiao Tong University, and a research grant (No. 52078290) from National Natural Science Foundation of China. For someone who in his academic life has, by chance on most occasions, repeatedly 'served people' as department head and as dean, this sort of support from one's institution is, if I am to use a Chinese expression here, 'a sweet rain after a long draught'.

Dongmin, together with Shumi and Shuyi, has provided me with the purpose of life. Although she declined in the past to have a book of mine dedicated to her, for a book is a book belonging only to the author and his readers, I know I can count on Dongmin as my reader!

# *Prologue*

## I

The Chinese, with a sustained interest across three millennia, desired an equilibrium: enjoying an earthly life for what it's worth while maintaining a certain awe below Heaven's arch; participating actively in society and taking responsibility for one's family while snatching a moment away to indulge in life's pleasures, or retreating to one's inner world; and staying put in the house while letting the mind and soul roam freely beyond it.[1] They managed, somewhat nonchalantly, to do so in and about the confines of their encircled courtyard dwelling. The impoverished in rural areas and many in the city even in pre-modern times may never have lived in an actual courtyard, it is, as this book will show, an inspirational idea, especially for the gentry class.

Pitching in *the middle* was a way of living, as well as a state of mind, as preached by Confucius. (His grandson Zi Si 子思 even wrote a book, simply titled *The Middle Way – Zhongyong* 中庸 – to elaborate on this idea.) The Chinese gentry, along with the populace at large, held dear this doctrine, as an art of avoiding extremes and respecting the enduring in life. Since saints and the innate moral defects in humans are rare, the middle, in the Chinese mind, is virtuous, for it represents not a compromise, but a propriety that is humanly achievable, hence *reason*. Such is demanded by Heaven and Nature.

Heaven is also the sky, called *tian* 天 in Chinese, which according to Confucius is the same as Nature. The following two questions also are the ever-pertinent modern background against which this book is conceived: How did the most populous nation on earth manage to live a virtuous as well as pleasurable life without the blessing from awesome God? What was the moral bedrock of this largely secular civilization?

A way of living in this book therefore is less concerned with what the Chinese ate for breakfast in 500 BCE, and how they answered nature's call in the eleventh century. The primary aim, rather, is to explore the ways in which their house and city (both were courtyards, either physical or literary) represented their view of the world, and of themselves. Differently put, this book is about how the courtyard helped facilitate the often languid cultural and spiritual life of the Chinese. To the chagrin of the modern mind, despite their technological and scientific ingenuity developed over a long history,[2] the Chinese in building their courtyards paid little attention to housing the general miscellany of life, with consequent convenience and comfort.

The high-minded elsewhere, such as sixteenth-century Venetian and Veneto nobles, who escaped in summer from city politics and business to their country villas built by the Renaissance master Andrea Palladio, managed to hide food preparation and other necessary services for daily subsistence under the podium. But above the podium were the monumentally vaulted halls, the backdrop for literary and philosophical conversations. Goethe, though much impressed with the splendour of the Villa Rotonda, nonetheless thought that it was not quite homely as a family house.[3] In the next 500 years following the Renaissance, while the European bourgeoisie retreated further into the room and their inner world, they in the meantime pursued corporeal comfort to an extreme level of advancement, resulting in not only the supply of running water and concealed plumbing, but also the reclining chaise lounge with soft upholstery, lustrous velvet window drapes and over-heated rooms. Chinese furniture, on the contrary, already boasted supreme design and craftsmanship in the Ming dynasty (1368–1644 CE), but was made of hardwood with austere elegance for an upright sitting posture. The Chinese courtyard, though refined as a seamless 'complicity' of Chinese life, remained sparsely furnished, poorly heated and, too often, existed in the absence of sanitary plumbing and the supply of running water until the middle of the twentieth century.[4] The lack of corporeal comfort, nevertheless, did not in any way tarnish their art of living, finely tuned to the middle and in the courtyard.

Like the complex solar system concealed by its crystal-clear geometry, a courtyard appears as a rather simple composition: the perimeter – usually a square or rectangle shape – is occupied by the building, whereas the centre is a void, left open to the sky. A courtyard, essentially, is defined by its *vertical* orientation. A courtyard lets daylight and air into the building, but it was not the sole reason (which we moderns like to believe) for its existence, since light and air are easily gained by spacing apart free-standing building objects in the field, which we do in our suburbs and cities in modern times. Why did humans build courtyards in the first instance? It remains an enigma.

The period between 1099 BCE and 221 CE, generally regarded as the golden age of Chinese civilization,[5] was when its enduring intellectual foundations were laid. The first timeline was marked by the rule of King Wen 文王 – the Cultured King (posthumously honoured by his son King Wu as the founder of the Zhou dynasty), and the latter was when imperial China was formed under the Qin dynasty. During this period, both the Chinese and the wise mortals in the Greco-Roman world, incidentally, had already developed, even by today's standards and expectations, rather sophisticated courtyard houses. Though exceedingly simple as a building configuration, none of these people commenced their civilized way of dwelling in a courtyard. For the Chinese alone, it took them approximately three thousand years to transform the free-standing house, much the same as our suburban houses today, to a courtyard.

The remains of courtyard houses can still be found today in many parts of the world. But an entire city fabric woven by a vast tapestry of low-rise courtyards, like that of Roman Pompeii, had largely disappeared in Europe after the fall of the classical world. The longevity of courtyard buildings and cities in China, however, is nothing short of astonishing: the Chinese kept it, or rather, like a child never tiring of nursery games, inexorably played with it, for at least three millennia.

Chinese cities, such as Beijing in the north, Suzhou on the south bank of the Yangtze River, Kunming in the once remote south-west, or even Lijiang – the town of minority Naxi on China's south-west frontier, were all built by continuous matrixes of courtyard houses as late as in the 1950s (Figure I.1). There must be something about the

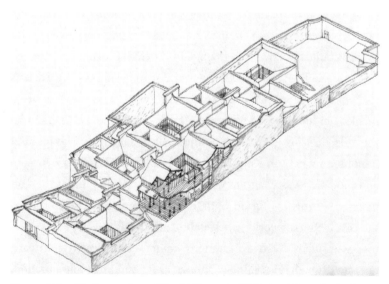

**Figure I.1a** *Bird's eye view of the Li House in Xi Baitazi Lane in Suzhou.*

extraordinary simplicity of this human dwelling, its puzzling longevity in China, and indeed the strangely persistent Chinese interest in it, that is worth knowing. That the Mediterranean and the Chinese, and the others too, came up with the same courtyard living makes its fall from grace in Europe curious. It is against this background I set out to answer: why its appeal lasted for so long in China, in what way it

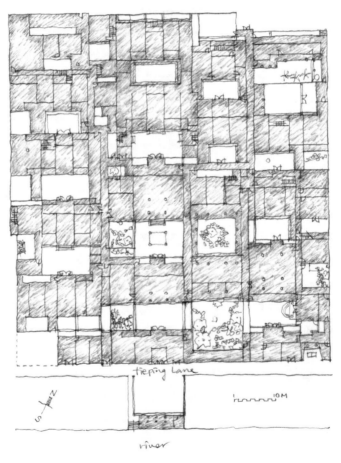

**Figure I.1b** *Figure (blackened as buildings) and ground (left white as courtyard voids) plan of Gu House in Tieping Lane in Suzhou, showing a fraction of the city fabric knitted together by continuous courtyard matrix.*

helped structure the Chinese world, and what it did to the Chinese life. This is the drive of the book.

To generalize at the outset, it would not be farfetched to proclaim that the Chinese courtyard, against the rich and diverse geography of the vast land, served as the very physical template of the Chinese world – the livelihood of its populace and their material subsistence, and, of more importance, the accomplishments of its artistic, intellectual and institutional life. Over the unbroken history (as conventionally regarded) of more than three millennia, the Chinese had endlessly reworked, rather than continuously reinvented, their way of living. To borrow a buzzword from the current wave of environmentalism, this was a remarkable case of sustainability. The Chinese house, too, remained largely unchanged in its meaning and anatomy until the turn of the twentieth century. What had been honed in the house, from the Golden Age through to the end of the Chinese empire, were the artifice of housing architecture and its associated art of living. The courtyard, as it transpired, was the universal architectural configuration that was used to accommodate nearly everything, like a magic wand. The Chinese saw no need to develop a particular building type to correspond to a special use, which the English took to an unparalleled level of specificity in the nineteenth century when work and living were separated, and assorted institutions emerged. A member of the Chinese gentry would be rather bemused, and perhaps even amused, to learn the existence of a room dedicated solely to gift wrapping in the house of a Hollywood movie star.[6]

For the Chinese, their entire built world from the city, the imperial palace, the temple, the market to the house was all configured in the courtyard. One could hardly distinguish, based on merely the look and the rather repetitive courtyard configuration of a building, a Buddhist temple from that of a Daoist, or even a mosque. On a market day, the expansive courtyard of a Buddhist or Daoist temple would be turned into *miaohui* 庙会 – temple market. A *shuyuan* 书院 – book courtyard (library or school), and a *fuxue* 府学 – government school, were effortlessly interchangeable. Any decent sized courtyard could be turned into a theatre – all that was needed was an open pavilion (sometimes a temporary marquee) protruding into the court. I should mention also, though this is not the focus of the book, the construction method of all Chinese buildings of different uses, and for both rich and poor, was essentially the same throughout. The technique employed was that of a lightweight timber structural framework for supporting the magnificent roof, along with non-load-bearing external walls on the perimeter and internal walls of divisions, built of rammed earth, masonry or timber. Whether it was built with refinement, ostentation or shoddily, the aim was to make the building more adaptive to human needs now and in this life, like a tent of the nomads. Permanency and solidity, as found in buildings of monumentality in European history, may help immortalize this transient life for a long time to come, but such an agenda is not usually registered in the Chinese mind.

# II

A historical examination of this peculiar Chinese persistency in their courtyard living has not been undertaken. But to add one more book, driven by a personal curiosity, about the longevity of 'things' Chinese (including ideas) does require some justification. Things Chinese, great or not, have withstood the test of their 'capacity to attract and retain the attention of others'.[7] Historian Jonathan Spence has charted a history of more than seven centuries of China in Western minds, from Marco Polo, Jesuit missionaries, Leibniz, to French and American searches for exotica, and even to literary and political luminaries such as Frank Kafka, Ezra Pound and Henry Kissinger.[8]

The Chinese writer Lin Yutang in the 1930s lamented with much cynicism a universal motive that drove the outsiders' interest – from the early Portuguese sailors, to Columbus and the more recent 'Old China Hand' – as simply 'gold and adventure'.[9]

Spence has avoided the temptation to generalize because 'individual experience rarely matches the allegedly universal trend'.[10] Since he does not see himself 'in the business of assigning blame or praise', what he has presented before the reader is a smorgasbord of negative (often) and sweet (at other times, but from those remaining 'in a state of blissful self-denial, regardless of other levels of reality that swirled around them') stimulus. Both of which, curiously, make others drawn to the Chinese world. Spence at the outset forewarns the reader that much of the assessment from 'these sightings' spanning seven centuries either reified or denigrated China,[11] which in itself is a common-sense statement that warrants no further discourse. At the end of his long and exhaustive list of curiosities, Spence provides this marvellous (and it seems to me, sincere) summary of the remarkably sustained Chinese appeal to the Western world:

> The curious readiness of Westerns for things Chinese was there from the beginning, and it has remained primed, over the centuries, by an unending stream of offerings. Precisely why this should be so remains, to me, a mystery. But the story we have traced seems to prove that China needs no reason to fasten itself into Western minds.[12]

But I for one, and for the reader too (dragon or non-dragon breed included, to paraphrase sinologist Simon Leys), do need a reason to warrant more search for an *understanding* of things Chinese and the endurance of their appeals. Leys himself was unambiguous about 'the deepest seductions of Chinese culture', and saw it as a 'conjuring power'.[13] He had his personal experience to illustrate the point: when Leys was a student of Chinese Classics in Singapore, he often visited a ramshackle open-air movie theatre showing old films of Peking opera. The theatre was named *Wen Guang* 文光 (Light of Civilization, or Written World, which are interchangeable according to Leys), whose name was written in magnificent calligraphy hung above the entrance. All the material existence of this shanty movie house dissolved into irrelevance when, under the starry sky and on the screen, the famous Peking opera singer, Ma Lianliang, gave a performance (I imagine) in his haunting voice, majestic and sublime. Leys recalled more of similar experiences when he slept in a bunk bed in a shared shelter with three young Chinese scholars in Hong Kong's slum town. The room, though shoddy and messy, was in the grand Chinese scholarly tradition named *Wuyong Tang* 无用堂 (The Hall of Uselessness, referencing the ancient Chinese classic *Yi Jing* 易经 – *The Book of Changes*, and also the words of Zhuangzi 庄子). Leys spent two 'intense and joyful' years in this shelter.[14]

But it is this lack of interest from the Chinese in physical forms and their appearances, and the careless Chinese attitude to distinguish material and non-material cultures, that have both fascinated and, more so, frustrated curious minds. Such frustration has contributed to so magnificently tenacious a misunderstanding of things Chinese – architecture included. The Chinese courtyard – the same as Chinese architecture – is, I suggest in this book, an important sleight of hand with a seductive conjuring power, for it is both physical and elusive at the same time. It is physical because the tangible configuration of a courtyard is necessary to be effective; it is elusive because the efficacy of a courtyard is not dependant on the countless shapes and dimensions that it can take. It is however the void in the middle that speaks to the core idea of the form, as well as a way of living that carries. The Chinese courtyard, therefore, is the basis of my overtly promised profit of this book at the outset – that is, a penetrating access to things Chinese that an *architectural* understanding may provide.

# III

Despite the above justification of Chinese curiosities, the courtyard included, I did not set out to write a book merely about China. The real spur for writing this book is the hope for, in the not-too-distant future, a response to, and better still a readjustment of, the inescapable distraction of the modern world and the consequential loss of one's inner life. Much of this, metaphorically speaking, has something to do with the loss of courtyard – that is, its celestial *verticality* and its insulation from the worldly horizon. Coastal dwellers desire to have a house with a harbour or ocean view. Elsewhere a distant mountain view will do. But a view from the house to the vast space is the allure of the capacious world out there that makes us relentlessly unsettled.

The French proverb *la forteresse assiégée* – fortress besieged – is often used to describe the dilemma of being strangled inside while the freedom of space outside is irresistible. Incidentally, the Chinese writer Qian Zhongshu used it as a metaphor for an unhappy marriage.[15] The modern world framed by a modern building made up by floor plates stacked on top of each other and sealed tenuously by floor-to-ceiling glass, or readily supplied with the screen of a television or smartphone, is by nature *horizontal*. Brilliant though it may seem, the external world lying tantalizingly beyond a thin layer of glass is an inescapable distraction. The Chinese aside, ancient Romans too would have been terribly puzzled as to why the moderns would want a view of the depressing distance. The well-to-do lived in introvert *domus* courtyards, while the poor lived in multi-storey apartments named *insula*. The poorest of all lived on the upper levels of the *insula*, with a view. The invention of the safety lift by Otis in 1852 has, up to now, reversed the vertical social pecking order in a multi-storey apartment building. For both the Romans in the *domus* and the Chinese, a slice of sky from Heaven's arch sufficed.

Abundant in pre-modern Chinese literature is the recurrent theme of melancholy caused by gazing into the space afar in a lofty building or on a mountaintop. A feeling of yearning in the European Romanticism, or 'pathos of distance' as coined by Nietzsche, evokes similar sadness and frustration to those in modern times.[16] This is a longing for wholeness and vast space that can never be reached (the possession of material goods too often has become the substitute). Such yearning has been growing in modern times. But in Christendom, the architectural manifestation of the Gothic structure seemed to fill the spiritual and moral void in medieval Europe, after the fall of the classical world and the disappearance of the courtyard. In this book I therefore knowingly wrestle with the Chinese courtyard as the representative of a largely lost celestial architectural *verticality* against the background of the horizontal modern world.

What then is the relevance of an *architectural* (in this instance a 'courtyard') understanding of the Chinese way of living, and the Chinese world? Highly pertinent! Let me speak to them one by one – that is, architecture and the universal modern world. First, let us pause for the moment to ask what we actually mean by architecture, and its seemingly intrinsic aesthetics. Consider our daily use of the word 'architecture', for the true meaning of it may be buried in our psychological substructure. Too often we hear the use of this word in politics: 'the architect of a visionary reform', or 'Does the prime minister have the necessary architecture to undertake this visionary reform?' So the way in which this word is used, in the English language at least, suggests that *architecture* is instrumental – it has some sort of power.

It is not quite the same connotation when we use the word 'architecture' to describe a building in our age. We mean, rather consciously this time, the aesthetics of a building. A starchitect (coined by modern writers to mean 'star architect') is someone who is able to invent a novel form for a building that is different from anything that we have seen before. The architect is therefore constantly under pressure to be avant-garde. Our modern fixation on the superficial (pertaining to the surface in the true sense of the word) – which we call aesthetics, is of course not confined only to the appearances of our buildings and cities (and how much of the brilliant world out there we can see from the inside of a building that we call 'view'). The superficiality extends to nearly all facets of modern life. It ranges from the tourist's interest in the picture-perfect postcard veneer of a place (not quite the 'inside experience' of its locals), to our relentless pursuit for youthful bodies and looks by hopelessly resorting to Botox and plastic surgery (rather than the cultivation of one's inner life), and even to our peculiar obsession with the presentation of food on endless television cooking shows that verges on voyeurism (and with only token interest in the taste and aroma of the food itself due to the limitation of the screen).[17] Consciously or unconsciously though, we assume aesthetics is always about something that is appealing to the eye. But we ought to be reminded of the root of aesthetics: 'aesthesia' is not just about beauty but connected with sensing – feeling and coming to life. The opposite of being alive is 'anaesthesia' – the dulling of the senses.[18] Aesthetics, therefore, is more than merely vision; it is also instrumental.

The modern assumption of the meaning of aesthetics, incidentally, rarely existed in the pre-modern Chinese world. The practice of art, including music, painting, poetry, calligraphy (or rather, 'the law of writing' is the true meaning of the original Chinese term) and, architecture, was simply an amateur pursuit of a scholar (often the salaried scholar-official) to cultivate one's inner life rather than advance one's career as we know it in our time. The desire to please with the beauty of form would, to a genuine scholar-artist, be a vulgar temptation to seduce, which was to be avoided.[19] Confucius detested eloquent glib talks, disliked superfluous embroideries, and even eschewed ostentation in rituals and ceremonies. The supreme measure of art, therefore, is that 'the great image has no form (大象无形)'. Artwork may be exchanged among those who were able to discern their inner qualities, but it should not be sold to an investor. Ultimately it is the artistic doctrine – 'the meaning surpasses the image' (意余于象) – where 'the sound exists outside of space (空外音)' in music, 'the meaning beyond the words (言外意)' in poetry, and 'a surplus of the momentum of the meaning (意势有余)' in the mind's eye beyond the image in painting, which Qian Zhongshu discovered in both Chinese and Western literary worlds. One startling example was the construal of a Chinese kindred spirit, Goethe: 'A word is like a fan in the hands of a beautiful woman that hides her face while revealing her eyes.'[20] Among all these maxims, the meaning beyond the form dwells in the space of imagination, readily provided by the void in the courtyard.

This book, with numerous errant sorties beyond its core subject matter, is about the indispensable efficacy of *architecture* in sustaining humanity, accompanied by a robust common sense in life. The Chinese courtyard happens to be the right material for such a book. In the background, the sense of purpose of architecture in the Western world has since the dawn of modern times been gradually thinned to surface, and in the meantime vision (and hearing too) have become more privileged than other senses, and more fatally, than mind.

# IV

But before I continue more of what might be easily dismissed as nostalgia of a past of little relevance by some readers of our time, I shall make an attempt to justify my call for returning to a *courtyard* understanding of the Chinese way of living. A surprising modern benefit based on a simple computation of land economy, strangely, has not caught much attention in our efficiency and data-minded modern mortals.

We build on a block of land, which, for the sake of simple comparison, is assumed as a square divided by 100 smaller squares – that is, 10 × 10. If we happen to decide to build a courtyard, we occupy the entire perimeter of two squares to achieve a 64 per cent building area with 36 per cent as open area left in the middle. The open area, judged by a prioritized reasoning in modern times, is needed for light and ventilation, which in this instance is a generous six-grid square. In addition, the thin building plate allows sufficient daylight penetration and cross-ventilation. But if we build in the middle, as we do in the suburbs of our age, the occupied floor area of the building and the open void are reversed. To achieve the same building area while occupying the middle, the open space is then left with only one grid (or the length of two grids in-between two buildings where a cluster of many is built). The core of the fat building plan is too deep for daylight and fresh air to reach, and may be further blocked by internal divisions as a consequence of the building depth; dark rooms that rely on artificial lighting and ventilation then become inevitable (Figure I.2).

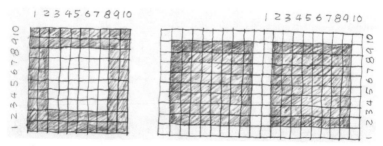

**Figure I.2** *Floor area comparison of courtyard and free-standing building placed on a 10-square grid.*

Some modern prophets of rational thinking, too, have discovered this miraculous land economy of the courtyard, though they presented it with a more elaborate building model in an urban context. Without any acknowledgement of this ancient form of building, a four-square urban gridiron is computed in two opposite ways: one, the grids themselves are filled up by four ziggurat towers; two, the perimeters of the same grids are occupied by the building of a similar flat-topped pyramid form, much the same as a cluster of courtyards (Figure I.3). The result of this study is surprisingly eye-opening for the moderns: '... the court form is seen to place the same amount of floor space on the same site area with the same condition of building depth and in approximately one-third the height required by the pavilion (tower) form.'[21] Following such rational computation, here then comes the sensational speculation: take a vast tract of Manhattan bound by Park Avenue (Fourth Avenue) and Eighth Avenue, and between 42nd and 57th Street, build it up with 36-storey buildings modelled on the iconic Seagram Building designed by the modern master Mies van

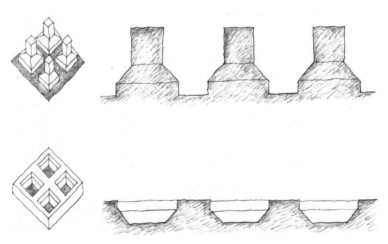

**Figure I.3** *Floor area and height comparison of court and pavilion (tower) forms placed on a 4-square grid.*

der Rohe in the same area, then rebuild the entire territory to achieve the same built volume but in courtyards – that is, buildings occupying only the perimeters of the grids with internal courts left as open space. The result: only eight-storey high buildings are required on the perimeters. Even better, the total area of open space is the equivalent to twenty-eight Washington Squares![22] But why did the rational moderns not build New York in courtyards? Even the clear-headed and authoritative Sir Leslie Martin of the above speculative computation had to concede, albeit ambiguously, to the power of fictional meaning and the symbolism of buildings: '... when high buildings and their skyline are being described, the talk is precisely about this and not about the best way of putting built space on to ground space.'[23] Any discussion of the rationale of 'court' versus 'tower' in our modern world is, still, likely to become fallacious.

The ancients had long worked out a most efficient land economy. But the ancients, alas, were not capitalists. Perhaps the rapture of reaching the ideal mathematics of dwelling in a courtyard could only be described as celestial in the Chinese mind, and divine in that of the West. Such divinity, unsurprisingly, was largely lost at a certain point in Western history when humanism, aided by modern science and capitalism in later times, expanded gradually and overthrew any human awe and humility left under Heaven's arch. But for more than three thousand years the Chinese kept their humanism in check under the watchful 'eye' of Heaven above their courtyards (and, it should be noted, in the absence of Judaism, Christianity, Islam and Hinduism). If Heaven was to the Chinese what God was to the Indo-Europeans, the use of anthropomorphic analogy here does not suggest that the Chinese showed the same enthusiasm as found in many other religions in humanizing God.[24] Quite the contrary, Heaven (*tian*) remained both awesome and wholesome, formless and abstract, hence the Christian theological solution of collective governance as Trinity in the heavenly kingdom would be ridiculously redundant to the Chinese. Rightly so, Confucius never gave Heaven a definition. This book, departing from celestial mathematics, embarks on a search for the meanings and shapes of Chinese life that, too, have been kept in check in the courtyard, largely secular but not materialistic.

# V

A peculiar character of Chinese civilization, quite the opposite of the Indo-European world, is that the Chinese have not radically changed their worldview, hence the ideal of the good life, ever since their intellectual foundations were entrenched in the Golden Age. At about the same time though, both the Greeks (the Romans too followed suit at a later time) and the Chinese turned skyward. In more than five centuries from the fourth century BCE to the second century CE, significant works of astronomy appeared in both high and popular literature in the Mediterranean world.[25] Like distant relatives, though vaguely knowing of each other's existence, the Mediterranean people and the Chinese nonetheless did not quite manage to contact each other directly, even though Chinese silk made its way to imperial Rome and it was worth its weight in gold. Still, our ancestors in both places found in the heavenly dome regularity, geometrical beauty and predictability that were absent from the earth. When laying out their cities, the Romans thought of it a 'heavenly' business, with clear references drawn 'in line with the course of the sun, while the cardines follow the axis of the sky', wrote Hyginus Gromaticus.[26] The Chinese simply built cosmic cities on the earth.

Quite expectedly, there emerged in both the Greco-Roman world and China courtyard houses, both with a slice of sky framed in the middle by buildings lining the perimeter. The difference, however, is that the Greeks, and the Romans too, sought in their *domus* courtyard towards zenith – the upward cosmos, in the imagined *axis mundi*, whereas the Chinese, relying on their courtyard, brought down the celestial sky – Heaven, to counterbalance their earthly life. But the signs of a parted future already existed: the pleasures and vices of civic life directly outside the Roman atrium – the courtyard fronting the street – posed horizontal distraction to the vertical celestial. Much of the similar however was artfully accommodated and contained within the four walls of the Chinese courtyard, which will be discussed in the chapters that follow.

The tightly knit urban fabric of courtyards, as seen in Pompeii and Herculaneum, was not to reappear in Europe after the fall of the Roman Empire. Life for most was harsh and even unbearable, but the heavenly kingdom of eternal happiness promised by Christendom was tangibly felt through the rays of shimmering light and colour in a Gothic cathedral. The Roman courtyards of atrium and peristyle were reincarnated as a matter-of-fact urban court for outdoor activities and sheer amenity of light and air in medieval castles, Renaissance urban palazzos and nineteenth-century multi-storey urban apartments. In the Renaissance countryside, and in the leafy suburbs of modern cities, the courtyard disappeared altogether to give way to the dominance of buildings as free-standing objects, and also the view from inside that commands the outside world.

Having had a long search for harmony in the human world, what was achieved by the Chinese during and a few hundred years after Confucius' lifetime (551–479 BCE) was the counterbalance between Heaven and Earth that was to be applied to the governance and rite of the state as well as everyday life. Earth is pertinent to society, family, the individual and, *tout court*, the earthly life. One example was the enduring complementation of Confucian thought (*ru* 儒) and Daoism (*dao* 道) in a long stretch of more than two millennia in China's pre-modern history. The first called for a stabilization of the family system as the foundation of the state, and active participation in society and human affairs within the confines of propriety and hierarchy. The latter allowed the emancipation of the individual's free spirit and even certain indulgence in abstract metaphysics. This may explain why, and how, the Chinese managed to live a largely secular, and occasionally even a little indulgent life on earth while maintaining a degree of awe and humility before *Natura naturans* and below Heaven. To hold onto the middle way, for the Chinese, therefore was the *golden mean* of the highest order.

The Chinese certainly were not the only people who happened to be enlightened by and profited from the salutary middle. Like the discovery of courtyard living, the sensible souls around the Mediterranean shores too sought the same wisdom. The ingenious craftsman Daedalus created wings held together at the base by wax so that he and his son Icarus could escape from Crete controlled by King Minos. He advised Icarus to fly in the middle to avoid the blazing sun above and the turbulent sea below. The impetuous young Icarus, alas, was fooled by his flying prowess and soared until the wax was melted by the sun. From Theano, Cleobulus, Socrates and Plato to Aristotle, the wise women and men in the classical world all advised of the benefit of moderation and the perils of excess and extreme. Buddha taught the middle, and the Chinese took up Buddhism with ease. The same golden mean found its place in Judaism, Christianity and Islam. Occasionally, some modern thinkers in their saner moments revisited the necessity of the middle, albeit in gnomic fashion. But the Chinese, in a prolonged span of nearly three millennia, sought not only the salvation of their mind but also their artistic living in the middle. More than that, the Chinese, as exemplified by their way of living in the courtyard, made *the middle* a moral bedrock through conscious cultivation, with which most of us ordinary mortals can be thoroughly imbued. Being reasonable, following common decency and humanity, therefore is the only virtuous way to live this earthly life.

\*     \*     \*

This book is modest in scale, not because there is only so much that can be said about this particular Chinese way of living accommodated by courtyard, which is only one among many patterns of housing in Western mind. On the contrary, there is an endless amount of material concerning the Chinese courtyard, for the entire Chinese life up until the turn of the twentieth century, was centred on the courtyard (if more an idea than the physical structure). But the author is impatient: after having made some cursory excursions into this topic, he is too eager to take the risk of making a vast claim here – that is, a good understanding of the Chinese courtyard (both the form and the idea) may afford one an effective tool to unlock the 'Chinese state of mind', and the meanings of things Chinese, ranging from everyday life to the edifice of culture, polity and society. The Chinese courtyard was the essential *architecture*, in the true primordial connotation of this word in many Western languages. It facilitated and animated a theatre of *Chineseness*, however elusive it may have appeared under different circumstances, but the courtyard has been strangely persistent a trait as testified by the sustained interest from outside China even after its physical disappearance.

Despite the seemingly fundamental uprooting and change in China's physical living environment, its unbroken culture and history up until the dawn of the twentieth century continues to haunt the present. But the Chinese world was too vast; the use of courtyard architecture nonetheless can provide us with a tangible vehicle with which to navigate towards, with some luck, a *fine* understanding of its complexity. In addition, against the rich and fertile ground of culture, we may enhance our chance to make alive China's architecture of a long past – the courtyard – beyond its abstract forms and shapes. I am of course aware that by making this claim I have inevitably raised an expectation that this small book cannot possibly fulfil. But I must admit that the joy of making discoveries in my own search for an understanding of the Chinese way of living, via its courtyard architecture in particular, gets the better of my fear of failing. Since I purposely fell down the rabbit hole, I have the urge to share my discoveries – gems or follies – with the reader. This is the justification of an ambitious and unmanageable title of a book backed by the modest undertaking of its author. The utmost goal of this book, therefore, is to seek the reader's rejoinder to an approach in which the Chinese world, material and non-material, is, in its form and meaning, understood as a courtyard. This, I hope, will trigger the reader's own exploration of the meaning of Chineseness, as well as a response to the unsettling character of the modern world arising from this intendedly salutary reflection.

*Part One*

# Heaven

## A Panacea from the Courtyard

# 1

# *What Makes the Chinese House*

King Linggong of Jin 晋灵公 (624–607 BCE), a notorious tyrant, ordered an assassin to kill the honest minster Zhao Dun 赵盾, who once witnessed the murderous behaviour of the King and protested in silence. The killer entered the main gate; it was unguarded. He then walked into the next gate; it was also unattended to. Into the courtyard, the assassin stepped up to the hall; not a soul was seen. Behind the hall through the passageway, the man peeked into the chamber: Zhao Dun sitting in the room was devouring a bowl of rice and fish. 'Ah, what a benevolent man!' sighed the killer. 'I entered the outer gate and did not see anyone; I entered the inner gate, no one was there. Walking up to the hall, still I spotted nobody. He is such an approachable gentleman. Even though he is a prominent minister of the state, he only eats rice and fish. How frugal and simple is he? The King has ordered me to kill this man, but I cannot bring myself to this task. As such, I will not be able to see the King anymore.' The assassin then knifed his own neck.[1]

This story from Chinese antiquity, in a nutshell, illustrates the spatial configuration and essential meaning of the Chinese house – that is, a dwelling comprising a series of enclosed courtyards with an axial progression, which includes a prominent hall raised above the ground on a platform. The Chinese, however, did not, from the very beginning, live in courtyards, let alone relying on them as the primary housing pattern for other activities. Free-standing houses sitting on piles are found among the minority groups in southern China, and they can be seen as the living example of the prehistoric Chinese house, as seen at the Hemudu archaeological site in today's Zhejiang province.[2] The living layout for these people, known in Chinese as 'front hall and back room' (*qiantang houshi* 前堂后室), corresponds neatly with the Banpo site, the Yangshao settlement ruins found near the modern-day Xi'an in Shaanxi province. The site is right in the middle of the Yellow River basin – the cradle of Han Chinese civilization. The Yangshao Culture 仰韶文化, from 5000 to 3000 BCE, was a significant period of the Chinese Neolithic era. The *tang* 堂, roughly equivalent to 'hall' in English, accommodated, in the primordial sense, almost all indoor activities from cooking, eating, domestic work to ceremonies; sleeping was only separated in the later period at the rear in an enclosed room, called *shi* 室. Such transformation mirrors partially what occurred in English housing history: evolving from the medieval English hall – where all sorts of domestic activities were congregated and different social classes mingled – to the eighteenth- and nineteenth-century English house in which separate rooms were dedicated to different purposes. But the Chinese, from antiquity through to the early twentieth century, never went beyond the differentiation between *tang* and *shi*.

On the contrary, the quintessential pattern of domestic living in a courtyard is typically described in the Chinese house as 'one bright and two darks' (*yiming liang'an* 一明两暗), meaning that the *tang* is relatively open and bright (open to the courtyard), which is sandwiched between two *shi* (or *fang* 房, also meaning room), the

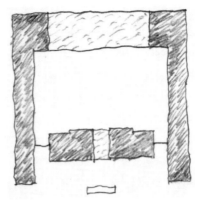

**Figure 1.1** *'One bright and two darks' courtyard pattern illustrated by a single courtyard example.*

partially enclosed, hence relatively dark rooms. In any courtyard, to use the prototype of the single-courtyard house to illustrate, this pattern lays bare the relations between the courtyard/bright and building/dark, and the *tang*/bright and the *shi*/dark (Figure 1.1). The attempted murder of minister Zhao Dun reifies precisely the bright and dark relationship in his courtyard house. Naturally this is the spatial pattern that can be extended to large multiple-courtyard houses, which cannot possibly be realized in ramified housing clusters by using a free-standing 'front hall and back room' configuration. But what exactly is the meaning of 'one bright and two darks' when it comes to the nature of Chinese life lived in the courtyard?

## The conceptual *parti*

To answer this question, we ought to find out what the Chinese house was like at a time when the enduring Chinese worldview was established. We unfortunately have no surviving buildings to assist us with the reconstruction. Material evidence from archaeological sites and ruins is not nearly as comprehensive as seen in Roman Pompeii, but we shall soon realize that the lack of surviving houses and archaeological evidence is not necessarily a problem. Before we look at the reconstruction of an early Western Zhou (1027–770 BCE) house based on the unearthed site ruins, let us first examine the 'prototype' derived from the literature. The Chinese house is an idea; it can be derived from the written world, which is precisely what the Qing scholar Zhang Huiyan 张惠言(1761–1802 CE) attempted, according to his study of the ancient Zhou text *Rituals and Etiquettes* (*Liyi* 仪礼). Zhang's intent was to give a concrete form to the scholar-official's (*shidaifu* 士大夫) house in the Western Zhou and the Spring and Autumn periods (770–476 CE).

Much the same as minister Zhao Dun's house in the above attempted murder case, Zhang's courtyard prototype is enclosed within a walled compound and centred on a symmetrical north to south axis marked by the front gate (Figure 1.2). The house itself, too, is centred on the axis, but it is detached from the compound wall and therefore free-standing. Due to the symmetrical and axial composition, the house is dominated by the south-facing central hall, the *tang*; other rooms wrap around the hall on three sides. A stone tablet, though isolated and small, is found at the centre of the compound, which appears as a powerful reinforcement of the symmetrical and axial composition. According to the interpretation of Zheng Xuan 郑玄 in the Han dynasty (206 BCE to 220 CE), the stone tablet in a regal residence was used as a sundial; it was the place of animal sacrifice for commemorating ancestors if placed in the ancestry temple (which too was a courtyard). A wooden substitute for the tablet was used in modest homes.[3] Zhang Huiyan, as we might expect, classified the central *tang* as the family's ritual and ceremonial room. Zhang's textual derivation might easily be dismissed as speculative hypothesis, since the drawing was schematic, without any sense of scale, and could hardly be regarded as architectural by the modern eye. A reasonably reliable reconstruction of an early Western Zhou (1027–770 BCE) house, based strictly on the ruins and construction reasoning, proves that Zhang's literature-based guesswork is not at all far-fetched. It is in fact the bony conceptual basis, almost like that of a mathematical formula, of the Chinese house and domestic life.

The discovery of the Western Zhou courtyard house ruin sites at Fengchu village 凤雏村, Qishan county 岐山县 in Shaanxi province

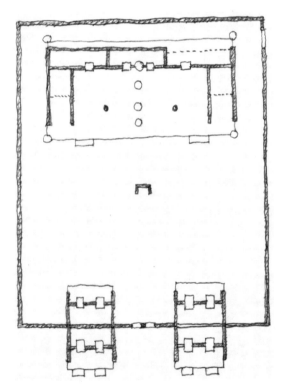

**Figure 1.2** *Western Zhou courtyard* parti *by the Qing scholar Zhang Huiyan.*

in the 1970s has provided for the first time the reliable material evidence of a sophisticated courtyard house dated almost 3,000 years ago.[4] The footprint of the entire courtyard, covering 1,469 square metres and rising above the ground to form a platform, is nearly intact. The elevated building footprint, therefore, is a truthful plan of the original courtyard compound. If Zhang Huiyan's diagram of the early courtyard is the universal mathematical pattern of the Chinese courtyard house, unsurprisingly, the Fengchu ruin site is nearly the exact scaled realization of the same idea (Figure 1.3). (Fittingly called *parti* in the Franco Beaux-Arts tradition for such a diagram is a clear choice made about the way of domestic living.) The walled compound in Fengchu is symmetrical and centred on the axis. The central hall (*tang*), on the highest platform, is fronted by the larger courtyard

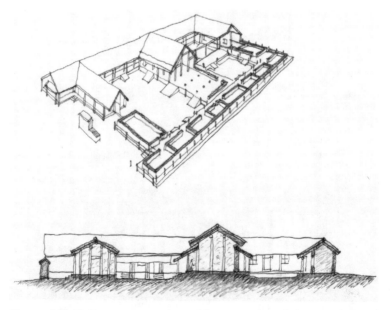

**Figure 1.3** *Bird's eye perspective with cutaway roof showing internal configuration, and longitudinal section of the Western Zhou courtyard house found at the Fengchu site.*

behind the central gate, which is protected by a free-standing screen wall outside the compound. The rooms (side room *wu* 廡 and back rooms *shi* and *fang* 房), as one would expect, form the edge of the compound and wrap around it. Except that there are two small and yet symmetrically arranged courtyards behind the central hall that did not appear in Zhang's diagram, the entire complex follows exactly the 'one bright and two dark' pattern. The meticulous reconstruction of the courtyard house by the architectural historian Fu Xinian 傅熹 年, with its scale and size carefully derived from the construction methods – rammed earth wall, timber frame and thatched roof[5] – presents us with an eerie image: it could have been a courtyard house built some 3,000 years later in Beijing (Figure 1.4)!

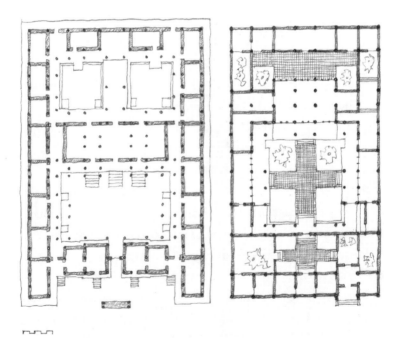

**Figure 1.4** *Plans of the Western Zhou courtyard and the Ming-Qing Beijing quadrangle juxtaposed.*

The Fengchu site and Fu's reconstruction of the house upon it show that Zhang's *parti* diagram is indeed a conceptual interpretation; the rooms (*shi*) in a real courtyard, for example, are not directly attached behind the hall (*tang*). There is, in fact, a small backyard between the hall and the rooms. This makes architectural sense for in this way the windows installed for the rooms receive light from the court. But their meanings remain the same as pronounced in the literature from Chinese antiquity. The symbolic connotations of the Chinese courtyard prototype, and especially what is entailed in living in a 'one bright and two dark' courtyard house against the background of 'front hall and back room', are well elucidated by the meanings of the house components. They have become the linguistic roots of numerous salient literary inferences in the Chinese language.[6]

## Confucius' courtyard

The courtyard house in which Confucius actually lived is nowhere to be found. Allegedly, Confucius' house was near the Temple of Confucius (孔庙) in today's Qufu in Shandong province. The temple, as it stands today, though a courtyard complex, is more akin to an imperial palace than a courtyard house for a failed politician and a self-proclaimed teacher, who did not even charge tuition fees as long as the pupil brought in some dry meat to his household. Confucius could not have possibly imagined, in the future imperial dynasties, his status as a sage and the state-installed 'Confucian school'; they would become barely recognizable to the Master himself. Nonetheless, Confucius during his lifetime, and after his death through to the end of the Han dynasty (the mid-third century CE), was held in high regard by his loyal followers, and was known to various royal courts due to his relentless preaching to kings and dukes in an attempt to secure a position. Confucius might not have wanted them, but after his passing, shrines and commemoration structures were erected near his house, with occasional attention paid to them from the early imperial courts. From the late Han to the mid-Tang (the mid-third century BCE to the mid-eighth century CE), a state endorsed sage assisting the imperial rule became a necessity, but the emperors were in two minds and alternated between Confucius and the Duke of Zhou 周公. The latter's ideas will be returned to in the following chapter.

In the meantime, the Confucian cult became widely spread in society, and the shrines of commemoration, now Temple of Confucius, grew in size and complexity. For the first time in Chinese history, the Song court in its early years (the late tenth century) took charge of the temple. From this point on and until the late nineteenth century, the sage status of Confucius was cemented in China and the Confucian school became a state ideology. In the early fourteenth century, the Ming court fully integrated the Temple of Confucius into the imperial empire. Beginning in 1411 CE, a major expansion of the temple was undertaken, and a decade-long restoration and reconstruction during the Hongzhi reign (1486–1505 CE) saw the elevation of the Temple of Confucius, in scale and status, to that of a palace, and second only to the imperial palace.[7] The temple however should not be mistaken for Confucius' courtyard.

Confucius' own courtyard house could not have been palace-like. The Master throughout his entire career was mostly unemployed; he had only sporadic and short-term official positions. Confucius nonetheless was not a destitute teacher. His main livelihood possibly came from his authoritative knowledge of ancient rituals and rites, hence was probably highly sought after as an officiant for kings, lords and aristocrats. In such 'consultancy business', Confucius at any one time would need a sizeable contingent of assistants who were his disciples and pupils. Legend has it that he had more than three thousand of them throughout his life. It is therefore quite plausible to imagine that Confucius in his heyday lived in a decent-sized courtyard complex. Yet the Master spent years on the road preaching to kings and dukes, and would have lodged in humble courtyards.

Through the lived experience of Confucius, the fundamental meanings of the Chinese courtyard, as a prototype, become legibly revealed. Starting from outside, at this point we can safely envisage, the screen (*ping* 屏) before the gate (*men* 门), which was known as *xiaoqiang* 萧墙 in antiquity (refer to Figures 1.3 and 1.4 in this chapter). The screen, now called *zhaobi* 照壁 (reflective screen), sometimes no longer stood outside the gate in the later periods, as seen in many Ming and Qing houses; it had become a 'shadow or mirror screen' (*yingbi* 影壁) inside the entry where the front gate was off-centred. In this instance, the screen was part of the small courtyard wall inside the front gate, and often was painted with a mural or adorned with a subtle landscape pattern composed with carefully selected marble slates. In antiquity, the use of *zhaobi*, like that in the more developed sumptuary laws in later periods, was restricted to the aristocracy. Xun Zi 荀子 (312–230 BCE), a Confucian philosopher, stated that only the emperor could erect a *zhaobi* outside his palace gate. Feudal princes must locate it inside the entry gate, whilst chancellors should use only curtains.[8]

In *Explanation of Names* (*Shiming* 释名), one of the earliest Chinese dictionaries allegedly complied by the Han scholar Liu Xi 刘熙 (believed to have lived around 200CE), *xiao* was interpreted as *su* 肃, meaning solemn, silent and respectful. The purpose of *xiaoqiang* was to hold the visitor in awe before entering the courtyard compound.[9] It was He Yan 何晏 (195–249 CE), a prominent politician and philosopher of the Three Kingdoms period (220–280 CE), who attempted to synthesize Daoism and Confucianism, and also spelled out clearly the meaning of *zhaobi* in antiquity: '*Xiaoqiang* is a screen. *Xiao* means *su*, hence it shall be applied to decorum required when a minister meets the emperor – a moment of silence and respect is created when the minister approaches the screen. This is the purpose of *xiaoqiang*.'[10] Reiteration of the same meaning can be found in the dynasties immediately following the Han. In *Notes of Things Old and New* (*Gujin Zhu* 古今注) by the Jin dynasty scholar Cui Bao 崔豹, the use of such screen was made plainly obvious: when a minster came to meet the emperor, after having entered the gate, he should pause behind the screen. In this way, he would have the opportunity to clarify his thoughts and consider very carefully what he should report to his Majesty.[11]

In *The Analects*, Confucius used the screen, *xiaoqiang*, as an analogy for defining the confined courtyard, hence the internal affairs of a family. When asked by two of his disciples for his opinion on a planned attack on a neighbouring state Zhuanyu by Lord Ji, Confucius replied: 'For Lord Ji, I am afraid, the real menace does not come from Zhuanyu, it lies within the *xiaoqiang* of his house.'[12] After Confucius, a literary analogy of internal crisis in the Chinese language became 'the trouble arising behind the screen of the house (*xiaoqiang zhi huo* 萧墙之祸)'. This of course is rather fitting, for Confucius always emphasized that stability and contentment of the family life was a necessary precursor to a harmonious society. In this way, a good society was ruled not by law, but rather by wise and cultivated gentlemen.

The front gate had three bays (*jian* 间), with the 'bright bay' (*ming jian* 明间) in the middle as the actual gate and two enclosed rooms on the sides for home schooling (*shu* 塾).[13] Behind the gate there was the central courtyard (*ting* 庭), and the central hall (*tang* 堂). Raised on a platform, the hall was open to the court without the enclosing wall on the south, or with full-height, translucent lattice and tracery doors that could be fully opened and even removed when necessary. This explains the scenario where the killer of minister Zhao Dun stepped up to the hall unobstructed. According to *Rituals and Etiquettes*, as seen in Zhang's diagram, there is supposed to be only two stairs leading from the court to the hall, but there are three found in the Fengchu ruins. The left-hand side was respected in Chinese antiquity, so the stair on the west was reserved for distinguished guests. When one was given the privilege to walk up from the western stair, to show respect and humility, the guest often insisted on using the eastern one. Since there was no front wall, the two ends of the hall's side walls, called *lian* 廉，were exposed, hence must be straight. Naturally, 'straight *lian* (廉正)' in the Chinese language means honest and incorruptible.

Sedentary furniture was not yet developed in the Spring and Autumn period; no chairs and tables appeared in the Chinese house before the seventh century. When the blind musician Mian called in, Confucius paid him the utmost respect by showing him the way up to the hall: 'When Mian reached the steps, the Master said: "Mind the steps." Taking him to his mat, the Master said: "Here is your mat." When everyone was seated, the Master explained: "So-and-so is here, So-and-so is there."'[14] This must have been the taken-for-granted and yet legible sequence: stepping up to the hall, being allocated the appropriately positioned mat, and sitting down to converse while facing the lower courtyard. The hall was reserved for the distinguished, while the lesser must remain in the courtyard. To rise to the hall without invitation from the owner therefore was an offence. In the royal palace, the emperor, sitting on an elevated platform in the hall, would give audience to his ministers who remained standing or on their knees (in the Qing dynasty). This was called *chao* 朝. In later periods, *chao* and *ting* together meant the imperial court – *chaoting* 朝庭.

Being in the elevated hall was the sign of authority. Such authority would not take any effect without the lower court before the hall.

Confucius, as recorded in *The Analects*, only offered advice to his own son Li 鲤 twice for he did not want to favour him more than his other disciples. On both occasions, the Master was standing alone while the son tiptoed quickly across the courtyard. When spotting Li, Confucius asked: 'Have you studied the *Poems*?'[15] The next time when this happened, the father asked: 'Have you studied the ritual'? If one did not know the *Poems*, one would not be able to hold a conversation; if one did not master the ritual, one would not be able to take a stand in society, explained the Master.[16] Ritual, *li* in Chinese, is the representation of social decorum and moral principles. It is safe to assume that at that very moment, Confucius was standing in the hall (which as we have learned had no wall on the south, hence was open to the courtyard), and could see his son walk past in the lower court. 'Courtyard lecturing' (*tingxun* 庭训) in Chinese, therefore, means the teaching given to the son from the father. In the imperial court, the emperor's audience offered from the hall to the ministers in the courtyard naturally signifies the supreme power, hence 'against the courtyard' (*buting* 不庭) in the Chinese language describes the situation of disobeying the authority. The significance of being promoted to the hall is prevalent in the Chinese language: 'hall-like royalty' (*tanghuang* 堂皇), for example, is great brightness and splendour.

The rooms (*shi*) were in sequence behind the hall. Though in reality they were separated from the hall by another courtyard, one must in the first instance be allowed to step up to the hall before going into the rooms. So the room was more akin to the meaning of a private chamber. But the chamber, the ultimate inner world of the Chinese courtyard, normally was not open to a guest. When Boniu 伯牛, a disciple of Confucius, was seriously ill, the master went to see him. 'Holding Boniu's hand through the window (*you* 牖)', Confucius said: 'He is lost. Such is fate, alas!'[17] Confucius regarded Boniu a man of high moral integrity. Even in these circumstances, the master did not enter the chamber: he talked to his disciple through the window. In later periods, the two partially enclosed rooms, known more often as eastern and western *fang*, completed the 'one bright and two darks' formation in the hall.

Confucius indeed was a master in fashioning analogies out of the meanings of a courtyard house. Commenting on the zither playing of another disciple Zi Lu 子路, he relied on the inner nature of the chamber: 'Zilu has ascended to the hall; he has not yet entered the chamber.'[18] Differently put, Zilu's music was not quite yet 'at home'. So when one ascends to the hall and also enters into the chamber (*dengtang rushi* 登堂入室), his learning must have reached a level of supremacy. Inside the rectangular chamber there are, needless to say, four corners, called *yu* 隅. Again Confucius played with housing analogies and their meanings: '. . . After I have revealed one corner of a room, if the student cannot discover the other three, I do not repeat.'[19] The south-west corner, *ao* 奥, was the most respected, therefore not supposed to be occupied by the son when the parents were still alive. The seating position on the west facing south, naturally, was the most privileged. The seating arrangement in one of China's most memorable banquets in history – the Feast of Hong Gate (*Hongmen yan* 鸿门宴) – was a vivid representation of the symbolic meanings of hierarchy and orientation in a room, which, to this day, is still ingrained in the Chinese consciousness.

The banquet was held in the third century BCE. Among all the resurgent forces against the Qin state, Liu Bang 刘邦 and Xiang Yu 项羽 were the most prominent. Though the size of his army was much smaller than that of Xiang Yu's, Liu Bang first took control of the Qin capital Xianyang and occupied the Guanzhong region in late 207 BCE. Displeased by Liu Bang's rapid foray ahead of him, Xiang Yu with his estimated 40,000 strong army pushed towards Guanzhong. A defector of Liu Bang's army, Cao Wushang 曹无伤 spread the rumour that Liu Bang was going to declare himself the King of Guanzhong. This further fuelled Xiang Yu's fury: he then decided to attack Liu Bang. Knowing his army of 10,000 men was no match to that of Xiang Yu's, Liu Bang resorted to subterfuge with the help of Xiang Yu's uncle Xiang Bo 项伯 by making an empty promise to marry his son to Xiang Bo's daughter. In return, Xiang Bo served as the messenger to assure Xiang Yu that Liu Bang had no regal ambitions and was willing to submit to him.

Liu Bang took 100 men with him to see Xiang Yu: he first apologized for taking over Guanzhong, and then attributed his success to sheer luck while extoling Xiang Yu's military prowess. Xiang Yu was convinced and revealed to Liu Bang that he learned the rumour from Cao Wushang. Being magnificently unguarded, Xiang Yu entertained Liu Bang and his men with a lavish feast at Hong Gate. The seating arrangements, as recorded in *Records of the Grand Historian* (太史公书, also known as *Shiji* 史记) by Sima Qian 司马迁, the 'grand historian' of Han Wudi's court and China's ur-historiographer, at around 94 BCE, was as follows: on the west and facing east sat Xiang Yu and his uncle Xiang Bo. The guest Liu Bang, according to the symbolic pecking order, should have been asked to sit on the east, hence facing the host Xiang Yu on the west. Instead, Liu Bang sat on the south to face north, the humblest place of a minister before the emperor. Xiang Yu's counsellor, Fan Zeng 范增 was on the north, facing south while Zhang Liang 张良, another adviser of Xiang Yu's, sat on the eastern side, facing west, in a servant position and yet occupying the position of the guest. The connotation of the seating configuration could not have been more legible to everyone involved: Xiang Yu assumed himself the position of the ruler, whilst Liu Bang, by sitting facing north, was a sign of willing submission. Fan Zeng nevertheless was clear-headed: he was sure that Liu Bang was not genuine, hence must be eliminated.

At the banquet, Fan Zeng tirelessly signalled and gestured to Xiang Yu to act, but all were ignored. He then took matters in his own hands, and ordered Xiang Zhuang 項莊, Xiang Yu's cousin, to entertain the diners by performing a sword dance so that Xiang Zhuang would conveniently kill Liu Bang at the banquet. The plot became apparent to all; Xiang Bo then intervened by joining the dance to protect Liu Bang. Liu Bang made a timely escape with the excuse of withdrawing to answer nature's call. The rest is history: four years later, Liu Bang defeated Xiang Yu, declared himself Emperor Gaozu in 202 BCE – the first emperor of the Han dynasty. Xiang Yu in defeat committed suicide in the River Wu. With the historical event such as the Feast of Hong Gate, how could any Chinese not take seriously the symbolism of positions and orientations in a courtyard?

To summarize, the spatial sequence of the courtyard – pausing before the screen, entering the gate, descending to the open courtyard, and rising to the hall, being allocated to an appropriate seating position, and eventually penetrating into the inner chamber – represented, for the diligent and fortunate, in both scholarly and official careers (*shitu* 士途), a life-long accomplishment in the Chinese world. These, in short, were the fundamental meanings of the Chinese courtyard, which the Chinese endlessly saw to with interpretations and reinterpretations in the next two thousand years, never quite willing to abandon them.

There is however a curious discrepancy between Zhang's *parti* and the Fengchu ruin site: there did not seem to be a stone tablet that occupied the centre of the front courtyard in the Western Zhou house. But since there were two small, symmetrically arranged backyards, the *tang*, monumentally raised on a platform, was the objectified part of the central ensemble, including the quadrangle courtyard. In this instance, a table altar, as we shall see in the surviving courtyards in the

Ming and Qing periods, occupied the inner centre of the *tang*. On the altar the ancestor tablet was displayed often in combination with popular gods of longevity, along with ritual provision of food (periodically refreshed if they were not permanent wax fruits), incense, candles and occasionally an ancestor's portrait, much like a shrine. This tendency of building up the central void was in the Han dynasty given an exuberant expression in brick reliefs (*huaxiang zhuan* 画像砖) and clay house models (*mingqi* 明器, the spiritual article) as a multi-storied tower; the tower in this instance was in the centre atop the hall. We will soon find, this was not necessarily skyward, and it did not survive beyond Han (if it existed in reality in the Han dynasty). In later times the centre reverted to a much-subdued fashion as seen in the Western Zhou period. But the centre in the Chinese courtyard never quite became 'solidified' fully: when Confucius entertained the blind musician Mian, and when the emperor gave audience to his court ministers, they both sat in the hall that was open to the lower court as well as Heaven above. All was under the watchful eye of Heaven's arch; the vertical void of the courtyard indeed was celestial, though not paramount.

The Chinese house, it is commonly believed by both the ordinary mortal and the scholar, 'has neither purpose nor meaning without the family that makes it a home'.[20] The transformation from tribal societies to that of family and clan-centric, marked the turbulent times of the Spring and Autumn period. The *li* 礼 (rite and representation of moral principle) and *yi* 义 (decorum and propriety), promulgated by Confucius, were to become the cornerstone of this harmonious, secular Chinese world, which in the first instance must take effect within the family. When the authority of the paterfamilias in the family was respected by the son with his filial duty, the necessary distinction of man and woman was established, the decorum of the entire household and family was observed, society could then function with a hierarchy analogous to the emperor, his ministers and subjects.

Such *li* and *yi* must be practiced with *yue* 乐 (music, sociality) and *ren* 仁 (benevolence, being human), which could only be facilitated and animated with the help of *architecture* – the courtyard in this instance. Although Heaven kept a watchful eye on the courtyard from above, humans were left to mind their own business in their walled compounds. Complex human relations were therefore contained within the limits that were set by various *li*. But to obey only the *li*, Confucius warned, one would fail to achieve the harmonious golden mean. *Li* was only useful to mark distinctions, much like the symmetry and hierarchy in the courtyard house, and of father and son, man and woman, as well as master and servant. But to enable one to stay content in the right place, the common interest ought to be identified to ease any conflicts within the family hierarchy. The way to realize this harmony was through sociality within the family; no conflicts should be larger than what can be identified as the family's interest. *Yue*, music, fittingly, was the analogy of this sociality. But *li* and *yue* together then must be guided by *ren* and *yi* (benevolence and decorum). *Ren* was human; being benevolent was, quite naturally, being human with necessary affection and empathy. Without such basic morality, *li* and *yue* would be rather empty. But none of them was to be applied without *yi* – the appropriate decorum. *Li* and *yue* were the surface – the exterior; *ren* and *yi* were the essence – the interior, which, without question, was the Mandate of Heaven (*tianyi* 天意). All of which, as we shall discover, was fully staged in the courtyard house. Once the family and the house were in this harmonious communion by reaching the golden mean, the larger world – the cosmic city and the later imperial empires, followed suit. The Chinese cosmic city, like everything else in the Chinese world, material or non-material, was in its spatial pattern and meaning, a courtyard.

# From object to void

But the Chinese house did not originate from the 'one bright and two dark' pattern as a Heaven-given mandate. The Chinese took the trouble and time to search for the courtyard. Consider the Banpo ruins in the present-day Shaanxi province, which still is among the earliest material evidence found on the Chinese dwelling. Two distinctive features can be recognized: first, dwellings are free-standing and detached from each other; second, house F3 of the ruins, and even more so in house F1, show a clear 'front hall and back room' pattern of enclosed internal divisions, with the hall having a central fire pit (Figure 1.5). Most of the houses are approximately 3 to 5 metres in diameter, but the plan shapes vary from square and rectangular to round. A larger than normal house – more than 20 metres long and 12.5 metres wide – has been discovered on the same village site, which has more room-like compartments inside, divided by partition walls. This could well be the sign of a higher social status of the owner, and consequently a greater need for segregation and even privacy, which the Chinese have never quite cultivated to the same degree as in the West. I shall return to this point when the coexisting ideas of segregation and gregariousness in a Beijing quadrangle are discussed.

Situated on a river terrace and high above the riverbed, the village at Banpo has a modest size of two hundred metres north to south length and one hundred metres east to west width. The placement of the houses follows the rather universal pattern that can still be seen in pre-industrial rural societies throughout the world – that is, the houses encircle the communal hall and the village square in the middle of the site. Built with a wattle-and-daub wall reinforced with wooden posts and thatched roof, the houses are semi-subterranean, with plastered floor and the central fire pit.[21] Although the Banpo

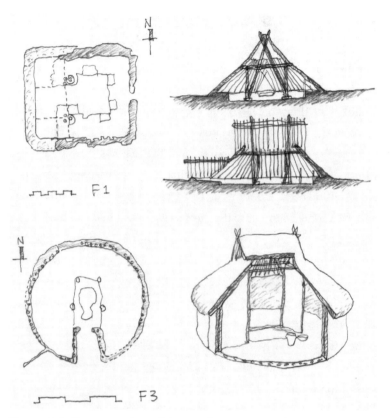

**Figure 1.5** *Reconstruction of Banpo houses F1 and F3, showing the configuration of the 'front hall and back room' pattern of internalized rooms.*

house is grounded in land, in terms of its implications of domestic life and society, it shares more affinity with the elevated pile-built dwellings belonging to the ethnic minority groups in southern China (Figure 1.6), and the wide spread of this pattern in South-East Asia and even on Pacific islands. Though built on piles to be elevated above the ground and dated 1,000 years earlier than Banpo, the house plan of Hemudu was the same 'front hall and back room' configuration as that of Banpo. The southern ethnic minorities in China essentially

**Figure 1.6** *A cluster of Dong house plans in Maʾan village, Sanjiang region in Guangxi province, showing free-standing buildings with 'front hall and back room' pattern.*

have maintained the relatively small two-generation family as the primary building block of a tribal society, which is not unlike that of the demographically grouped suburbs and 'urban villages' in a modern Western society. They are spontaneous and yet loosely determined by income level, education and political conviction, hence are fittingly supported by this particular housing pattern.

Archaeological evidence of houses found belonging to the proto- and Longshan Culture 龙山文化, the later Neolithic era from 4900 to 4100 BCE, in the lower reach of the Yellow River in Shandong province do not show much difference from that found at Banpo. The Longshan houses, reconstructed based on the ruins, are still round or square, semi-subterranean with entrance ramp, lime plastered floor, wattle-and-daub and perhaps a conical thatched roof,[22] except that a Longshan village appears to have a rammed earth wall encircling it. The Yin-Shang civilization associated with the Shang dynasty (from approximately the seventeenth century to the eleventh century BCE) is generally characterized by its bronze metallurgy, patterns of warfare, the use of horse chariots, currency and writing, along with more developed urbanism, class distinctions and a political system.

In urban as well as village settings, within the encircling city walls there were the living and administration centres, but commoners' houses, the cemetery, craft workshops and farming fields were outside the city wall. The city centre became more ceremonial with designated buildings and raised earth altars. One new feature emerging at this time can be seen in the house foundations of bronzesmiths and potters; they are stamped earth raised above the ground. But in the same area outside the city wall, peasants still lived in semi-subterranean houses, which lasted well into the Eastern Zhou period (770–221 BCE). A house on a raised platform indicates that the bronzesmith most likely enjoyed a higher social status than the common folk. A royal house foundation of the Shang dynasty, found in Xiaotun 小屯 of Anyang 安阳, proves that houses of nobilities were now raised above the ground, whereas others lived in semi-subterranean pit houses.[23] This could well be the first major transformation in Chinese housing history when a house erected on a raised platform symbolized the ranks of the upper echelon, which had become a consistent character in the later courtyard houses.

The more radical change is the transformation from the Banpo 'front hall and back room' pattern of domestic living to that of the 'one bright and two dark', which became a precursor for the emergence of the courtyard. 'Bright', in this instance, signifies void hollowed out of solid objects. Like a long overdue decluttering of superfluous thoughts in the mind, the *bright* empty space carved out, in the name of courtyard, foreshowed a fatal enlightenment in Chinese life. The change, of course, did not happen overnight: the above archaeological evidence proves that the semi-subterranean houses, as seen in Banpo, lasted at least three thousand years. The crunch is believed to be the five hundred years between the Western Zhou and the Spring and Autumn period (1099–476 BCE).[24] The last leg of this period happened to coincide with the lifetime of Confucius, who, as it transpired, became a chief synonym of Chinese civilization for the next two and half thousand years, though the authenticity of his mellowed thought and his sage-like status placed on a pedestal by successions of imperial states are not always corelated.

# 2

# *Heaven and What Is Below*

## The Chinese *tian*

That the Chinese were left alone to mind their own business in their courtyards for more than three millennia was paradoxically due to the celestial origin of the courtyard. The Chinese word *tian* was not from the very beginning related to sky and Heaven. Scholars of Chinese history generally agree that it originated from *da* 大 – the ideogram of a grown-up person as opposed to a child, hence the word also means large. The addition of a round cap in the eleventh and tenth centuries BCE, and its transformation to a horizontal line in the ninth century BCE brought it to the form of 天 (*tian*), as an acknowledgement of a higher being above humans. In the eleventh century BCE, *tian* was already the supreme deity that would provide the legitimacy for the king's rule, and the subsequent concepts of 'mandate of Heaven (*tianming* 天命)', 'Heavenly Thearchy (*tiandi* 天帝)', and the king as 'son of Heaven (*tianzi* 天子)'.[1] This was also the result of a slow transformation of an anthropomorphic deity of ancestors a millennium or so ago to a more abstract notion of a Supreme Being. Incidentally this was contrary to the trend of humanizing god in Indo-European cultures.[2]

From the eleventh century BCE to the middle of the Zhou dynasty in about the seventh century BCE, *tian*, and also the notion of 'nature (*ziran* 自然)', began to be related to the heavenly sky of celestial regularity and predictability proven by the movements of stars. The Chinese fascination with their appearance and disappearance was recorded in the *Book of Changes*, or *The I Ching* (*Yi Jing* 易经, compiled in the ninth century BCE). The depiction of *tian* as the residence of Heavenly Thearchy appeared in the *Book of Odes* (*Shi Jing* 诗经). There also appeared the early form of astrology known as 'patterns of Heaven (*tianwen* 天文)'.[3] *Yi Jing*, since it was renamed from its early title of *Zhou Yi* (*Changes of the Zhou*) by Emperor Wu of the Han in the first century BCE, has been regarded by the Chinese as the origin of all classics. On the surface, it is a book about oracles with sacred hexagrams explained in obscure languages: there are a total of 64 hexagrams with each configured by six stacked unbroken (*yang*, male) or broken (*yin*, female) lines. Allegedly authored by the legendary sage Fu Xi 伏羲, King Wen, his son the Duke of Zhou and Confucius, it is a book of a special kind of divination, for it carries moral weight by advising what should be done to the outcome of a hexagram. It is this conferral from heavenly destiny to human responsibility on earth that speaks to the peculiar Chinese character of divination. Though it may be more a book of statecraft and wisdom of life, it can only be used by those with tranquil and ethical mind.

The title of the book itself is a paradox. *Jing* are the principles of universe and life. For the Chinese, Heaven and Earth together constituted cosmos; yet Earth concerned only human affairs, family and society. *Yi* on the other hand is either the image of a flying bird or a lizard; the latter especially is characterized by its ever-changing camouflage. The ideogram itself is the combination of sun and moon;

another meaning of *yi* is easiness, all of which leads to constant movement, hence change. When the outcome of cleromancy, random in nature, is consulted in association with the hexagram and its explanatory texts in *Yi Jing*, the reconciliation of 'principle and change' always reverts to the harmonious communion of Heaven and man (or Earth) and their associated analogies, such as *yin* and *yang*. The agrarian and deeply earth-bound Chinese for the first time were distracted by the irresistible eternity of the sky in its cosmic grandeur. But unlike a wayward child who is preoccupied by his daydream, the Chinese were too realistic to become completely devoted to celestial beauty.

Heaven (*tian*) in the Chinese world, from this point on, was first and foremost the celestial arch – the sky, but its many other roles, as the supreme deity, a pantheon of deities, a land of immortals, and as a cosmic force,[4] and later as the representation of an ethical cosmic order, were never quite settled by the Chinese with much clarity. All encompassed, 'what is below Heaven (*tianxia* 天下)' therefore means, quite naturally, the Chinese empire as well as the civilized world. The debate between the absolute mandate of Heaven and a more secular, and to some degree humanized Heaven that 'helps those who help themselves'[5] occurred very early in China's Golden Age between the Duke of Zhou and the royalists, who eventually forced him to retire from his role of King's regent.

The Duke of Zhou's position, however, was of no righteous and absolute heaven mandate either. In the chapter titled 'The Grand Pronouncement' (*Da gao* 大诰) in *Venerated Documents* (*Shang shu* 尚书, also known as *Classic of Documents – Shu jing* 书经), the young King Cheng pleaded with his old and wise counsellors to support the mandate of Heaven given by the oracles to fight his rebelling uncles:

'Alas! I, the humble son, dare not ignore the mandate of Heavenly Thearchy. Heaven bestowed his benevolence on King Wen and enabled our small land of Zhou to prosper. Back then, King Wen used only the turtle-shell divination, so that he was able to receive the mandate of Heaven. Now Thearchy is helping the people. Is this not the prophecy from the turtle-shell divination? Ah! The great brightness of Heaven must be held in awe, you ought to support this grand endeavour.'[6]

Although this appeared as the speech from the young King Cheng, the Duke of Zhou, who masterminded the second campaign to the East, must have been in this case an advocate of obedience to Heaven's will. The famous feud between the Duke of Zhou and Shao Gong 召公 in the chapters of *Jun shi* 君奭 and *Zhao gao* 召诰 in *Venerated Documents*, however, revealed a very different Duke of Zhou. On the contrary, he asserted that 'Heaven cannot be trusted (天不可信)' and, the king therefore shall seek wise counselling from his able ministers in order to prevail. Resorting to the lessons of antiquity, the Duke of Zhou went so far as to suggest that it was the teaching of these ministers who enabled King Wen and King Wu to profit from the wisdom of Heaven.[7] Such was the seed planted in China's intellectual foundation in its Golden Age that was to grow into a ubiquitous equilibrium between celestial divinity and the everyday life of pre-modern Chinese history. The Chinese world, though largely secular, was therefore never fully materialistic.

Heaven's prowess was duly acknowledged and, indeed, used too often by the ruling class to justify the new sovereignty gained by force. Mencius (372–289 BCE), while interpreting Confucius, made this explicit. The Chinese by and large, however, always trod a little askance anything that seemed to be beyond their reach. They, for example, never developed the belief in a singular creator, and lacked a complete faith in Thearchy. Scholars suspect that the Chinese myth of creation – Pangu 盘古, separating Heaven from Earth, – was fashioned as a late making to meet the desire of outsiders who wanted a creation story. It possibly originated from India, or even from the legends of ethnic groups of Miao and Yao of Southwest China and South-East Asia.[8]

The Pantheon was the Roman emperor Hadrian's homage to both Heaven and man, but man was contained within and, subordinate to, the internalized cosmic building. Though gods were many in classical antiquity, Heaven especially was to be held in awe. The coffers in the dome (Figure 2.1), shrinking gradually in size towards the oculus, and still the largest unreinforced concrete dome in the world after some two thousand years, are, in the mind's eye of a modern philosopher a chorus of angels ascending upwards to Heaven.[9] The *atrium* courtyard in a Roman *domus*, narrow and skyward (Figure 2.2), was in the same spirit of the oculus in the Pantheon; it was the vertical axis mundi. Rain, snow and occasionally hailstones, fall from the oculus. But this is the divine sublime. Even to this day, a cascade of ruby rose petals descends from Heaven's eye (the oculus) on every Pentecost. Raphael, one of the few human souls cemented in the Pantheon with god-like status, rests in a chapel that is often piled with roses. The Pantheon itself, tellingly, was only saved when it was turned into a Christian church in 609 CE.

But the Chinese left their Heaven unclaimed and in blandness. In their cosmic cities, palaces, temples, and also in their courtyard houses, *tian* in the Chinese mind, less sacred and divine and certainly less vertical than the axis mundi, was at best a vague god, who too was responsible for regulating the unchanged and the enduring, such as the four seasons and the lunar calendar. In the cosmic city, and in the courtyard house, *tian* therefore was the expansive void framed by the buildings lining the courtyard (Figure 2.3). The Chinese copulation of Heaven and Earth is nonetheless tilted more to the secular than the divine. The hexagram of Peace (*Tai* 泰) in *Book of Changes* appears

**Figure 2.1** *The coffers in the dome of the Pantheon, shrinking in size towards the oculus.*

like a conundrum: three broken lines representing Earth atop three unbroken lines representing Heaven (坤上乾下). This however is the only way, for the tendencies of heavy Earth descending and light Heaven rising ensure the two are thus bonded together.

The profundity of hexagrams is never meant for the young and the impetuous. Confucius, who allegedly wrote the commentaries known as '10 wings' (*shiyi* 十翼 ) following each hexagram, once remarked: 'Give me a few more years in life, I shall study *Book of Changes* after I turn fifty, so that I can avoid making big mistakes.'[10] Incidentally, the age of fifty, according to Confucius, is the time when one should know the 'will of Heaven'.[11] The commentary following this particular hexagram, if indeed written by Confucius, offers no surprise: 'The small departs, the great arrives. Great fortune and auspiciousness. Heaven and Earth are inseparable, peace and prosperity descend upon all living things. Those in high places and the lowly communicate with each other with understanding and a common sense of purpose descends upon a harmonious society.'[12] The supposedly sacred communion of Heaven and Earth as such is quickly skewed to the profane – the ultimate Chinese pursuit on earth to emulate the heavenly order.

When fallen leaves in the imperial courtyard were spotted, the emperor was informed about the arrival of autumn. Women and children cut golden leaves in various shapes and stuck them on their sideburns . . . a long forgotten Chinese custom known to have existed in the Song dynasty.[13] Heaven's pulse, in this Song celebration of autumn, was felt through the framed sky from the courtyard, but its true meaning remained on Earth – that was, the connection of the emperor – son of Heaven – with his subjects.

The Chinese worldview, *yuzhou guan* 宇宙观, meaning cosmic view, is a housing analogy, for *yu* 宇 is the eaves and *zhou* 宙 is the ridge beam.[14] Together they are atop a house. In addition, *yuzhou* is

**Figure 2.2a** *The atrium in the House of Menander, Pompeii.*

space and time,[15] as well as Heaven and Earth.[16] Was the Chinese courtyard, like a mathematical pattern, the Chinese worldview cemented in bricks and mortar? Or putting it differently, in what way was this harmonious, secular Chinese world made legible and effective in the Chinese house?

The Chinese version of Heaven did not include an identifiable god to start with; later it became more a cosmic decree of ethics. Heaven, as for the Greeks and the Romans, was likewise to be held in awe,

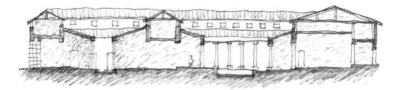

**Figure 2.2b** *Section through the House of Pansa (now identified as* insula *Arriana Polliana, property of Cnaius Alleius Nigidius Maius, with upper floor rental apartments wrapping around the* domus *of atrium and peristyle), Pompeii, showing the verticality of the Roman courtyard.*

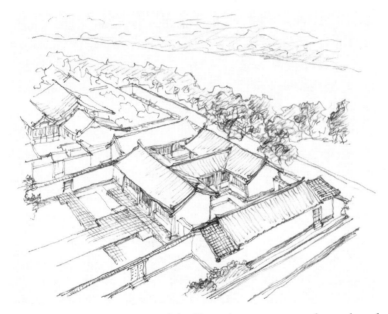

**Figure 2.3** *A reconstruction of the Yuan dynasty courtyard complex of Houying Fang* 后英房, *showing the expansive voids framed by the courtyard.*

but for Confucius there must be acute human humility before it since Heaven, in a nutshell, not only was the equivalent of nature's rules, but also, quite naturally, demanded human benevolence and appropriateness. In his quintessentially fatalistic cheer, Confucius would brush off any awkward situation; the people of Kuang Kingdom suffered much from the robbing and killing of Yang Hu of Lu Kingdom. Confucius, due to his unfortunate resemblance to Yang Hu, once was mistakenly jailed in Kuang. Instead of blaming and whingeing, Confucius laughed: 'King Wen is dead; is civilization not resting now on me? If Heaven intends civilization to be destroyed, why was it vested in me? If Heaven does not intend civilization to be destroyed, what should I fear from people of Kuang?'[17] Heaven therefore was to remain rather intimate and hence concerned with human affairs, and yet a little elusive. So the Master concluded: 'I wish to speak no more.' Zigong, one of his disciples, asked in puzzlement: 'Master, if you do not speak, how would little ones like us still be able to hand down any teachings?' The Master replied: 'Does Heaven speak? Yet the four seasons follow their course and the hundred creatures continue to be born. Does Heaven speak?'[18]

The Chinese did not really want to settle with crystal clarity what exactly they meant by Heaven, but they nonetheless did not forget about what was below. They took the trouble to decide the Earth's primary composition so that they could weave a complex, yet legible world of physical and symbolic interconnections. In the courtyard, much of the meaning and significance invested in the axial composition and characteristic orientations of the buildings mirrored this composition, as seen in the architectural reconstruction of a Western Zhou courtyard house examined above. To gain further understanding, we ought to make sense of the Chinese cardinal directions and their associated meanings that appeared as early as in *Venerated Documents* as 'five phases, or elements (*wuxing* 五行)'. In the chapters of Ganshi 甘誓 and Hongfan 洪范, Qizi 其子 introduced the 'five elements' theory to King Wu in order to enable the king to govern properly all that was *below Heaven*.

The five elements are: metal (*jin* 金), wood (*mu* 木), water (*shui* 水), fire (*huo* 火) and earth (*tu* 土). In the Hongfan chapter, the grand theory was summarized as 'the mixture of five elements giving birth to all things (五行相杂以成百物)'.[19] Table 2.1 shows not only the cardinal association with the five elements, but also seamless and symbolic links with the seasons and the human body as well as sensual and conceptual faculties, virtues, medicine, agriculture and, essentially, all 'that is below Heaven'.

The five elements and the grand theory of the make-up of the world must have been the most fundamental guiding force in Chinese life. Confucius, for example, remarked rather naturally: 'Happiness of the wise is like a bubbly stream; joy of the benevolent is like an uplifting mountain (智者乐水, 仁者乐山)'.[20] This simply illustrates the connection between two of the five virtues to their corresponding primary elements. It does not even seem farfetched to associate the wider geology of the Chinese soils with the five elements and their cardinal direction: the yellow soils from the central loess plateau, the bluish grey water-logged soils on the eastern seaboard, the reddish iron soils of the south, the whitish soils of the western deserts, and the black organic-rich soils of the north.[21]

It should be no surprise that this grand system, made of five elements and through their cardinal dispositions, became legible and found their efficacy in the Chinese courtyard. I shall return from time to time to this meaningfully interconnected Chinese world when some of the components are scrutinized in the courtyard.

# The King's City

The Chinese made their cities a cosmic world of vast courtyards. The fragmented remains of the early Chinese cities fail to give a reliable and integral picture of their physical configuration and structure. The earliest city noted in the literature, however, can be traced back to

**Table 2.1**

| | Metal 金 | Wood 木 | Water 水 | Fire 火 | Earth 土 |
|---|---|---|---|---|---|
| Five Elements 五行 | Metal 金 | Wood 木 | Water 水 | Fire 火 | Earth 土 |
| Five Directions 五方 | West 西 | East 东 | North 北 | South 南 | Centre 中 |
| Five Mythological Creatures 五神兽 五方兽 ? | White Tiger 白虎 | Azure Dragon 青龙 | Black Turtle 玄武 | Vermilion Bird 朱雀 | Yellow Dragon 黄龙 |
| Five Virtues 五德 | Righteousness 义 | Benevolence 仁 | Wisdom 智 | Propriety 礼 | Faithfulness 信 |
| Five Colours 五色 | White 白 | Green 青 | Black 黑 | Red 赤 | Yellow 黄 |
| Five Sounds 五音 | Shang 商 | Jiao 角 | Yu 羽 | Zhi 徵 | Gong 宫 |
| Five Tastes 五味 | Acrid 辛 | Sour 酸 | Salty 咸 | Bitter 苦 | Sweet 甘 |
| Five Facial Features 五官 | Nose 鼻 | Eye 目 | Ear 耳 | Tongue 舌 | Mouth 唇 |

(Continued)

**Table 2.1** *Continued*

| Five Internal Organs 五脏 | Liver 肝 | Spleen 脾 | Kidney 肾 | Lung 肺 | Heart 心 |
|---|---|---|---|---|---|
| Five Faculties 五事 | Speaking 言 | Appearance 貌 | Hearing 听 | Seeing 视 | Thinking 思 |
| Five Seasons 五季 | Autumn 秋 | Spring 春 | Winter 冬 | Summer 夏 | Midsummer 长夏 |
| Five Crops 五谷 | Rice 稻 | Wheat 麦 | Bean 菽 | Millet 黍 | Grain[22] 稷 |

Fu Xi, believed to have been born about 2900 BCE and living for 197 years. He was one of the legendary rulers, and his capital, Chen, was located at the present-day Kaifeng. The legends and the later recorded histories backed by archaeological evidence show each new king or emperor would found his capital on a new site, often near the previous one. For more than four thousand years, Chinese cities, from the imperial capital to provincial, prefectural and county towns, like the courtyard house, were conceived and built with essentially one consistent idea.[23] There were inevitably variations in form and size, but the underlying pattern has nonetheless remained remarkably unchanged even in the present-day Beijing after more than half a century of 'radical' transformation in the second half of the twentieth century. This seemingly static idea began with the secularization of the cosmic world: a walled, four-sided, square enclosure, which was the Chinese universe. Indeed, the Chinese word for city, *cheng* 城, in early times was used as a verb – that is, 'walling a city'.

The earliest and the most complete planning regulation for a 'King's City (*wang cheng* 王城)', can be found in the official book of the Qi Kingdom in the late Spring and Autumn period, called the *Record of Trades* (*Kaogong ji* 考工记), which is widely regarded as the written evidence of the King's city planning methods and regulations in the Western Zhou period. Much debate among modern scholars has been centred on whether or not later cities were planned according to the rules laid out in *Kaogong ji*, given the fact that the forms and sizes did vary significantly in the following two millennia. The centre of the quarrel is this section in the *Record of Trades*:

> The building official plans the King's City. The city is based on a square of nine *li* on each side, and each side has three gates. In the city there are nine north-south and nine east-west avenues. The north-south avenues are installed with nine carriage tracks in

width. On the left (to the west when facing north), there is the Ancestral Temple, and on the right (to the east), there are the Altars of Soil and Grain. The Hall of Audience is at the front, and the markets are behind (Figure 2.4).

Strangely, pre-Tang dynasty cities did not follow exactly the advice from the *Record of Trades* (Figure 2.5). Taking the principle of 'Ancestral Temple on the left and Altars of Soil and Grain on the right' as an example, there was an exact realization of it in the Yuan capital, perhaps due to the serious attempt by the Mongol rulers to emulate things Chinese. There was once more a near-following of this rule in Ming and Qing Beijing. However, the number of gates and the width of the avenues in built cities in the lengthy Chinese history did not follow strictly either the formula established in the *Record of Trades*; even the position of the imperial palace was occasionally off the central axis. The expansive and yet walled void before the ceremonial Hall of Audience, nonetheless, was the consistent *parti* of any Chinese

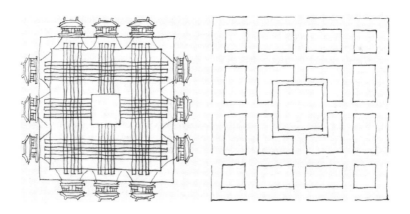

**Figure 2.4** *Diagrams of King's City from* Sanli Tu 三礼图 *by Nie Chongyi* 聂崇义 *(left) and* Kaogong ji Tu 考工记图 *by Dai Zhen* 戴震 *(right), showing schematic interpretations of* Kaogong ji.

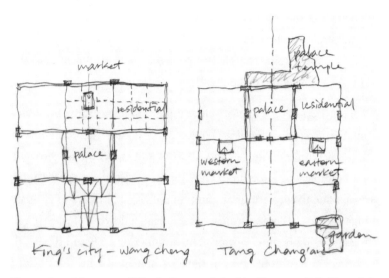

**Figure 2.5** *Diagrams of King's City as advised by* Kaogong ji *(left), and the Tang Chang'an (right), showing similarities and discrepancies.*

city, where the emperor's secularized divine right to rule, in his capacity as the son of Heaven, was cemented in the ideal of the Chinese cosmic city. Although taken for granted, the palace courtyard as the centre of a Chinese city, only materialized when the Han capital Chang'an was founded. This principle had since been kept throughout the entire imperial history. The three-layered courtyard city – the palace city core, the inner city and the outer city – in the Song capital Bianliang 汴梁 (today's Kaifeng) set the precedent for a city of walled compounds, one within the other, which was followed in the Ming and Qing dynasties (see Figure 7.5).

The mirror of this centralized royal power in the family hierarchy was the *tang* (hall) in the courtyard, where the role of paterfamilias was actualized as an architectural idea. In this way, anyone, from the emperor to his subjects, could go about doing one's daily business without having to worry too much about worshipping the divine order, for it was brought down to earth as 'rite, sociality, benevolence and decorum (*li yue ren yi* 礼乐仁义)', ably summarized by Confucius. These human traits naturally were to be followed, for they were the kind of human goodness demanded by Heaven (Nature). To compensate for the lack of heavenly zeal, one could afford to be a little forgetful on Earth, hence we have this self-portrait of Confucius: 'He is the sort of man who, absorbed in his learning, forgets to eat, immersed in his joy, forgets his sorrow, and is oblivious to old age creeping on him.'[24] Such was this harmonious and legible Chinese cosmos, which, as we have seen thus far, began in the family courtyard house.

## The built world and the literary world

The Chinese courtyard, beginning as a house, was extended to the entire Chinese built world – from cosmic city and royal palace to many different temples. It is, however, a little startling to realize that the Chinese peculiarly did not invest much faith in the permanency of the built world. Chinese civilization, and its long-lasting Chineseness, however abstract it may still seem to be, had its inception at a time when the written world was well established, which can safely be dated between 2000 and 1500 BCE. The precise time of the invention and the development of the Chinese written language can always be challenged with new archaeological findings. The Shang civilization of 1500 BCE, already consciously aware of itself as a 'central kingdom' and a high culture, was featured by sophisticated writing, bronze technology and chariot warfare.[25]

In fact, neither the Shang nor the following nine hundred years of the long reign of the Zhou dynasty was characterized by its built world – cities, palaces and houses. Only the faintest traces of them can be found. Indeed, the last centuries of the Zhou, a time marked by the birth of Confucius (551 BCE) through to the conquest of the Qin dynasty (221 BCE), commonly regarded as the Golden Age of Chinese thought as discussed earlier in the book,[26] was represented chiefly by the written world.[27]

In addition to what was alluded to in the Prologue, more, still, can be said about this curious lack of interest in an immortal built world, including the relentless Chinese fixation on the visceral pleasure that has led to their disdain for aesthetic properties by cultures that privilege vision and its associated visuals. A synthesis of the Chinese visceral interest in both things and literature was most pertinent in the garden house, to which I shall return in Chapter 6. A case in point is the fundamental difference between the Chinese way of garden making and that of the Japanese, despite the latter's Chinese parentage.[28] Without resembling the rigid symmetry of the European garden of the Renaissance, the Ryoan-ji, a Zen temple in Kyoto for example, may look like a meandering Chinese garden, confined by walls and attached to a temple, a government building or a house. The rocks in the garden, organically composed in a 'pool' of pebbles, may or may not be symbolic, but the pebbles are combed to shape like frozen waves and cascades of water. Though enclosed within four walls, the garden is a composition of vistas. Even plants and verdure in Japanese gardens are dwarfed or manicured to be looked upon.

The Chinese garden, with the same open veranda galleries, building halls, rocks, plants and water, on the contrary, was meant to be occupied and used: wandering in a Chinese garden, one is embraced 'in its soft charms and intricacies'.[29] In essence, the Japanese garden is more akin to Western tradition of garden making with the sole aim of creating awe-inspiring views. Relying on openness to form vistas, parterres, marbles, staircases, cascades, terraces and rows of cypresses, together they contributed to a splendid composition that can only be viewed by a nurse on the second floor, as remarked by Louis XIV's gardener André Le Nôtre (1613–1700 CE).[30] And yet Le Nôtre did exactly that in the Palace of Versailles. The asymmetrical look and the encircling walls are deceptive: the Japanese gardens follow only two patterns, that is formal and informal, and hilly and flat. The garden walls are sufficiently low to allow viewing over them from high vantage points. The Japanese were not faithful pupils of the Chinese, for they took on only certain Chinese techniques but honed them into supreme craftsmanship, which the Chinese would consider obsessive and beyond the wisdom and the morality of the middle ground. This may explain why the modern worlds in both the West and Japan have found their affinities, with much mutual admiration, in the visual arts of painting and architecture. But the frustration, from the cultures that privilege visual and material, at China's indifference to 'aesthetics'[31] and stylistic taste is simply futile, if not merely naïve, for none of the forms of Chinese arts, painting and calligraphy for example, not to mention courtyard architecture, were ever considered as a form of the visual arts. All, however, was regarded as inexorably literary and was practiced only by those who received considerable cultivation in literature and belonged to the gentry class of scholar-officials.

One consequence of this lack of enthusiasm in a permanent built world is that the earliest surviving houses are dated only in late Ming dynasty (1368–1644).[32] Any Chinese house dated as a Ming house has inevitably undergone numerous rebuilding cycles through to the present day. In comparative terms, a Ming house was considerably recent given that some large scale built fabric of European antiquity can rather reliably be reconstructed, and both the Parthenon and the Pantheon still stand. The Europeans staked their hope for immortality on architecture that was erected with their full devotion, talent and resources, hence were built to be long-lasting. More than that, painstaking and ongoing restoration effort has been spent to keep them standing. Consider only the Gothic cathedral, where the glorification of God and the solidification of human existence were magnificently carved in stone.

Not that the Chinese were unconcerned with the transience of human existence, and the possibility of it being immortalized in stones, but they preferred rather to represent it via the literary world, and the written world in particular. The Chinese in this regard might occasionally find a few kindred spirits in Europe. Victor Hugo in the nineteenth century suddenly woke up to the fact that the birth of the printing press in fifteenth-century Europe had killed architecture. Hugo, nonetheless, still asserted that 'he who is born a poet is an architect'. The material of stone may have been killed, but not the thoughts that the stone embodied. This, incidentally, represents the true Chinese mentality. It therefore should not be any surprise that the Qing scholar Zhang Huiyan's literature-based guesswork of a Western Zhou scholar-official courtyard house, corresponds seamlessly with the ruins of a Western Zhou house.

Since the near-complete cast of the Chinese worldview in the Golden Age, in the long period of the Pan-Chinese empire of 1,800 years that followed, from its inception in the Qin dynasty (221 BCE) through to the late Ming dynasty (the early seventeenth century), there have been no full-scale surviving houses found or unearthed to this date. The Chinese house, in vivid and meticulously detailed fashion, however, has been represented in the literary world, including poetry, painting and all sorts of forms of artefacts. What these representations tell us about are the lives that lived in these houses, which cannot be readily deciphered from a skeletal surviving house. Even if the literati and artists have embellished and exaggerated the reality (too often this was bound to be the case), the literary world that has been circulating to this day should represent 'the optimum level of performance of the house', to use the data-driven jargon of our age, which, if it is to be fashioned in the spirit of this book, is the pursuit of the *golden mean* in life.

Such is the good life, less dependent on fulfilling any saintly moral high ground of the time or zealous religious devotion, but more about pitching in the middle to seek harmonious coexistence, albeit dynamic, fragile and even tenuous at times, with the demands of this earthly life and, occasionally, the heavenly calling of a free-spirited 'floating life'. This pull from the desire for the freedom of space was Daoist in nature, and was persistent especially among the gentry. The Chinese, however, mellowed at an early age to settle on a long-lasting worldview that was skewed towards earth and this earthly life. A 'floating life' indulging in individual idiosyncrasy, life's pleasures (including the acquisition of luxury in the form of goods and craftsmanship), anarchy and metaphysics, as the chapters that follow will show, was largely lived in imagination. Even so, a ubiquitous moral examination was always simultaneously applied to contain it, most effectively, through the physical and mental confinement of a courtyard. The efficacy of courtyard architecture lies more in its idea, and less in its various forms and shapes of gardens, houses and cities, not to mention the fact that many never lived in courtyard.

Even more puzzling, to the European mind, is that the enduring fame of a building could be derived from its history of numerous uses and associations with the people who occupied it, rather than the physical features of the building itself. Famed schools which were called 'book courtyards', such as Yuelu Shuyuan 岳麓书院 and Beiludong Shuyuan 白鹿洞书院, littered Chinese history. Yuelu Shuyuan, for example, dates back to the Tang dynasty with its inception as a Buddhist temple school founded by Monk Zhixuan 智璇. Its original physical form could not possibly be traced. The record of its official establishment as a courtyard school in the Northern Song dynasty in 976 CE, nonetheless includes a vague description of its size – five lecture halls and 52 dormitories. Future extensions in 999 CE saw the addition of libraries and ceremony halls. The plaque bestowed on Yuelu Shuyuan by Song Emperor Zhenzong 真宗 in 1015 CE sealed its reputation as one of the four greatest courtyard schools in China. While extensions were added in the next three centuries, distinguished scholars (including Zhang Shi 张栻 and Zhu Xi 朱熹) visited Yuelu Shuyuan, and numerous schools of different philosophies were founded in it.

In 1275 CE the Mongols attacked the school and burnt down the entire courtyard complex; the pupils and the masters defended the school with their lives. But the school endured and was rebuilt serval times in the Ming dynasty respectively in 1432, 1469, and from 1494 to 1496, and again in 1514, when its historical glory was fully restored, though the scale and form of its architecture were scarcely recorded in literature. The actual schools of thought and noted scholars cultivated by this magnificent courtyard school, were nonetheless clearly and meticulously documented, including the famed philosopher general Wang Yangming 王阳明 and his followers. This history continued throughout the Qing dynasty until the courtyard school was turned into a modern university between 1897 and 1926. The vast comprehensive Hunan University today prides itself as part of the continuous lineage of Yuelu Shuyuan, as a cultural legacy rather than a physical building.

This peculiar lack of overt interest in actual building form as well as things material in general – a point I will return to later in the book – inevitably led the Chinese courtyard to become a site of mind games, which the Chinese obstinately, and yet a little waywardly, played in the hope of reaching the *golden mean* between Heaven and

Earth. They did so in the confinement of the courtyard where an ambient synthesis of sensual pleasure too was much enjoyed, but they were quite oblivious of two particular senses – vision and hearing, that gradually gained the ascendency elsewhere after the European Renaissance. In the chapters that follow, I shall attempt to reveal this mind game.

*Part Two*

# Heaven and Earth

## Equilibrium in the Courtyard

# 3

# *The Divergent Tower*

The Qin dynasty (222–207 BCE) lasted only fifteen years. During this period the ruthless Qin Shi Huangdi ruled for twelve years. Shi Huangdi, meaning the First August Supreme Ruler (usually rendered as emperor in English), was a self-given title by the former King Zheng of Qin 秦政王 himself. For the first time in Chinese history, the emperor replaced the various kings of the feudal states, and the pan-Chinese empire was established. The unification included the introduction of a definite style of writing, the standardization of weights and measures, and the gauge of the tracks for wagons to enable a convenient country-wide transportation.

But the 'unification' of thought was not to be easily achieved. Shi Huangdi in the end had to resort to a holocaust of scholars and philosophers, and the burning of books. Allegedly, only wicked alchemists were persecuted; the palace book collection was kept and the emperor was sane enough to spare books on agriculture, medicine and technology. The elite class were able to discourse and debate freely on different schools of thought. This was only part of the hefty price paid for the unification. There was also the mercilessly forced labour to build the infamous early Great Wall for the defence of the north, as well as the emperor's stupendously extravagant palace and his desperate pursuit of the elixir for immortality, both of which eventually drained the empire's coffer. A few years after the death of Shi Huangdi, the young princes were dethroned to give way to the great Han dynasty (207 BCE–220 CE).

Neither literary nor material evidence of a Qin house has survived. A wealth of unearthed artefacts across the long reign of Han – brick reliefs (*huaxiang zhuan* 画像砖) and clay house models (the spiritual article, called *mingqi* 明器) – have been unearthed. They show not only the meticulous details of the Han house, but also the vivid domestic life within the house (Figure 3.1). There were particular social and economic reasons behind the boom in churning out the house models.

The first Han emperor Liu Bang, the wise Han Gaodi, decided to let his long-suffering subjects 'rest' so that they could recover from the bloody rule of the Qin. During his reign of seven years, Han Gaodi laid the fine building blocks for more than a century of prosperity (the early and the middle Han), which plateaued under the reign of Han Wendi. In the early days, the first thing Han Gaodi did was to recruit 'decent and talented scholar-officials' (*xian shidaifu* 贤士大夫) to fill roles in his court bureaucracy. Though modest, they were given titles, land and houses. The gentry were content since the emperor himself could not afford a chariot drawn by horses of the same colour. Han Gaodi also contained the greedy merchants by imposing a heavy tax, a limit on their luxury living, forbidding private army and slavery. Politically, the astute emperor made peace with the northern nomads Xiongnu. He awarded generously those ministers and generals who were gratified enough to stay as the supportive aristocracy and purged those who were sufficiently ambitious to declare independent, separate kingdoms. Above all, a light tax on peasants and reward for bearing children enabled a steady recovery of agricultural production and the economy.

In the early Han, although Han Gaodi restored the orthodox role of Confucianism, the intellectual conflicts between Confucianism

**Figure 3.1** *Examples of unearthed clay house models* (mingqi) *of the Han dynasty, with one showing a tower atop the courtyard house (excavated in Wuwei county, Gansu province).*

and other schools of thoughts were at work. Politically *huanglao xinming* 黄老刑名 and *yinyang* were more dominant. *Huanglao xinming* is a quasi-branch of Daoism but in the name of the legendary Yellow Thearchy – Huangdi 黄帝, which was more akin to the legalism when it came to governing and action. It was not until Han Wudi established the official school of Confucianism that the conflicts between *ru* 儒 (Confucian) and non-*ru* ceased to exist. This, however, was not an encouragement for 'a hundred schools of thought to contend' as seen in the Spring and Autumn, and the Warring States periods. The pan-Chinese imperial empire was now in full swing. The consolidation of the Confucian school, though debatable in terms of its authenticity, for much was lost in the previous Qin dynasty, had brought the true inception of a prosperous society of gentry for the next one thousand years.

# The emergence of the individual and metaphysics

Economic prosperity and strategic establishment of the gentry cliques in the Han cultivated the right milieu for self-reflection, individual experience and even a nonconformist spirit that were readily supplied by Daoism. All were in fact well developed in Confucius' time. This was the philosophical strand of Daoism that was much valued by the high-minded. There was also the religious bent of Daoism, zealously vulgarized to promise elixirs for supernatural powers and immortality for the emperor and, not unexpectedly, the impoverished masses.

The gentry however were in two minds. *The Classics of Dao and De* (*Dao De Jing* 道德经), reputedly authored by the sage Laozi, was the theoretical foundation of philosophical Daoism. Sima Qian 司马迁,

though riding on the archival work of the previous generation (his father too was appointed to the position of court historian), could not quite determine the identification of Laozi as a real person, and the authorship of *The Classics of Dao and De*. He then coined the term *Daojia* 道家 (Daoism) to allow different versions to coexist and, of more importance, to define Daoism as a school of thought. *The Classics of Dao and De* therefore was most likely to have been developed over time by multiple authors.

Laozi, as a real person named Li Er 李耳 (or known under his posthumous name Li Dan 李聃), was a contemporary of Confucius and served as the archive keeper of the Zhou court. Confucius allegedly paid a visit to consult with the venerable record keeper during his lifetime. But Laozi probably remained a less prominent figure at a time when Confucius was taking a stand through his teaching to preach his ideas. That the courtyard of the Western Zhou was the materialized Confucian world is testimony to the certain acceptance of his thought at the time. But the doses of counter intellectual trajectories were by then well prepared, if not yet fully served. Daoism, in its inception, was in a nutshell an antidote to Confucianism, and yet Confucius himself held Laozi in high regard as one of the key founders of this indispensable school of thought. The Daoists ridiculed Confucians, often in light-hearted spirit and with good humour (a point to be returned to later), but the thoughts promoted were nonetheless meant to complement, not conflict with Confucianism. *Ru dao hubu* 儒道互补 (Confucianism and Daoism complementing each other) has perhaps since the Han dynasty become the principal philosophy of life of the high-minded gentry, the scholar-officials, and to this day an average Chinese mortal of reasonable education. The Confucian and the Daoist infused as one was the ideal, whilst the more conservative were fearful of the potential danger posed by the complete Daoist who advocated anarchy.

For the high-minded, it was the acute awareness of the individual that supplied the salutary compensation to the Confucian world. Both Confucianism and Daoism desired harmony. Such for a Confucian was, in the first instance, to be attained through a delicate balancing act between the family and society (for he was a social being), and then a harmonious coexistence with nature ought to follow. But for a Daoist, first and foremost, one was to obtain the wonderful ease of an individual with nature. To do so, one must withdraw from society, because the rules that were laid out for structuring this perfectly harmonious world made one feel a little tiresome, and his spirit a little suffocated. The technique of the highest Daoist accomplishment was not necessarily a physical withdrawal, but was manifested via the whim of one's emotion, intuition and even eccentricity. This may explain the deliberately obscure language deployed in *The Classics of Dao and De*, which has for centuries yielded endless interpretations and translations with no definitive explanation.

The key concepts of *dao* and *de* remain elusive: is *dao* the Way, or some sort of archetypal force that is formless, colourless, soundless and limitless, hence Heaven's Way? Is *de* virtue, or natural efficacy that comes from *dao*? The very first sentence in *The Classics of Dao and De* is forever a conundrum, with both its meaning and musical rhyme irresistibly appealing: *Dao ke dao ye, fei heng dao ye* 道可道也，非恒道也; *ming ke ming ye, fei heng ming ye* 名可名也，非恒名也. Among the endless versions of interpretations, here is one from Arthur Waley that has reached a wide audience: 'The Way that can be told of is not Unvarying Way; The names that can be named are not unvarying names.'[1]

Confucius, it should be safe to conclude, was anything but a Confucian himself, for he would have detested any rigid parade of rituals and mindless followers of rules and propriety. He would have also sneered at the 'cult of Confucius' and Confucianism as a state religion prompted by the emperors in later dynasties. He would have given us a wry grin if he learned that his 'system of thought' was used by a modern state for a successful marriage between 'authoritarian politics with capitalist prosperity'.[2] Confucius was not a saint, and he did not talk and act like a saint either. He was simply a good-humoured and warm-hearted human being with deficiencies. He promoted the good and the moral, and the necessary propriety for a civilized society, but he did not go so far as to defy the existence of human weakness. In *The Analects*, Confucius declared more than once: 'I have never seen anyone who loved virtue as much as sex.'[3] Confucius should have been the perfect Daoist himself. It is highly plausible that Confucius was a great admirer for the free-spirited Daoist soul (maybe he did take the trouble to call in and seek the advice from Laozi), but he would not have endorsed anarchy and a complete withdrawal from society and family. What would be the point of turning into an anarchist if one could reach the golden mean of harmony in one's courtyard, or better still the *courtyard* of one's mind?

A pervasive and yet misleading image of the Daoist ideal of life is this tiny figure of a graceful scholar-official, who, after having retired from the office, has retreated to his thatched hut in the splendid isolation of the idyllic Chinese *shanshui* 山水 (landscape of mountain and river). The true Daoist, although he may have withdrawn from society and even from his own family, still must have been a Confucian at the same time, for he could not possibly have survived in his occasional hermitage in the great mountains without being surrounded by a few kindred spirits, and of more importance, a small contingent of servants. Without the acceptance of societal decorum and propriety, much lauded by Confucius, the servants would not have been content to stay in the place where they belonged to in the stratified social hierarchy. It was art, not the actual hermitage, that provided the Han gentry and the later scholar-officials with the effective avenue of escape to reach an *internalized* salvation for the soul. Much has been said about poetry, painting, calligraphy and music, but it was the courtyard architecture that enacted a potent internalization of Chinese thought and life that might have begun in the Han period.

A startling contribution from Daoism is its crystal-clear philosophical validation of the importance of void out of substance, as seen in a courtyard building. Laozi offered his explanation with the sharpest and most legible analogies:

> We put thirty spokes together and call it a wheel; but it is on the space where there is nothing that the usefulness of wheel depends. We turn clay to make a vessel; But it is on the space where there is nothing that the usefulness of the vessel depends. We pierce doors and windows to make a house; And it is in these spaces where there is nothing that the usefulness of the house depends. Therefore just as we take advantage of what is, we should recognize the usefulness of what is not.[4]

It is reassuring, albeit still a little surprising, that Confucius expressed almost the same idea in *The Analects*. A disciple asked Confucius: 'Master, can you teach me gardening?' The Master replied: 'You had better go and ask an old gardener.' The obedient disciple left to find an old gardener. 'What a moron!' said the Master to his other disciples. Early in *The Analects*, the Master already lamented: 'A man is not a pot!'[5] This was a vivid illustration of Confucius' expectation of a cultivated man, who should not be a utensil with only a single use. For the Daoist, however, such down-to-earth explanation perhaps was too real and appeared too much like robust common sense, hence lacked the thrill of speculation and the mystique of metaphysics. A century or so later, Zhuangzi (*c.* 369–286 BCE), the delightful and acerbically witty advocate of Daoism, used riddle-like prose to give Laozi's analogies, and dare I say, the same idea as that of Confucius', a philosophical summary: 'Everyone knows the usefulness of what is useful, but few know the usefulness of what is useless.'[6]

Though not without parody, Zhuangzi admired Confucius. In his anthology simply named *Zhuangzi*, Confucius was frequently used almost as a literary protagonist. When Confucius first appeared, he was quoted by his disciple Qu Quezi 瞿鹊子 as being dismissive of the student's categorical understanding of the behaviour of the saints, who were imbued with the *dao*. The interlocutor Zhang Wuzhi 长梧子 in this instance expressed his doubt as to whether or not Confucius truly discerned the *dao*, for those who did, such as Huangdi, would even pretend not to understand the question, hence avoid offering any commentaries. Later in the book, Confucius became a supreme Daoist: when his pupil, the ethical and earnest Yan Hui 颜回, was determined to go to the Kingdom of Wei to right the wrongs of its tyrant king, Confucius advised him not to go and get slaughtered. While reminding Yan Hui of the lessons from history, Confucius did not mean to teach his student to be street smart. In a long stretch of didactic preaching, Confucius, as intended by Zhuangzi, unexpectedly pointed out to Yan Hui his self-grandiose moral superiority which was above the *dao* and nature's rules. The way out of it, advised the Master, was to clear even the slightest traces of self-interest and awareness through a profound 'fasting of the heart' (*xinzhai* 心斋)'. This was how the wise ancient kings reached the harmonious communion between Heaven and Earth.

When Confucius emerged again in the book, Zhuangzi painted the picture of a teacher who, after having placed incremental demands on his pupil Yan Hui through meditation, finally sat up to realize that the student had achieved a higher level of the *dao* than that of the Master himself. Yang Hui first managed to delete from his mind the concept of benevolence, then forgot rites and decorum, and finally reached a state of 'sitting forgetfulness', in which the corporeal self was fully detached from the true self that was completely merged with the forces of cosmos.[7] Confucius, in the mind of Zhuangzi, was no pedantic guardian of Confucian doctrines of rite and morality.

# Immortality and freedom imagined

Neither Confucius nor Laozi had faith in the rule of law as the precursor of good government. The difference however was that Confucius, perhaps rather naively in the mind of a true Daoist, hoped for a *xian* 贤 – a cultivated gentleman of high morality – as the ruler, so that the king could govern by example instead of resorting to legislating peoples' behaviours. This, alas, was a high hope, and Confucius too often was bitterly disappointed: he himself only managed to become a court official after he turned fifty, but the high position did not last long because it transpired that the King of Lu was no gentleman of integrity at all. Laozi, on the contrary, avoided the problem of ethics and sought a philosophical solution, for the good could only be defined against the background of the bad, and virtue against evil. The solution was to follow one's own nature (not the demand of the benevolent Heaven) to reach a complete state of freedom, that is, the ultimate Daoist ideal of *wuwei* 无为 – doing nothing, no activity, passive achievement, hence no need to do anything and yet nothing is left undone. But Laozi could not resist using the example of governing the state to illustrate his philosophical contemplation. On the surface, he advised that in order to restore peace the ruler should not praise those of high morality, then there would not be any jealousies; if we stopped treasuring rare goods, there would be no thieves. The key was not to excite peoples' desires so that their hearts were not disturbed. The golden rule for the Sage, *tout court*, was: 'emptying peoples' hearts, filling their stomachs, weakening their ambitions, and strengthening their bones and sinews. In this way, the masses would have no knowledge, no desire. Even those crafty ones would not dare to interfere. By exercising no action, nothing will be left ungoverned.'[8]

By lowering his philosophical speculation to the mundane, Laozi left his thoughts wide open not only for the devious to turn them into shrewd tactics of survival, but also the legalists in the Qin and Han to validate autocratic rulers, and posterity to use as political strategies. The vulgarization of Daoism as a popular religion went hand in hand with the pursuits of supernatural powers and immortality. For the most impoverished, the promise of an afterlife of eternal happiness provided some compensation for the suffering in this life. For the emperor, the aim was to become an immortal, and then ascend to Heaven. Qin Shi Huangdi sent extravagant expeditions of thousands of virgin boys and girls to search for the land of immortals, Penglai Island 蓬莱岛, to no avail of course.

Han Wudi did the same and tried the architectural approaches to build pathways to reach Heaven. While he patronized Confucians and enjoyed their support of his rule as the Son of Heaven, he desired more than just the Mandate of Heaven to rule; he wanted to elevate to immortality as the legendary Yellow Thearchy. The 'master of methods' (*fangshi* 方士) Gongsun Qing 公孙卿, knowing the frustration of the emperor of having met no immortals on the east coast, promised to Han Wudi that the immortals liked to live in towers.[9] The emperor in a desperate undertaking then ordered the Tower of Wind and Cinnamon (*feilian gui guan* 蜚廉桂观) to be built in the capital, Chang'an, the Tower of Longevity (*yiyan shou guan* 益延寿观) in Ganquan, and in Ganquan Palace, the Terrace Leading to Heaven (*tongtian tai* 通天台). Based on the assessment of the earth mounds on the site of the Ganquan Palace, and the watchtower appearing in the murals of unearthed tombs, historians speculate that these structures would consist of rammed-earth terrace bases with wooden towers atop them. Even with dry meats and jujubes, the immortals were never enticed to call in. Han Wudi in a last-ditch effort, built Jianzhang Palace 建章宫 as a vast imitation of the land of immortals, and not surprisingly, with numerous towers erected in it. The highest, according to the Han record, soared to 115 metres.[10]

The patriotic and romantic poet Qu Yuan 屈原 (allegedly living between 341 to 283 BCE) of the Chu State, while in exile and seeing the imminent fall of the Chu and the taking over from the Qin, wrote his monumental elegy *Heavenly Questions* (*Tian Wen* 天问). While he questioned the notion of heavenly justice, Qu Yuan was also attracted to the fantastical land of immortals and the possibility of someone like himself ascending to Heaven. The Han gentry, too, undoubtedly were allured to an afterlife in the heavens, for there must have been wishes that could not be fulfilled in this life. But they, after all, were Confucians who were more concerned with the earthly life. Also, they would be aware of the doubts in Heaven's prowess shown by the Duke of Zhou in antiquity. In the absence of either ardent religious fever or the vast means of the emperor, towers of different sorts, either in reality or in artistic imagination, nonetheless appeared in the courtyards among the Han gentry. But they must have been acutely aware of their slim chance of reaching Heaven via these towers; there ought to be other reasons behind their enthusiasm in producing the towers while they stayed put in their courtyards.

Much as Confucius had advocated, the establishment of the new gentry in the Han dynasty was based on the idea of family as the primary building block of society. Many of these families might have sprung from the Zhou aristocracy. This was the remarkable strength of the long-lasting ruling elite in China, which was to remain for the next millennium. Individuals might fail, but life was bound to overcome vicissitudes, and the gentry in the bureaucracy helped each other to endure simply due to the fact that they were bonded together by blood and marriage. After some fifty years of 'rest', and by the time of the reign of Han Jindi (156–149 BCE), the provincial granaries were full, and so was the court food store, where surpluses were left to rot on open ground. The imperial safe, too, was packed with monies, and the officials could not be bothered to count them when the strung coins were let loose. The new gentry, quite expectedly, benefited most from this prosperity, and were by now sufficiently affluent to emulate the life of the old aristocracy.

An Eastern Han brick relief unearthed in Chengdu, Sichuan province in the 1950s, shows a leisurely domestic scene in a family dwelling of the gentry (Figure 3.2). This was a four-square grid checkerboard courtyard compound, but the hierarchy among the courtyards was clear. The top left court was the centre that was flanked by the *tang* (hall) on the north. The master of the house and a guest, sitting on the floor to a pot of tea, were entertained by peacocks fighting (or perhaps phoenixes?) in the open court. The habit of sitting on chairs would not have been cultivated by then. Sedentary furniture only became wide spread in the Tang dynasty under the influence of the cross-legged chair, used by the northern nomads since the first century, and known as 'barbarian bed' (*huchuang* 胡床). The two front courts were subordinate to the main one in size and use; the entry court on the bottom left was dotted with domesticated animals (chickens perhaps). The court on the bottom right could be plausibly designated as the servants' quarter for food preparation, clothes washing and drying since there was a well, a clothes-hanging rack and a stove in it. The top right court, which appeared to be the extension of the hall on its side, is curious for it was occupied by a multi-storey tower.

This was unprecedented: there was no sign of a tower in the Western Zhou courtyard, nor was there any evidence found about its

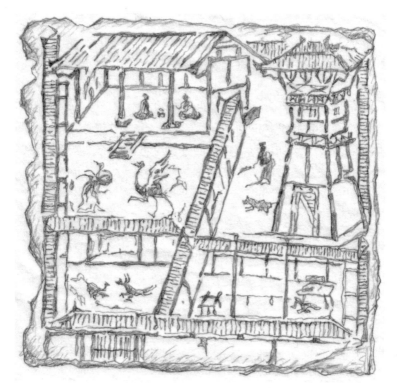

**Figure 3.2** *An Eastern Han brick relief unearthed in Chengdu, Sichuan province.*

existence beyond the Han. Based on some of the more recent names of towers in Chinese architecture, such as *guan* 观 (meaning watch, but it was used in the Han dynasty for tower) and *wanglou* 望楼 (watchtower), the tower in a Han courtyard, supported the reality of a fortified courtyard compound and might serve defensive purposes. *Wang* 望 means gazing afar but also has the closely associated connotation of 'yearning', 'looking forward to something' and 'hoping' (which often induced a bout of melancholy in the literature as discussed in the Prologue).[11] Historians are also tempted to speculate that the tower in the courtyard was used to store treasure,[12] or even for worshipping the Buddha,[13] since Buddhism by that time had already been imported into China. In addition to 'gazing afar' for the leisure of the family members, some historians assume that this tower in the courtyard served a double purpose of providing an emergency escape when the courtyard compound was ambushed by bandits.[14] Such a scenario would only happen if the courtyard compound was in an isolated and thinly populated area. Then this would be a self-defeating proposition for the nature of a tower offers a trapped destination rather than any escape.

But the Han gentry would have lived in the vast courtyard of the King's City, knitted together by densely packed courtyard houses within its city walls. The tower engraved in this brick relief, nevertheless, was situated in the servant quarter: in the open yard, a servant was sweeping the floor and a dog was barking . . . it was behind the kitchen and laundry court, in parallel with, rather than on, the main axis. It would have been more prominently placed in the courtyard if its purpose was to entice the immortals to visit. Dominant the tower might seem, with various purposes accommodated such as storing treasure, housing a Buddha, defence or even reaching Heaven, but all, after all, were subservient to the main axis – the Confucian world of the Chinese family.

The sheer number of unearthed Han *mingqi* pottery houses seem to suggest that multiple courtyards, often asymmetrical, and with towers in the courtyard, were recurring features of the Han house, though some of that might belong to artistic exaggeration or even imagination (Figure 3.3, also see Figure 3.1).[15] But *mingqi* pottery houses were buried in the tomb as funerary artefacts in the Han dynasty for the dead to continue to enjoy the same life as already lived on earth. Nonetheless, it would not be too farfetched to assume that the living wished that the dead would enjoy a better life through this representation. *Mingqi* were popular among the gentry who, in the

**Figure 3.3** *Elevations of an Eastern Han* mingqi, *with a tower in the courtyard complex.*

Han dynasty, were an assortment of recruited and appointed scholar-officials. This was the time of tremendous transition in Chinese history: bureaucrats were elected in a fluid mix of hereditary aristocracy, and examination or recommendation-based meritocracy. The true establishment of the imperial examination system to elect the scholar-officials for the entire imperial bureaucracy occurred later in the Sui dynasty (581–618 CE). The Han gentry, still, were below the aristocracy in terms of their means. *Mingqi* were produced to cater to their needs: they came as a kit of parts, which could be assembled in different combinations to catch the owner's fancy.

This may explain why most of the *mingqi* combinations were asymmetrical and appeared rather free in configuration. It was partially due to the convenience of using the economical kit of parts to make the *mingqi*, but also because the afterlife could be let loose a little from the high demand of Confucian ethics. Among the examples, towers usually appeared at the corner (see Figures 3.3 and 3.1), rather like the watchtower that provided the opportunity for the gentry to expand their horizon, but the tower was at the margin of the Confucian world. It was the escapist instrument for cultivating the nonconforming, and, in the Daoist fashion, the light-hearted individual, although he might half-heartedly and occasionally wish for a path to Heaven via this tower. More likely, though, this was the scholar-official who amidst his duties as the official and as the paterfamilias would occasionally indulge his artistic fascination, or even ridicule himself in the spirit of Zhuangzi, in the secluded and yet lofty place hidden away from the general miscellany of everyday life beneath his feet. In the extreme case, the tower occupied the centre court (Figure 3.4). The tower in this instance, however, was built atop the hall, which commanded the centre of the court. The centre of the courtyard, therefore, was both solidified by the hall and reified by the void open to the sky. The tower in the courtyard might have never existed in reality in the Han house, but it nonetheless is nothing short of striking that, in the early days of the static Chinese empire, the gentry already started seeking the individual freedom through the tower, even though it probably only appeared in their artefacts for life in nirvana.

**Figure 3.4** *A Western Han* mingqi *courtyard model (from Tomb No. 1 at Yuzhuang in Huaiyang, Henan province), showing a towering building atop the hall as well as a corner tower. Museum of Henan Province.*

The tower is all too familiar to our moderns as a potent symbol of modernity: its coming of age began as a shock of the new in the late nineteenth century when the Eiffel Tower was erected in the centre of Paris. One way of perceiving this marvel is to focus on the fact that it occupies a small parcel of land, which can be possessed through wealth, and which itself was once generated solely from land. But the Eiffel Tower – the miraculous child of nineteenth-century engineering prowess – commands the sky, which was a privileged position; from it the promise of expansive space and the freedom of movement in the new world and the upcoming twentieth century could be tangibly felt.[16] The true effect of the Eiffel Tower, unlike a medieval church spire or Renaissance dome in an European city, which can be seen from many vantage points in the city (and in the case of the Eiffel Tower, it can be seen from almost anywhere in Paris), is that one can climb up it to inspect the horizon. This was a time before air travel became an everyday experience. Flying in a hot air balloon would be a rare thrill for a few. Overcoming gravity, the command of distance and space from the air, the sheer sensation of levitation, and the freedom of moving in space which once was only imagined in the mind's eye by the strong-willed individual, have now become an everyday reality.

The well-to-do Romans, content with a vertical axis mundi in their atrium, did not see the need to climb high in their house; the poor (not the destitute) occupying the upper levels of multi-storey apartment *insula* sought neither thrill nor consolation from their high vantage point. Even in coastal Pompeii, only the rental apartments atop a bath house, named by modern archaeologists after its river valley view, as Sarno Baths, were exposed to capacious space and distance. Not that the ancient Romans were blind to vistas and expansive ocean views; they separated their celestial vertical atrium from the places where distant vistas were offered. A villa on the outskirts of Pompeii was positioned to have an ocean view, but the external *exedra* (where the views were gained) was separated from the internal *atrium* and *peristyle* that opened only to the sky. Atriums, after all, existed in both singular houses for the rich and the multi-storey rental apartments, as found in Rome and Ostia. Whether or not gazing afar towards distant views caused the Romans similar emotion of sadness and melancholy as found among the Chinese, we have no evidence.[17] With the exception of the true watchtower in the fortified medieval castles and manor houses, it took the Europeans nearly two thousand years to reach this point of fulfilling the desire for the freedom of space.

Such was the freedom of space only occasionally contemplated by the scholar-official of the Han gentry: he certainly was not able to live up to the expectation of Zhuangzi to practice the life of a complete anarchist and a nonconforming individual, though the sage did not really preach an ascetic life that required one to become, spiritually at least, homeless. So a tower in the courtyard, either in the imagination of the Han gentry for the afterlife or in reality, was as far as they would go to strike the golden mean in life. It was not a tower for the worldly leisure of all family members, for the ecstatic sensation caused by the view of vast distance, and its associated connotation of freedom of space, were not yet registered to the mind of the Chinese. The tower was reserved for the scholar-official paterfamilias for his momentary and solitary escape, either physically or mentally. But the tower in the house, either in art or in reality, was not to be seen again after the Han.

Surviving buildings from the earliest dates in the Tang dynasty, for example the main hall of Nanchan Monastery 南禅寺 in Mount Wutai, Shanxi province, 782 CE, are largely horizontal with the exception of Buddhist towers, among which the earliest surviving one is the timber pagoda in Fogong Monastery (1056 CE ) in Ying county,

Shanxi province. Surveillance towers, named *qiaolou* 谯楼 as part of the city wall fortification, and independent *zhonglou* 钟楼 (bell or drum towers), were built throughout Chinese history. Minority groups in the mountainous southern China, such as the Dong and the Miao, still build striking multi-eaves drum towers (though only occasionally is a drum found in the top pavilion loft). But there are no floors in these towers, and they certainly are not intended for one to climb up to inspect the horizon (Figure 3.5). The Qiang, an ethnic minority group in Sichuan, did indeed build tall and slender watchtowers for defence and emergency escape. In the late nineteenth and early twentieth century, overseas Chinese labourers sent money back from America and Canada to build multi-storey masonry towers. They were erected, in a grotesque fusion of Western and Chinese stylistic façades, in the labourers' home villages in Kaiping, Guangdong province. Rather unprecedented, these isolated fortification towers, known as *diaolou* 碉楼, stood in the open field like treasure houses to announce their raison d'être – preventing damage from floods and deterring robbers and bandits. None of these towers were similar in purpose to those in the courtyard houses of the Han gentry.

The technique promulgated by Zhuangzi is that of concentration through relative insulation from everyday concerns: there was a foolish man who disliked his own shadow; he tried to leave his shadow behind by running away from it. The faster he ran, the closer his shadow seemed to chase him. The fisherman sage then had a piece of advice for the busy man: all he needed to do was to take a break under a big tree and his shadow would disappear immediately![18] Supposedly, this was a piece of advice that the wise fisherman gave to Confucius, for the fisherman pitied Confucius' vain persuasions to the corrupted kings. A student of Confucius once heard a gatekeeper describing his master as someone who kept pursuing what he knew was impossible.[19] But Confucius was a tireless activist without self-interest, who, with

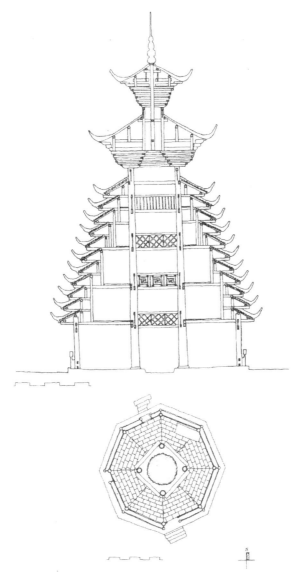

**Figure 3.5** *The section and plan of the Zengchong drum tower in the Congjiang region, Guizhou province, showing the tower centred around a fire pit on the ground without any upper floors. First built in 1672* CE *(early Qing dynasty), this drum tower is considered one of the oldest surviving examples in the whole Dong region.*

no grudge whatsoever, submitted himself to Heaven and the *dao*. Zi Lu, by using the teaching of Confucius, once lashed out bluntly over the disappearance of a hermit: 'A gentleman has a moral obligation to serve the state, though we already know that the *dao* will not prevail in politics.'[20]

Wasn't the tower in the Han courtyard the seamless materialization of Zhuangzi's tree? Since Han gentry only sought a temporary suspension from the Confucian world, the tower of *dao* on the periphery would be sufficient to compliment the courtyard of *ru*. After all, relative contentment dwelt on pitching in the middle to reach the golden mean, as advised by Confucius himself. The Master, however, saw such middle way as a moral problem: 'The doctrine of the middle way is supreme morality, but it has been lacking in people for too long.'[21] Even so, and since those who steer the middle course were hard to find, Confucius, himself aspiring to *the middle* as the supreme moral high ground, would be happy to settle on the crazy and the pure, for the crazy had the virtue of being progressive and the pure, the virtue of prudence.[22] Such is the salutary common sense of the middle.

# 4

# *Secluded World and Floating Life*

From the fall of the Han to the reunification of the Sui – a period of nearly 300 years of turmoil, there is very little remaining written or material evidence of housing at our disposal. But one thing is certain: Buddhism, assisted with more accurate and sophisticated translations of its texts, had begun to have profound imprints on Chinese life, polity and, inevitably, architecture. Arriving along with Buddhism were other foreign and exotic influences. The later periods of cultural renaissance in the Sui and Tang dynasties bore marks of this cosmopolitan spirit; Confucianism, Daoism and Buddhism coexisted. One example of its material existence is the Great Buddha Hall in Nanchan Temple (mentioned in Chapter 3), built in 782 CE. It is China's oldest standing timber-frame building, and a superb early specimen of the distinctive Chinese eaves bracket system, *dougong* 斗拱, which supports the roof like stem and receptacle holding up a half-bloomed flower bud[1] (the preferred *middle* rather than full bloom, I shall add).

Neither *mingqi* nor brick reliefs have been found to provide us with the vivid scenes of domestic life in those house models as seen in the Han dynasty. Literature and some surviving paintings on the other hand are the principal sources. The gentry class and the Confucian school were much suppressed in the Sui, but Tang Gaozu, the second and the truly wise emperor of the Tang dynasty, reverted to what Han Gaodi did: he consolidated the imperial examination system to select the scholar-officials and prompted Confucian learning through it. The gentry benefited from the unprecedented affluence of the imperial empire. Since the emphasis of the imperial examination was placed on classic learning and literary accomplishment, the gentry, who by the Tang period were largely installed through the imperial examination to hold the positions in the bureaucracy, pursued leisure in literature and painting, and poetry composition in particular.

Tang poetry, together with the *ci* poetry in the succeeding Song dynasty, was the supreme pinnacle of Chinese literature that, arguably, has not been surpassed by that of the later periods. It became the primary avenue to win fame, respect, reward, and occasionally even official positions. The gentry also used it to invest in a predictable sense of immortality – quite different from those fervent pursuits of ascending to Heaven by the emperors in the Qin and the Han periods. Li Bai 李白 (701–762 CE), the ingenious and flamboyant poet, detested the imperial examination. During the splendidly prosperous time of emperor Tang Xuanzhong, Li Bai managed to live almost his entire life as a hedonistic nomad: for a period of more than thirty years, the poet, allegedly riding on handsome horses and escorted by beautiful singsong girls, was hosted by local officials with lavish banquets and stately abodes wherever he stopped over to pay a visit. At the age of forty-two, and on the recommendation of a Daoist priest, Wu Jun 吴筠, he was bestowed with the title of *hanlin* 翰林 by the emperor, a kind of laissez-fair official who worked as the emperor's confidant and adviser. It was a serious position under the reign of Tang Xuanzhong for it could be elevated to the role of the emperor's primary counsel. In the case of Li Bai, it was a sinecure as he served only as the emperor's literary critic. But Li Bai fell out of the emperor's favour after three years. Remarkably free from everyday concerns, Li Bai was exceptional among the gentry literati: when his poetic aptitude was flattered by the fellow poet He Zhizhang 贺知章 as a divine gift,[2] he had the illusion of being a descendant of the immortals. But then he was never quite fully convinced by it. To overcome the fear of his inevitable mortality, Li Bai's only remedy was to resort to a state of forgetfulness – the fantastical world of poetry with the help of wine.

## The middling hermit

But the more earthly Confucian mortals, no matter how talented they were, had to establish a harmonious communion among the many conflicting demands made on them. The modern writer Lin Yutang had this to say about a quintessential member of the Chinese gentry: '. . . every Chinese is a Confucianist when he is successful and a Taoist (Daoist) when he is failure. The naturalism of Taoism is the balm that soothes the wounded Chinese soul.'[3] Neither of them, however, ever wanted to go so far as to seek the state of being ascetic and homeless. The courtyard, as it happened, was the instrumental template on which such a golden mean was artfully held. The Han gentry, we have learned, showed some tangential divergence, away from the Confucian world, through a tower (imagined or real) on the margin of the courtyard. The poet Bai Juyi 白居易 of the late Tang (772–846 CE) was one of those who sought to resolve these conflicting demands through, not only his poems, but also through the *courtyard* dwelling.

Bai Juyi, exceedingly gifted as a poet, was also an early bloomer in the imperial examination. Although he was successful in his early career as a scholar-official, he was not shrewd enough to bite his tongue as a court counsel. His official career peaked prematurely in his forties. But unlike Li Bai, he did not, like a true Daoist, let it go. He served various marginal positions – often self-ridiculed as a 'leisurely official' (*xian guan* 闲官), but not quite a sinecure for he did what he could to fulfil his responsibilities, and lived a life for what it's worth. Though an innate Confucian, Bai Juyi branched out to become a devoted Buddhist, often combined with a touch of romantic Daoist spirit. The hope for immortality, too, was a major concern: he knew only too well the potential eternity of the written world, hence placed his five volumes of poetry, each with 3,840 poems, in safe hands, one with his grandson and four in different Buddhist temples. Whilst the business of immortality was taken care of, the leisurely scholar-official promulgated an ideal way of living – that is, the 'middling hermit' facilitated by the courtyard: an oasis amidst the hustle and bustle of street life.

When Bai Juyi began his mandarin career in 803 CE, he was a junior secretary responsible for proofreading the classic literature collected in the court library (校书郎), so he could afford to rent only a thatched roof courtyard of four to five rooms, two servants and one horse. Being still single at the time, the poet-official cared only for the shadows of bamboos seen from his window and the wine that accompanied him when composing and reading poems. Though humble and even shanty-like, this was a secluded garden house. Before he was demoted to Jiangzhou (the present-day Jiujiang in Jiangxi province), Bai Juyi climbed the bureaucratic ladder a little in 815 CE to reach the advisory role for the royal prince (太子左赞善大夫). But it was a lowly paid position of no particular importance. He rented a larger courtyard in a sparsely populated part of the capital where he could, over the low courtyard walls, borrow the view of the distant mountain and walk out to the fields of blossomed trees. The seclusion in this instance was more the result of a deserted location of the house chosen deliberately. After the exile, Bai Juyi in 821 CE managed to resume a position of the same rank but of more substance and he became a writer of royal decrees (中书舍人). This time, with his savings, he finally bought a large house featured with bamboos and pines in its courts. Bai Juyi restored this courtyard house of more than thirty rooms, including storage and stables, for his by now quite large household of chefs, servants, concubines and singsong girls. He also built, at the rear of the house, the 'Southern Garden' where, with bamboos planted on the north of the hall in the garden, he would entertain himself in summer with musical ensembles played by servants and a chorus of singsong girls.[4]

In his old age, Bai Juyi took more than ten years to rebuild and tweak his beloved house and garden in Lüdao Li Lane 履道里 in his hometown Luoyang. This courtyard has become one of the most noted private garden houses in the literature, even though the physical traces of it are nowhere to be found. According to his own description, the actual house occupied only one-third of the entire compound; the area of water filled one-fifth, and the bamboo forest one-ninth. In the garden, islands, trees, bridges and pathways alternated. There were three islands, which were connected to each other by bridges. A pavilion was built on the middle one. Along the lake there were pathways, beaches and streams running over the rocks. A library, a study and a zither pavilion were dotted across the garden … water was even channelled to the front steps of the master bedchamber in the house. There were water lilies, but above all, the bamboos growing in the water were the main feature of the garden.[5]

Bai Juyi was most fond of music and bamboo. Playing zither himself did not bring him the greatest satisfaction, so Bai Juyi would order his servant band to play as an ensemble in the island pavilion. The distant music, either intense or sparse, was brought to the shore by the wind, the poet was already intoxicated and would fall asleep on a piece of garden rock before the music ended.[6] The symbolism of bamboo in Chinese life is rich and far reaching. For one, it is a symbol of longevity and of old age because it is evergreen and immutable, and it is gaunt like an old man. This may explain why Bai Juyi, in his old age, retired from his honest and robust counselling to the court, was particularly drawn to bamboo. He once came up with these memorable lines: 'Everyone has worries in time of drought: for my part, when it is dry, I am anxious about pine trees and bamboos.'[7]

What was life like for a middling hermit in a courtyard house? Bai Juyi spelled this out fully in a poem:

| | |
|---|---|
| Supreme hermits live in the imperial court, | 大隐住朝市， |
| Petty hermits retreat to the country. | 小隐入丘樊. |
| In the country life is somewhat quiet, | 丘樊太冷落， |
| In the court it is too exuberant. | 朝市太嚣喧. |
| Why not become a middling hermit, | 不如作中隐， |
| Veiled behind a sinecure. | 隐在留司官. |
| As if serving, as though withdrawing, | 似出复似处， |
| Neither busy, nor indolent. | 非忙亦非闲. |
| Wear out not your mind and body, | 不劳心与力， |
| But spared hunger and cold. | 又免饥与寒. |
| No official duties throughout the year, | 终岁无公事， |
| Yet comes the monthly pay cheque. | 随月有俸钱. |
| Fond of climbing high, | 君若好登临， |
| Autumn Mountain is to the city south. | 城南有秋山. |
| Prefer loafing about, | 君若爱游荡， |
| Spring Garden is to the city east. | 城东有春园. |
| Keen to become tight, | 君若欲一醉， |
| Frequent feasts. | 时出赴宾筵. |
| In Luoyang gentlemen abound, | 洛中多君子， |
| With them you may indulge in interlocutions. | 可以恣欢言. |
| Rather sleep on thick pillows, | 君若欲高卧， |

| | |
|---|---|
| Shut yourself deep inside your house. | 但自深掩关. |
| No guests in carriages then, | 亦无车马客, |
| Turn up without invitation before the gate. | 造次到门前. |
| Only one life to live in the world, | 人生处一世, |
| Hard to have both ways. | 其道难两全. |
| Humble brings cold and hunger, | 贱即苦冻馁, |
| Noble grows worry and fear. | 贵则多忧患. |
| But only the middling hermit, | 唯此中隐士, |
| Live a life of propitiousness and peace. | 致身吉且安. |
| Defeat and success, wealth and poverty, | 穷通与丰约, |
| He is right in the middle of the four.[8] | 正在四者间. |

A courtyard, secluded from the hassle of everyday concern, with a garden behind it, would suffice for the life of a middling hermit. This was the idea of a 'floating life' (*fusheng* 浮生) which by the Tang and Song dynasties was being tweaked by the Chinese gentry from its meaning of the transcendental character of life to that of a more house-bound middle ground. Zhuangzi said: 'Being alive is like floating; being dead is like resting.'[9] In later times, floating life meant more of a transient life, hence this memorable line from Li Bai: 'That the floating life is like a dream, how long is the happiness?'[10] The literati of the Song had the same yearning, but the remedy was Daoist: one should not take this life too seriously, so that one could tease about life and death. Regardless, the conservative house was not the burden to the Chinese floating life as long as it was a courtyard. The key, as we will soon find out, was an artful transition from the street to the inner courts, which made the Chinese courtyard different to that of the Romans'.

The need for a levitating escape into a tower, for a scholar-official, was by the Tang dynasty well met by the garden attached to the court: the Confucian world compensated by the Daoist garden, and occasionally spiced with the metaphysics of Buddhism. For the middling hermit, the true meaning of a floating life was to 'snatch a moment away for half a day's leisure' (偷得浮生半日闲). There was endless pleasure in courtyard domesticity. The Qing dynasty humble scholar-official (and a wine merchant later in life) Shen Fu 沈复, though living a simple and humble life with his wife Yun 芸, revealed with much loving care the leisure in their daily routines in a book titled *Six Chapters of a Floating Life* (浮生六记); the topics in the book include the boudoir, the state of melancholy, travel and health. But Li Bai, one of the very few audaciously homeless souls in Chinese life, would have detested this oblivious lack of imagination of space and time beyond the earth-bound Confucian world.

Before courtyard garden appeared, in the house of antiquity, thorns (ji 棘) and locust trees (huai 槐, also known as Chinese scholar trees) were planted in the imperial courtyard before the hall. They were also found in scholar-officials' houses in later periods. Tang dynasty Buddhist murals in Mogao Caves in Dunhuang show dotted trees in various courtyards (as well as a vivid iteration of the meaning of the Confucian courtyard centred by the elevated *tang* opening to the lower court) (Figure 4.1). The earlier Sui painting, Spring Outing (*Youchun tu* 游春图), allegedly regarded as one of the earliest surviving Chinese paintings by Zhan Ziqian 展子虔, depicts courtyard houses in the idyllic mountainous landscape (Figure 4.2). Judging from the way the houses were located – a courtyard here and there nested rather artfully among trees and rocks, they were not likely to be farmers' houses.

The Portrait of a Superior Gentleman Scholar (*Gaoshi tu* 高士图) by the late Five Dynasties painter Wei Xian (Figure 4.3), portrayed the domestic scene of the Han dynasty hermit Lian Hong and his wife, who famously raised the food tray above her eyebrow. It was a gesture, which later became an expression known as *ju'an qimei* 举案齐眉,

**Figure 4.1** *Two examples of Tang dynasty Buddhist murals in Mogao Caves in Dunhung, showing dotted trees in the main courtyard before the tang, as well as its elevated position and openness to the lower court.*

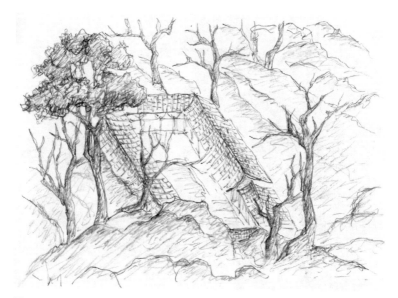

**Figure 4.2** *A courtyard house in Spring Outing* (Youchun tu 游春图) *by Zhan Ziqian* 展子虔, *showing courtyards artfully nested in the idyllic mountainous landscape.*

showcasing respect between wife and the husband, as if one were treated like a house guest by the other. The house was situated in the landscape, but it was no wilderness. The fence between the house and the cultivated landscape beyond seems pointless, for the trees and the rocks in both the foreground and the background look like the tamed ones in a scholar-official's garden. A few centuries before these paintings were produced, especially from the Wei and Jin periods (220–420 CE), the Chinese gentry, like the well-to-do Romans and Renaissance nobles, indeed built country villas.

Pursuing metaphysics and free spirit through indulgent discourses and withdrawal to nature, following the tradition from the Han period, was in vogue at the time. Compounded with the Daoist desire to break away from the confinements of Confucian doctrines, retirement from official positions to retreat to the country appealed to

**Figure 4.3** *The Portrait of a Superior Shi* (Gaoshi tu 高士图) *by the late Five Dynasties painter Wei Xian.*

scholar-officials at a time of political uncertainty. There was also the advantage of acquiring large tracts of land due to the privilege of being a retired official; the life of a 'petty hermit' in the mountains and by the water was in fact rather comfortable. Notable country villas from the literature were large estates that were not only paradisiac abodes of garden houses, but also productive orchards, herbal nurseries and fish ponds. Xie Lingyun 谢灵运 (385–433 CE) of the Southern and Northern Dynasties, the founder of the genre of landscape poetry, wrote an essay, titled *Living in the Mountain* (*Shanju fu* 山居赋), to describe his stupendous villa *Shining bieye* 始宁别业, where views of the mountain were framed by windows, and building and landscape embellished each other.[11] Despite the undertone of romantic naturalism in the depiction, there is no reason to suspect that the buildings were not clustered in courtyards nested in the landscape, as seen in the painting Spring Outing.

The house in the Portrait of a Superior Gentleman Scholar, however, was no country estate well catered for with food supply and servants; it was simply one of those idealized but misleading images of a hermit escaping deeply into nature in the Daoist fashion. If it ever existed, it would have been an exceptional case. By the late Tang dynasty when security and prosperity had been maintained for centuries, the refinement of the garden attached to the house in the city should have made the country villa largely unnecessary, if not improbable. With the development of sedentary furniture and a high level of corporeal comfort, the middling hermit, rather than the great, or petty ones, struck the golden mean between *rushi* 入世 (engaging in the official duty and society as a responsible social being) and *chushi* 出世 (retiring to the life of a hermit) – the perpetual paradox facing the Chinese scholar-official. The middling hermit indeed was in accordance with a long-established Chinese tradition of 'city hermit' (市隐), which was made possible by the Chinese courtyard with a garden attached to it.

Bai Juyi was not original in coining the term 'middling hermit', nor was he the first to come up with the three classifications of hermits. Yet he sealed the middle one in the mind of scholar-official with his poem, as the ideal golden mean for life, pertaining to the courtyard as its most effective apparatus. Of course he also practiced what he preached with the building of his own courtyard garden house. The Chinese saying of 'petty hermits escaping to wilderness, middling hermits retreating in the city, and great hermits hiding in the imperial court (小隐隐于野，中隐隐于市，大隐隐于朝)' and its various versions have been prevalent in Chinese history. The earliest version possibly appeared in the Jin dynasty (265–420 CE), but with no mention of the middling hermit.[12] Retreating to one's home to live a simple life in the idyllic country, rather than being homeless and hedonistic, has always been edified by both the gentry and the general populace as a morally heroic act, even if it could not have been seriously followed, like our admiration for a saint.

Tao Yuanming 陶渊明 from the same period (between the fourth and the fifth century) occupies a towering position of both literary accomplishment and moral integrity in Chinese history. But it was the latter – his decision to resign from the bureaucracy after serving just over 80 days in his last job – that has made him a household name. In his poetic essay Returning Home (归去来兮辞), Tao Yuanming recorded his home-coming journey with a touch of melancholy, and yet a joyous anticipation of a simple life in country seclusion. Tao Yuanming's humble home in the country was no extravagant villa of Xie Lingyun calibre, but there is nothing petty about Tao Yuanming's hermitage, for he is known as someone who would not 'bow to a corrupted' senior in return for five pecks of rice' (为五斗米折腰), which was the equivalent of a magistrate's annual salary.

The idea of great hermit was promulgated by the court minister Dongfang Suo 东方朔 of Han Wudi. 'One can escape by hiding in the court, so why bother disappearing in the mountains and under the thatched roof?'[13] Being erudite, discerning and self-made, Dongfang Suo nominated himself to Han Wudi. In order to gain direct access to the emperor and provide him with honest counselling, Dongfang Suo used the profound Daoist conjuration – that is, the greater wisdom appears as if it was stupidity in the first instance, in the philosophical sense of losing the burden of too much self-awareness in order to become part of *dao* for gaining greater knowledge. Such, however, was used by Dongfang Suo as a political tactic. Acting like a jester and appearing foolish, he managed to lie low and find opportunities to persuade the emperor to do the right thing. Legend has it that Dongfang Suo, fond of wine and often profoundly tight, once was caught answering nature's call in the emperor's audience hall, hence lost his position. It was his wit that not only spared his life, but also made the emperor sit up and reconsider those decisions made out of emotional impromptu. Here was one such occasion: a maniac killed a deer in the imperial sanctuary, and was sentenced to death by the official. Dongfang Suo remarked before the emperor: 'There are three reasons that this person deserves to die. One, he has made Your Majesty kill a person because of a deer; two, he has led all your subjects to know that Your Majesty values a deer more than a human life; three, when Xiongnu (a nomadic tribe that lived in the north) invade, we will need deer horns to kill their soldiers.' The emperor turned silent; the man's life was spared.[14]

The price that one might have to pay for being a great hermit, in addition to the risk of losing one's head by giving the emperor coded advice, was to be mistaken as a court clown, hence not taken seriously. The assessments of Dongfang Suo's behaviour and political accomplishments have unsurprisingly been divided in Chinese history. Bai Juyi, alas, was not an unequivocal Daoist, but a quintessential Confucian, Daoist and amateur Buddhist infused as one. Neither petty nor great hermit allowed this harmonious communion of the two extremes in life that the Chinese gentry pursued. The position of a 'leisurely official' and a courtyard garden house in the metropolis sufficed for all the delicate balances necessary for being a 'middling hermit'.

The demarcation between the courtyard and the room, over which even Confucius felt reluctant to cross, was not clearly defined in a Chinese house. Much of the internal domestic life occurred in the courtyard. A rare depiction of indoor activities, not seen elsewhere, appeared in the scrupulous and painstaking Night Revels of Han Xizai (*Han Xizai yeyan tu* 韩熙载夜宴图) by the talented figure painter Gu Hongzhong 顾闳中 in the tenth century (the Five Dynasties). A plausible version, among many, of its story goes like this: the Southern Tang emperor Li Yu 李煜 (937–978 CE), a highly accomplished poet and painter in his own right, but a rather hopeless ruler, suspected that the court minister Han Xizai had political ambition. Knowing this imminent danger, Han Xizai decided to trick the emperor by pretending to be an indulgent pleasure seeker. He hosted, night by night, lavish revels of singsong girls to entertain his friends (Figure 4.4). Anecdotal reports reached the court, but the emperor was not convinced. He therefore sent two painters (one of them was Gu Hongzhong) to investigate the truth. The splendid long scroll recorded what Gu Hongzhong witnessed at Han Xizai's night parties. There are five scenes in the scroll: Han Xizai and his guests listening to the *pipa*; Han Xizai, standing and beating a drum to the rhythm of a dancer, and the guests are entertained by the dancers; Han Xizai, along with a few singsong girls, retreating to a large bed-like couch to wash his hands; Han Xizai, changing into a night gown, and the guests listening to the singsong girls in a flute ensemble; and Han Xizai seeing off guests, while some of them are still flirting with the girls. The configuration of the rooms, in typical Chinese fashion in painting, disappears into the bland background, but the interior furnishing was remarkably

**Figure 4.4** *The first scene in Night Revels of Han Xizai (Han xizai yeyan tu* 韩熙载夜宴图*) – Han Xizai and his guests listen to the pipa.*

sophisticated. There are chairs, tables, bed-like couches and free-standing screens of all sorts, signs of using elegant bent wood (this was to be developed into a high art form later in the Ming dynasty),[15] comfortable upholstery with soft padding for chairs, stools and beds, fine fabrics and the overall sartorial refinement. All gives the impression that the figures were fully content to stay put in the room.

Indeed, they were oblivious to the outside world. This must have been an exceptional, if not just a passing moment in the Chinese house, for the conscious sense of being in an artfully confined room only appeared in Europe from the seventeenth century onwards: the domestic scenes in seventeenth-century Dutch paintings and the highly confined rooms in the eighteenth- and nineteenth-century English houses. By and large, the sense of being inside a room was rare in the Chinese house. Even with such a high degree of internalization as seen in the Night Entertainment, the protection provided by the architectural apparatus (of flimsy window panes of paper and translucent lattice doors) would still be defenceless if the ambition of the 'hermit' was not contained within the solid walls of his courtyard. For the middling hermit though, the relations between the street, the courtyard and the garden would be a leitmotiv in the centuries that follow, albeit circumstantially and subtly different.

# The artful transition

The unprecedented flowering of urban economy and culture in the Song dynasty has left us with a vast amount of literature and some material evidence of architecture. In addition to some surviving buildings, there is *Yingzao fashi* 营造法式, the first comprehensive set of official building standards compiled by Li Jie 李诫 (1035–1110 CE) in the Northern Song (between the eleventh and twelfth centuries). This was a tremendous achievement: through a series of graphic illustrations of the Chinese timber construction standards and detailing, it served the purpose of regulating the entire building trade from initial budget estimate, to the types of trades and construction organization to standards control.[16] But, still, no Song houses have survived to this day.

It may be that the building construction and standards had been well looked after by *Yingzao fashi*, houses of the Song period, as portrayed in paintings and literature, show, at first glance, more flexible and even organic configurations. The quintessential scene of a boisterous and fructifying street life, and the houses behind it, were meticulously and vividly portrayed in perhaps one of the most prized Song paintings, Qingming Festival on the River (*Qingming shanghe tu* 清明上河图) by Zhang Zeduan张择端 (1085–1145 CE). The literature of the same period, Meng Yuanlao's 孟元老 *Dong jing meng hua lu* (东京梦华录, the Song invention of the *biji* genre of short essays on a miscellany of literature, art, politics and daily life), prove that street life in the Northern Song capital Bianjing (today's Kaifeng) was truthfully reflected by Zhang's painting.

Zhang Zeduan's long scroll, 248 mm in height and 5,280 mm in length, is a panoramic painting showing, from right to left, the country scenery, a river, boats, scattered street buildings along the river, the magnificent 'rainbow bridge', the more densely packed buildings and streets, the city gate and, lastly, the street life and buildings within the city gate. In the entire painting, there are 814 humans, 28 boats, 60 animals, 30 buildings, 20 vehicles, 9 sedan chairs and 170 trees. Much has been deciphered about the figures and the narratives: peddlers, jugglers, actors, begging paupers, alms-seeking monks, fortune tellers and seers, doctors, innkeepers, teachers, millers, metalworkers, carpenters, masons and scholar-officials, with characters from all ranks included. The houses behind and in between the shops, taverns and restaurants seem to follow the configuration of the street and the river rather than the rigid courtyard pattern as we have seen thus far. But this painting is deceiving. Despite the bustling commercial life known as a feature of the Northern Song capital (by then, the Tang dynasty legacy of designated markets, enclosed residential wards and the associated night curfew were abandoned), the courtyards, though some of them were turned into hotels, shops, restaurants and clubhouses, remained intact even as the urban fabric was partially encroached along the major commercial arteries (Figure 4.5).

The invasion of commercial activities into the impeccable King's City was recorded as early as in the Tang period. The capacities of the designated east and west markets were inadequate to meet demand, hence shops appeared in residential wards in the Tang capital Chang'an. Provincial cities, such as Kaifeng during the Tang period, were even more out of control in terms of the chaotic commercial encroachments on the Confucian regulation of the Chinese cosmic city. That Bai Juyi thought of the ideal life of a middling hermit is the proof of the existence of the bustling street life in a Tang city. In his touring of Kaifeng, Emperor Sui Wendi was singularly unimpressed by the disorder of commercial activities in the city, hence appointed a minister to gentrify Kaifeng by eliminating the peddlers and forbidding residents to place their doors directly onto the street frontage.[17] This must have been a recurring event in Chinese history, for fissiparous Chinese commerce and the Confucian order were in constant negotiation flux. Fortuitously, by the time of the Northern Song, the mix of social class and activities in the street was not only accepted but also celebrated as seen in the Qingming Festival on the River.

The Song rulers however struck a different kind of golden mean – not just the communion between the worldly Confucian and the escapist Daoist for the gentry, but more so between the life of the

**Figure 4.5** *The centre-left section of Qingming Festival on the River* (Qingming shanghe tu 清明上河图), *showing the hints of enclosed courtyards behind the layer of shops fronting the street.*

salaried gentry and the free and robust merchants. The Song rulers were moderate in exercising power. The emperor was called *guanjia* 官家 (administrator). One emperor in the early twelfth century was even known to have said that 'I do not regard the empire as my personal property; my job is to guide the people'.[18] The entire Song ethos was geared towards the interest of the gentry and the merchants. On the one hand, there were highly developed rules and regulations for the stratified society, such as the sophisticated building manual *Yingzao fashi*. Other regulations even included dress codes: each class had its own dress code of special colour and material so that the social status of a person was clearly recognizable. The houses of the different layers of the social spectrum, too, were differentiated by the type of tiles, front door and gate ornaments, and the size of the hall; the form of tombs for each social class was also prescribed in detail.

The poor, it was believed, must be sufficiently looked after, for they were the foundation of the Song prosperity. There were the equivalent of social housing and medical care: Buddhist monks took charge of caring the sick; homes were built for the old and the destitute; even the burials of the poor were taken care of; and cheap grains were sold to the hungry from the state granaries. Not surprisingly, the eleventh century was the most culturally active time enjoyed so far by the gentry in Chinese history, with Song painting and porcelain production surpassing the artistic accomplishments of the previous centuries.

In addition to the lively street life and the harmonious social cohesion that were much celebrated in Qingming Festival on the River, the subtle depiction of life within the courtyard house should not be overlooked, for it was the remarkably static courtyard, as both a place and a way of living, that provided the long-lasting continuum of the pre-modern Chinese culture. 'It is evident anyway that the Chinese as a nation are more philosophic than efficient,' so the Chinese writer Lin Yutang said, 'and that if it were otherwise, no nation could have survived the high blood pressure of an efficient life for four thousand years. Four thousand years of efficient living would ruin any nation.'[19]

To return to Qingming Festival on the River, the focus of Zhang Zeduan's painting was on the outskirts of the city. The scene beyond the city gate on the right occupies the majority of the more than five metres long scroll. This was a busy area of various burgeoning trades, especially silk production, to cater to the demand of the upper class in the city. The organic and vibrant street life no doubt was artistically embellished by the painter through the effective organization of the street fabric. In reality the street fabric at the outskirts of the city would have been formed largely by makeshift buildings. Within the city gate on the left, though the exuberant street life continued, we see, on the bottom left, a bearded man sitting quietly reading in his upper storey study (see Figure 4.5). Unaffected by the hustle and bustle of the street, this upper level room was secluded inside a walled compound – the courtyard oasis. Judging by the banner hung on the flag pole, this is a hotel, where a provincial official attending a royal audience or an aspiring scholar sitting through the imperial examination would have stayed. Further to the left in the top corner, almost at the book end of the long scroll, we see more clearly a courtyard house, intact and secure. There was the hint of a screen behind the front gate with its doors ajar. Further into the capital city, we could envisage, the courtyard still must have been the primary building element used to weave the larger city fabric. Pingjiang tu 平江图, the city map of Suzhou (known as Pingjiang in the Song) engraved in a stone tablet in 1229, clearly shows that the courtyard, from official residence to government house, was the archetypal pattern of the entire urban morphology, which in itself was also a form of enclosed courtyard. The mechanism which effectively ensured spatial seclusion, and the moral integrity of the courtyard world in this instance, was the simple screen, and by now it stood behind the front gate.

In one of the many versions of the Lady Wenji's Return to the Han (*Wenji gui han tu* 文姬归汉图, also known as one of the scenes in the long scroll of Eighteen Songs of a Nomad Flute 胡笳十八拍: The Story of Lady Wenji), a popular theme of the Song painting, Cai Wenji was the daughter of a prominent statesman of the Eastern Han dynasty (25–220 CE). Around 194 CE, a civil rebellion brought Xiongnu mercenaries into the Chinese capital and Wenji was abducted, along with other hostages, into the northern frontier. During her captivity, Wenji became the wife of the heir apparent *Zuoxianwang*, and bore him two children. Twelve years after her capture, the powerful minister Cao Cao (155–220 CE), ransomed her in the name of her father, Cai Yong (133–192 CE ). When Wenji returned to the Han capital, around 206 CE at the age of approximately twenty-eight, she left her two children behind in the frontier.

The arrival of Wenji at the gate of her house was the centre of the painting (Figure 4.6): the demarcation between the busy street and

**Figure 4.6** *Details of one version of Lady Wenji's Return to the Han (*Wenji gui han tu* 文姬归汉图), showing a free-standing screen behind the first gate of the courtyard.*

the court behind the wall and the gate (the first of many courtyards of a large mansion) was facilitated by a free-standing screen behind the gate. The female members of the household and the maids were standing about the second gate to the inner court, while the coordinated male servants carried Wenji's trunks and stuff through the first gate into the house. The gradual sequence of the courtyards from the street to the utmost inner court is clearly hinted at in this painting. The story is from the Eastern Han, but this anonymous painter of the Song period must have modelled his painting based on the Song house, since no free-standing screens have been spotted in Han *mingqi* or from the brick relief engravings. In Chinese antiquity, as we have seen, and understandably, the screen stood outside the gate for there was no bustling street trades as such.

A complete record of a Song courtyard has not been found in the surviving Song paintings. In the Palace Banquet (the original Chinese title *Qiqiao tu* 乞巧图 says this is a painting about the festival celebration of the assignation of the Herd Boy and the Weaving Maid in celestial constellation on the seventh day of the seventh month), a detailed depiction of the rear quarter of a large courtyard complex was rendered with ink and colour on a silk scroll by an unidentified painter during either the Five Dynasties (907–960 CE), or in the later Northern Song (960–1127 CE) (Figure 4.7). To where exactly this section of the courtyard belonged, we can never verify. Judging from the title, it is plausible to read the scene as a preparation for the festival banquet by the women in this large household, either patrician or even royal. The prominent open pavilion on the corner terrace seems to prove that this was the place where the celestial reunion could be viewed and contemplated from earth. Layers of courtyards and doors do not line up in symmetrical or even axial manner, which suggests this was likely the portion of the courtyard complex where the Confucian world was gradually transformed to the pleasure garden at the rear.

**Figure 4.7** *Palace Banquet (the original Chinese title* Qiqiao tu 乞巧图*) by an unidentified painter during either the Five Dynasties (907–960 CE), or the later Northern Song (960–1127) CE.*

Willows, willowy trees and banana leaves were dotted in the
courtyards, but no bamboos, water lilies or library could be spotted.
This surely was not the garden of the likes of the Tang poet Bai Juyi.
Indeed, exotic lake rocks and peonies, which had since the Tang
period become the prized necessities of the house garden for the well-
to-do, were featured in the garden as the foreground of the painting.
The plump figures and their flowing sartorial outfits do suggest the
legacy of a particular Tang taste, which has made some art historians
to suspect that the setting was (or implied) the harem of the Tang
emperor Xuanzong (712–756 CE), who was notoriously obsessed with
his beloved consort Yang Guifei, and lost his reign as a consequence of
his negligence of state affairs. Even if this was painted in the twelfth
century, the use of eaves brackets – *dougong*, the tracery pattern of the
balustrade, and the placement of prized lake rocks and peony flowers
in the garden, like the courtyard itself, suggested that life had remained
largely unchanged for the next 800 hundred years.

Although the nature of the courtyard and the identities of the
figures will remain unverified, the change from the more rigid
Confucian court in the background to the more organically organized
courts and buildings in the garden is apparent. The seclusion of the
courtyard complex itself is uncompromising, for the world beyond
the rear gate was left blank by the painter. The artful transition from
outside to the inner courts, as evidenced by the multiple gates in
between the sequences of layered courts, should be agreeable with
that of the front gate as hinted at in Qingming Festival on the River
and Lady's Wenji's Return to the Han. The effect of the courtyard
house in striking a delicate and ingenious middle ground, regardless
of what needed to be harmonized at the time, was consolidated by the
Song dynasty as the most instrumental template for the Chinese life.
In this way, the kind of 'floating life' desired by the free-spirited
Chinese was well provided by the artifice of the secluded courtyard.

# 5

# *A Deceiving Symbol*

The 88 years of the foreign rule of the Mongols left some architectural traces of a cosmopolitan society – that the Tibetan pagodas are still dotted about today's Beijing is the living proof. No remains of credible Yuan courtyard houses are still standing today, but there is no reason to believe that there was any radical change in the continuity of the courtyard in the Yuan dynasty. Scattered literature and houses portrayed in paintings all attest that the Chinese courtyard continued in the Yuan.[1] The founding of the Yuan capital Dadu 元大都 (1264–1368 CE) by the Mongol rulers was based on the cosmic city prototype of the King's City, which in itself was a vast courtyard. Memories of their nomadic past were incorporated in the urban fabric, such as the choice of the wetland site itself for the capital and the man-made lakes in it; they enriched, rather than derailed, the idea of the courtyard city. I shall return to Yuan Dadu later in the book.

As one might expect, the Mongol rulers did all they could to ensure the privileges of the Mongols themselves, and even granted foreigners more rights than that of the Chinese. Nonetheless, they ran a bilingual bureaucracy and left the Chinese gentry alone, except that the gentry were banned from being part of the administration. The accounts of Marco Polo (if he actually set foot on the soil of Mongol China) and other travellers could well be skewed towards portraying a civil and harmonious cosmopolitan society, partially because of the privileges the travellers enjoyed, while the reality of impoverished peasantry was neglected. Though there was land-grabbing of vast tracts by Mongol nobles, especially the agricultural land in the north that was turned into pasture to feed their horses, the Yuan rulers were sane enough to allow the wealthy landowners in the fertile Yangtze region to continue agrarian production. This region became the food basket of the capital Dadu in the north, which, in addition to its vast administration, was also a cosmopolitan trade centre. Perhaps because the Mongols had no Confucian teaching in their blood, they did not discount trade and commerce. Some nobles ran trading businesses themselves and amassed large profits. Since allied foreigners were treated better than the Chinese and were given privileges, international trade thrived. One privilege was tax-free business for foreign merchants, hence potential tax money went abroad and Yuan commerce, as a consequence, did not benefit the empire.

The Mongols did not force the Chinese to change their way of living; they admired it and attempted to emulate it. Certain forms of arts, opera and theatre for example, prospered as a result of royal patronage and the enthusiasm of the Mongol nobles. The urbanized nomads and their offspring lived in courtyard houses and palaces. Such a comfortable sedentary life crippled the future generations of Mongol soldiers – they eventually lost their military ferocity that landed their forefathers the Chinese empire in the first place. Perhaps life in the Chinese courtyard never quite suited the nomadic Mongols. When the Chinese peasant uprisings spread across the country, the Mongols had already lost their interest in running the vast and impoverished empire. They fled back to Mongolia without putting up much resistance.

The first emperor of the Ming dynasty (1368–1644 CE), a peasant, Zhu Yuanzhang continued the absolute monarchy: the economy reverted to land-based endeavour without much encouragement of trade and commerce. Indeed, private trade of salt and tea, and private foreign trade were banned in the first half of the Ming; the only revolutionary trace left from the peasant uprising were the laws directed against the rich. Like the Mongol rulers, the new emperor started off by sending decrees to pay large pensions to the imperial family. But several pressing problems competed for resources: the remote northern and south-western frontiers needed army protection; the long eastern coastline was constantly assaulted by Japanese pirates, which was a persistent nuisance that the Ming court failed to respond to with much effect. Extravagance beyond the monarchy's means, too, helped to drain the coffers of the empire quickly: they included the display of imperial splendour, the increasingly large and complex administration, the zealous rebuilding of the Great Wall, and the heroic naval expeditions led by eunuch Zheng He, with the world's largest and most advanced fleet, to Indo-China and the coast of Africa. The forced labour of craftsmen and heavy taxes on the peasants could only go so far. There was however, one economic lever designed to encourage the merchants to help run the country: in the early days, in order to feed the military colonies (*ying* 营) spreading from central China and the east coast to the deep frontiers of south-west China, the court issued salt certificates to merchants who transported grains to the military colonies. The merchants were then permitted to sell salt at higher prices outside the state monopoly.

Driven more by demand and necessity, much less by any deliberate planning manipulation and incentives offered by the imperial court and its administration, the Ming period saw a continuing agricultural revolution based on a better irrigation system that allowed alternating crops to avoid leaving productive land idle, fast-growing rice that yielded two harvests each year, cotton cultivation and the associated textile production. The tremendous increase of agricultural produce coincided with larger and more concentrated urbanization in the first Ming capital Nanjing, and also in the surrounding area of the lower reaches of the Yangtze River. Following the lifting of trade bans, commerce inevitably resumed to support these trends; the merchants, too, came from the same region. Those who specialized in salt, for example, were from the Huizhou region, the south-eastern corner of Anhui province, which was close to Lianghuai 两淮 region (located in the central-north and north of today's Anhui province) where large quantities of salt had been traditionally produced since the Tang dynasty. The early incentives generated by salt certificates did not last long. The court terminated its monopoly of salt trade in the middle of Ming (1492 CE) because the salt merchants amassed handsome profits by inflating salt prices. In addition, after salt deregulation, heavy land taxes imposed on Huizhou during the Jiajing period (1522–1566 CE), which continued in the Longqing period (1567–1572 CE), further deterred the Huizhou merchants from the land-based trade of tea and lumber, which they were known for in the past.

# The travelling merchant and the oddity of their courtyard

A Ming courtyard would have been consistent in supporting the largely unchanged Chinese family life. But a Ming courtyard found in Huizhou and also in western Zhejiang and northern Jiangxi provinces, appears to be an oddity: its narrow and atrium-like courtyard void and the often centred front entry are reminiscent of a Roman *domus* (Figure 5.1). They are, however, the camouflages of an unchanged Chinese courtyard, and in this instance more of a symbol than a living house. Although any standing Ming house to this date would have gone through various renovations and even rebuilding, a sizeable number of

**Figure 5.1** *A Roman atrium-like void in Hongcun, Yi county of Huizhou.*

Ming houses in the Huizhou region have been discovered and dated by a group of Nanjing-based Chinese architects.[2] Huizhou is mountainous and its villages and hamlets nest in river valleys. In the Ming dynasty, this region was particularly known for its diligent and successful merchants who travelled to other places to establish their business in trading salt, as well as timber, lacquer, tea, and running pawnshops.

Salt trading by Huizhou merchants had a long history dating from the fourth century of the Eastern Jin. In later times when wealth was 'translated' into better education for their offspring and more refined cultural taste, the locally produced 'four treasures of the scholar's studio' – fine rice paper for calligraphy and painting, writing brushes, ink sticks and ink grinding slabs – became a significant part of their business. They were known simply as travelling merchants (*keshang* 客商) or merchants from Huizhou (*huishang* 徽商).[3] The merchants sent money back to the home village to build fine houses and ancestral halls. The reasons these capable men abandoned their rice paddies, wives, children and elderly parents to seek mammon elsewhere were not conclusive, but a plausible cause, in addition to the sudden heavy land tax in the middle of the Ming dynasty, was the chronic lack of cultivable land, hence the difficulty in feeding the increasing population from the yields.

A cursory examination of Huizhou houses and villages reveals, to the modern eye, a strangely restrained and yet elegant austerity: high, white-washed masonry walls enclose a two-to-three-storey house, which is crowned with black roof tiles (Figure 5.2). The footprints of these houses are small without the expansive courtyards that are normally associated with the Chinese house. There are, nonetheless, small voids in the houses, which are fittingly named as 'skywells' (*tianjing* 天井) (Figure 5.3). The raison d'être of the skywell often is

**Figure 5.2a** *The village centre of Hongcun, Yi county of Huizhou.*

attributed to climate: since a Chinese house was to face south, the shallow void would minimize heat gain from both west and east; compounded with this was the scarcity of level land in those mountainous river valleys. The narrow skywell, though appearing like the atrium in a Roman *domus*, was not overtly skyward; its lack of expansion could not be readily linked to the above-mentioned practicalities: the little need for a social template in the courtyard without the presence of paterfamilias was the true cause. The occupation of a Huizhou house, more associated with ancestor commemoration and past generations, proves that the meaning and the workings of its *parti* still were quintessentially those of the Chinese courtyard. The thrust of it, however, was the heavy price that the men

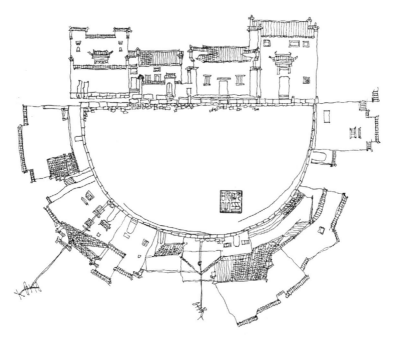

**Figure 5.2b** *Fieldwork sketch of building elevations surrounding the crescent-shaped pond in the village centre of Hongcun, 1988.*

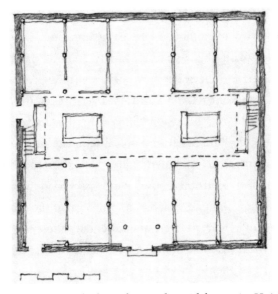

**Figure 5.3a** *The ground plan of a single void house in Huizhou, with dotted line showing the size of the void in the roof.*

had to pay for the solace of their nomadic soul, rather than for those who actually lived there – the wives, the children and the elderly.

There are four different types of houses in Huizhou, but they are essentially derived from the same courtyard pattern: the *ao*-shape (凹) is the one with shallow void at the front, surrounded by rooms on three sides and a wall on the fourth; the *kou*-shape (口) is the one with the narrow void in the middle, surrounded by rooms on four sides; the H-shape is the one with two shallow voids at both the front and the rear; and the *ri*-shape (日) is the combination of *ao* and *kou*, with a shallow void at the front and a narrow void in the middle (Figure 5.4). The choice of a particular type was simply determined by the actual sizes of the site and the family. One feature, which was not seen elsewhere, was common among all the Huizhou houses: a dedicated ancestral hall was placed on the upper level right above a

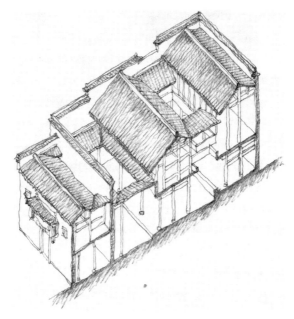

**Figure 5.3b** *A cutaway bird's eye view of a three-void Huizhou house.*

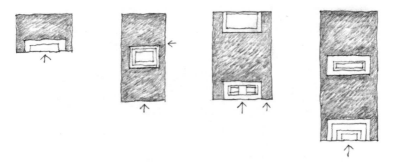

**Figure 5.4** *Diagrams showing the four types of Huizhou courtyard.*

common activity hall on the ground. Centred about this ancestral hall – *mingjian* 明间, provision for day-to-day living took the form of a lean, homogenous, and almost mathematical, division of gridded space with no recognizable distinctions of activities and social hierarchy in the family.

Gardens were either non-existent or trivial – a small fishpond in the skywell, and occasionally a makeshift vegetable patch in the rear yard. This was nothing like the convivial Chinese life as seen in a Han brick relief, nor the wise literati official's garden oasis amidst the buzz of street life depicted in Tang poems and Song paintings. A striking and yet eerie resemblance of a Huizhou house plan is that of a Mies van der Rohe's sleek glass and steel house in the twentieth century: there is a complete lack of any corporeal warmth and traces of messy daily life (Figure 5.5). Apart from the purpose-built ancestral clan halls, more monumental and extravagant in scale, a Huizhou house itself was more a shrine built for the family ancestor, but not so much for the living souls.

A hardworking travelling merchant from Huizhou would start his apprenticeship at an early age, as early as twelve or thirteen. By the time he reached the age of marriage, he was obligated to return to Huizhou to wed the bride chosen by his parents. Huizhou sons married

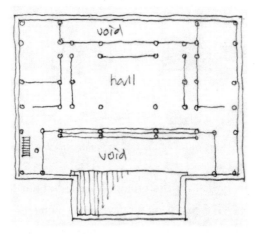

**Figure 5.5a** *Diagram of the upper floor of a Huizhou courtyard, showing the homogenous divisions of rooms surrounding a large ancestry hall (with ground floor hall for daily activities half of its size).*

early – usually at about sixteen (and just over fourteen for girls). It was
not unusual for the young merchant to leave home shortly after the
wedding to resume his travelling business in the major metropolis
centres, such as Hangzhou and Yangzhou. Stories of this kind were
widely circulated in popular novels and recorded in local village
gazettes. Only two months into their honeymoon, a stern father Pan
scoffed at his son Pan Jia: 'You two indulge in love, and face each other
day in and day out. Would you rather waste the rest of your life in this
way? Why can't you venture out to do business?' Pan Jia felt helpless,
and spoke to wife Di Zhu. The newlyweds spent a sleepless night
crying to each other. But father Pan still forced the son to leave home
on the following day.[4] Three to four years was the interval for these
Huizhou merchants to visit their wives, children and, of more
importance, to perform their filial duties to their elderly parents and
family ancestors. The children and the wife, needless to say, spent most
of the time of a twenty- to thirty-year period without the presence of

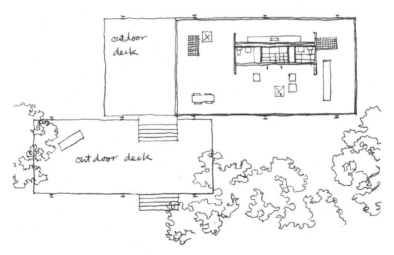

**Figure 5.5b** *Diagram of Farnsworth House – a weekend retreat for a
medical doctor, by Mies van der Rohe, designed and built between 1945 and
1951.*

the father and the husband at home. A Western traveller in the early nineteenth-century witnessed a rather peculiar and non-sentimental return of a travelling tea merchant to his home in Huizhou:

> After traveling 40 li, we arrived at the dwelling of my fellow-traveller. He had been nearly two years away, and I was curious to see, under such circumstances, what sort of reception a Chinese father of a family would meet with on his return home; on arriving at the village, one or two persons recognized him, but without stopping to converse, he passed on to his own dwelling. Entering this, he found his younger brother, who had been left in temporary charge of his abode, and to whom was entrusted the out-door work connected to this little farm, sitting in the front room, engaged in shelling some beans. This man, on recognizing his brother, merely gave him a nod, after which he rose up, cleared away the beans, and proceeded to sweep the floor, which much needed it. The wife then came in, and without any salutation proceeded to wipe the table, and spread the tea-cups. The daughter, a young woman of eighteen, was equally indifferent; and both she and her mother seemed only anxious to know what fine things he had brought with him. His baggage not having arrived, they were obliged to wait for the gratification of their curiosity.[5]

The merchant obviously did not expect a warm and sentimental reception after two years of absence; neither did the wife and the daughter wish to show any emotion. There seemed to be mutual understanding of this situation that looked puzzling to the Western traveller. But the Western traveller should soon puzzle it out: the travelling merchant would have taken a second wife in Yangzhou; he would have, if his amassed fortune allowed, built a lavish courtyard house with a pleasure garden attached to it. Such a scenario could well be an ideal escapist haven for the travelling merchant, and maybe for the wife too: the kind of animosity between husband and wife in a traditional Chinese marriage could never be quite resolved under the normal circumstance when the husband actually lived at home.

# Women in Chinese marriage and household

Whether in the Ming Huizhou or anywhere else, prior to or after this time, the wife was chosen by the son's parents, often with the help of a matchmaker, according to the equal status of the families. The Chinese expression for this – *mendang hudui* 门当户对 – is an architectural metaphor: *mendang* were the pair of carved stone blades placed at the two ends of the front gate threshold; *hudui* were the round or hexagon wood plugs projecting out from the front door lintel. The shapes of *mendang*, drum or lion like, and the number of pairs of *hudui*, indicated, based on sumptuary law, the official rank of the family. But this was only on the surface; many of the marriages were more for economic benefit than that for social rank. A woman from a family of proper status, therefore, must be married into another equal household through 'open matching making and formal wedding' (*mingmei zhengqu* 明媒正娶). Naturally, there was no guarantee that a marriage of this kind would result in any genuine affection between husband and wife, for they hardly knew each other before the wedding date.

After a glorious and rowdy wedding was drawn to the end, the dust would settle, and the wife would soon be confronted with mammoth, if not impossible, tasks. Her job was to take care of the husband and the parents-in-law, and to run the household. But the wife's job was much more than taking care of the daily needs of the husband; she was entrusted with the responsibility of making sure the husband would succeed, be it the preparation for the imperial examination, the job in the office or the family business. In the case of Huizhou, like anywhere else, the career path via the imperial examination to become a mandarin was preferred. Failing that, the next choice for a young man in Huizhou was to become a travelling merchant. Any failure of the husband, not unexpectedly, was blamed on the wife. Too often, the mother-in-law, who herself was in the same position, would, almost with no exception, accuse the daughter-in-law of many inadequacies such as bringing bad omen or being too flirtatious, hence distracting the husband from concentrating on his pursuits. The wife, besides fulfilling her duty to produce the male heirs for the family, had to make every attempt to encourage the husband to abstain from excessive carnal pleasures so that he would succeed in his career.

Once children were born, the relationship between husband and wife would simply become an alliance with the upbringing and the education of the children as their common mission. Any reasonably successful husband, by now, would have earned the right to take a concubine (*qie* 妾). The second wife was also called, literally, 'the second room' (*erfang* 二房). The life of a *qie* was, on the one hand, tough: she was on the open stage of a courtyard house and must obey the first wife and the elders, without enjoying much status and dignity. On the other hand, her life was simpler and could even be pleasurable: the only reason for her existence in the family was to please the husband behind the door in 'the second room'. Here then was the birth of the chain reaction series of some old Chinese sayings, which began with 'a wife is inferior to a concubine (*qi buru qie* 妻不如妾).'

A *qie* also was taken with an agreement of the first wife, and sometimes was a gift from the parents. One of the virtues of a wife, often embellished in the wishful thinking of the Chinese literati, was not only the agreement of, but also an initiative from, the first wife to find the husband a young concubine. The impoverished Qing dynasty scholar Shen Fu in his moving tribute to his beloved wife Yun, *Six Chapters of a Floating Life* (as mentioned in the previous chapter), recorded this fantasy-like scenario:[6] A relative of Shen Fu showed off his newly acquired beautiful concubine to Yun. The unguarded Yun commented in his face: 'Yes she is quite pretty, but she lacks charm.' The annoyed relative then challenged: 'If your husband ever gets a concubine, she then must be both beautiful and charming.' 'You are absolutely right!' replied Yun. She started an obsessive search, but they had no money. When Han Yuan 憨园, the daughter of a famous courtesan, appeared, she fitted both criteria. Shen Fu thought that he being a poor scholar should not even have such a dream; besides he and Yun were madly in love. Yun, however, smiled and simply said: 'I, too, like her. Leave this to me.' Following the teaching of Li Yü,[7] Yun managed privately to strike an intimate accord with Han Yuan and persuaded her to join in forming a 'sisterhood'. That Han Yuan eventually was taken away by the rich and powerful, and the event caused to a large extent Yun's death, alas, was a different story.

The reality in most cases of course would be the opposite of the exaltation of the Chinese literati, like the overt upper-class accent zealously acquired to hide one's humble upbringing. Having a *qie*, however, might not suffice for the husband, for a *qie*, quite often, was taken due to the failure of the first wife in producing a male offspring for the family. The husband and the *qie* might still be under certain pressure to fulfil their duty if a male heir was to be produced. The complexity of Chinese family life, however, did not stop here. If the husband still had much agony and frustration to be eased, it might be provided by a servant girl (*bi* 婢), who was accepted, though unspoken, by the wife and the concubine to serve this role. But for the cultivated literati, free love and understanding had to be sought beyond the house from the talented and literate singsong girls (*ji* 妓). The chain reaction series of sayings therefore continued: 'the concubine is inferior to the servant girl (*qie buru bi* 妾不如婢), but the servant girl ultimately is inferior to the singsong girl (*bi buru ji* 婢不如妓) ...'

# Behind good taste and refinement

Such, in a nutshell, was the charged theatre behind the encircling walls of a courtyard and on the public stage of the house. A travelling merchant from Huizhou and his anchored wife, in this odd and yet mutually accepted set of circumstances, both largely avoided facing life's day-to-day squabbles – a 'golden mean' in its most contorted and obscure form. The free love and decadence of the husband was not to be seen in the family house. The wife, though still the victim of a loveless life, had in a tragic way her anguish lessened by not having to put up with the husband's concubine and the servant girl at home. The house, as a consequence, was streamlined and refined to serve primarily the dead – ancestor commemoration. Filial duties were a matter of monumentalizing the house: the accommodation of the parents, wife and children on the other hand catered only to their subsistence, not the pleasures of day-to-day living.

But the Yangzhou garden house built by the Huizhou merchant in late Ming or Qing times, which may still stand to this date, was the recurrent juxtaposition of the Confucian world of courtyard and pleasure garden. Nonetheless, it would be vulgar in taste if compared to the house in Huizhou, which the same merchant built for his family. From the Ming through to the Qing, some of the wealthiest and the most prominent salt merchants in the Yangzhou[8] town came from Huizhou. For generations, the complex psychology of these travelling merchants – described as 'left Confucian and right business' (*zuo ru you gu* 左儒右贾, against the age-old doctrine of 'right Confucian and left business') – had meant that they used their colossal means to do essentially a few things that appeared to be contradictory to each other: supporting culture, and pleasing the emperor whilst bribing the officials. Apart from their generous patronage of culture, and despite their innate frugal character, they splashed lavishly on the two particular weaknesses that they were widely associated with – that is, 'black gauze cap' (*wusha mao* 乌纱帽, the metaphor for one's official position) and 'embroidered red shoes' (*hongxiu xie* 红绣鞋, the symbol of woman). Both, on the surface, were out of necessity: the first was spent on official and court protection, and the latter, being travelling merchants away from home, catered to their biological needs. And they undertook both with immense prodigality, especially after the middle period of the Ming when the travelling merchants from Huizhou dominated trade in south-east China.

Wang Daokun 汪道昆 (1525–1593 CE), the Ming scholar-official of Huizhou's She county, in his anthology *Taihan ji* 太函集 recorded much of the life and business of his fellow countrymen, including the decadent behaviour of the salt merchants: bells were rung when they returned home; carriages were prepared when they went out; revelry sprung up spontaneously whenever they had a spare moment; Yangtze beauties were held in their arms; and guests partied to their hearts' content, day and night. No known extravagance and ostentation in the world would surpass this.[9] This might be true for some, or exaggeration for the most, for the travelling merchants in general were known for their sagacity. Frequenting singsong girls, for the infamously calculating Huizhou merchants and their hard-earned cash, proved to be unsustainable. A cleverer way was to find a second wife in Yangzhou. Driven by this demand, mainly coming from the travelling merchants, a local business, known derogatorily as 'Yangzhou lean horse' (杨州廋马), thrived. Willowy young girls from destitute families, often caused by malnourishment, were bought with a penny by the madams to be taught in literacy, chess, music and dancing. When ready, they were sold to the merchants at vast profits. The travelling merchants, however, looked not only for the graceful posture and porcelain complexion, but also useful skills. So in addition, accounting skills with an abacus was also part of the training, for this second wife of the travelling merchant might also help with bookkeeping.

Since the second wife acquired in Yangzhou and the first wife staying put in the Huizhou family house were unlikely to ever run into each other, the second wife was not taken as a concubine, hence both were wives (两头大). This, technically speaking, was illegal in the Ming and Qing, for the status of wife and that of concubine should not be modified or overlap. Whilst the second wife in the city enjoyed the fruits of a successful business, the life of the first wife in the Huizhou courtyard in comparison was miserable. In the early days of the husband's sojourn in the city, funds had to be accumulated for business. This would include the dowry of the wife and her jewellery being pawned. Before the husband was able to send back home the business profits (if he was lucky enough to succeed), the wife fed the family through her embroidery work and tea leaf picking. There was no guarantee that the enormous sacrifice of this kind would pay off. The story of 'time recording pearl' (记岁珠) tells of the tragic tale of a Huizhou wife. Only one month after the wedding, the husband left his wife for business in the city. The wife exchanged her embroidery for food. Each year she bought a pearl out of her savings. She strung them together with a colourful silk string to mark the passing of time. When the husband finally came home, the wife had already passed away three years earlier. The husband opened her jewel case – there were twenty pearls on the string![10]

If the travelling merchants were shrewd in spending their coinage on 'embroidered red shoes', they did not hesitate when it came to receiving royal visits. Legend has it that in the Qianlong period (1735–1796 CE), in one of the emperor's numerous expeditions to the south, the monarch, though he enjoyed the extravagant garden Dahong Yuan 大虹园 (known now as Shou Xihu 瘦西湖) that the Huizhou salt merchants built for his amusement, was a little disappointed by its lack of a white Tibetan pagoda. Hearing this, the salt merchant Jiang Chun 江春 secretly bribed an official in the emperor's entourage to draw a pagoda because the merchant never saw one in his life. Jiang Chun and his fellow salt merchants then organized to have a white pagoda erected overnight. Quite expectedly, the emperor, when seeing this on the second day, was delightfully surprised, hence famously remarked: 'What greatness is the mammon capacity of the salt merchants!'[11] These house gardens, especially those built in the Qing to receive the emperor's expeditions, were more ostentatious in taste. In contrast to the 'black, white and grey' palette seen in their home region Huizhou, and also in Suzhou, the salt merchants pursued more gilding and novelty, and in later periods, even exotic influences as farfetched as what appeared to be the Baroque.

A Huizhou house, on the contrary, was renowned for its good taste in refinement and stark austerity, which, eerily reminiscent of the modern belief, was to uphold the image of the morally good. Not only was the pleasure garden nowhere to be seen, there was no hall for sitting and entertaining guests, no subordinate hall on the opposite side for the servants (*daozuo* 倒座), and no study, which were normally associated with the house in southern China. Behind the fortified envelope of high, white-washed, firewalls capped with black tiles, in effect tomb-like but now admired for their elegant austerity reminiscent of modern aesthetics (Figure 5.6), there was a collection of fine paintings, calligraphy, and Ming furniture. The latter, incidentally, is known to a modern connoisseur for its extraordinarily refined and sleek structure (Figure 5.7). Much of the mid-century Scandinavian furniture making, and that of the Danes in particular, sought inspiration from this Chinese era, for one is inclined to assume that Ming chairs and tables are the miniatures of the 'true to structure' timber building frames within the masonry building perimeters.

Amongst the things of austere taste in the house, the wood work, indeed, was paramount: rarely ornate and usually without any extraneous colour and paint, the finely carved timber panels, the window shutters, the balustrades, and the beams and columns were only oiled and allowed to weather naturally. An outstanding feature is the subtly arched 'crescent moon beam' (*yueliang* 月梁), which is interlocked with the columns and the intricate eaves brackets, which,

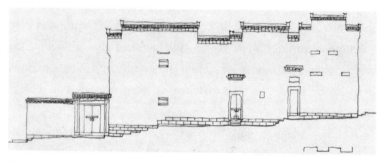

**Figure 5.6** *East elevation of house Jiushi Tongtang in the village of Zhanqi in Huizhou.*

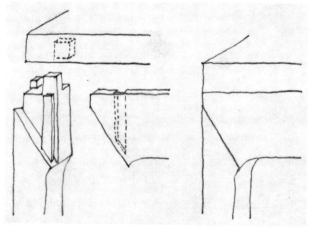

**Figure 5.7a** *A Ming table top and leg joint detail.*

up until the Ming dynasty, served to carry the roof load (Figure 5.8). But the eaves brackets in the following Qing dynasty were more ornamental. Only two examples of painted beams in Huizhou have been dated to the Ming dynasty, but they, though largely faded, are of a subdued colour ensemble of green, blue, white and black, with limited use of red. Ming sumptuary laws have been attributed to having brought in this accidental elegance. That in the fourteenth-century the sumptuary laws were principally concerned with the size and ornament of graves and mausoleums is startling a fact in this context. Huizhou houses might well be the surrogate tombs, and they certainly were beyond the bounds of these laws in the tomb category.

The refinement and austerity of Huizhou courtyards were anything but accidental. The merchant class, in China's social hierarchy, and in

**Figure 5.7b** *Horseshoe-shaped back armchair.*

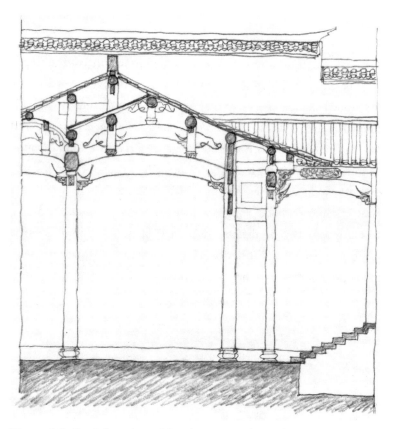

**Figure 5.8** *Partial section of Dunhe ancestral temple in the village of Zhanqi in Huizhou, showing the use of 'crescent moon beam'.*

Ming sumptuary laws, was the lowest of all classes. The ancient legacy, established before Confucius' time by the Chancellor of the State of Qi, Guan Zhong 管仲, set a clear pecking order of four major classes: scholar-gentry, farmer, artisan and merchant (*shi nong gong shang* 士农工商). The reasoning, consistent in the pre-modern Chinese psyche, was simple; the livelihood and the usefulness of the merchant relied on the production of others. The number of merchants in society must be limited to prevent society from collapsing.

Merchandising, though not forbidden, was never encouraged. In the preceding Mongol Yuan dynasty, the privileged merchant class consisted mainly of the Yuan aristocracy and allied foreigners. The first Ming emperor Zhu Yuanzhang, given his humble peasantry background, was known for his belief in frugality and its associated morality. The inaugural emperor was serious about restoring the ancient ideal of social stratification from Chancellor Guan Zhong. Like many of the previous founding monarchs, Zhu Yuanzhang in the early days of the Ming, was particularly zealous about issuing 'the luxury ban' (禁奢令). The merchants, despite their wealth, were forbidden to use gold utensils and wear silk, though such bans, including free trade of salt and tea, and foreign trade, were loosened after the middle of the Ming dynasty. The worldly success of the Huizhou merchant was no substitute for his desire to rise to the gentry, which could only be achieved through the imperial examination. The profitable trade of Huizhou merchants lasted for three to four hundred years, but the success rate of the imperial examination in the region, alas, was not high enough to be noticed. Magnificent ancestral halls and those rich merchants who built them were recorded in local county gazetteers, though not their worldly success and decadent life lived elsewhere. The desperate sojourners would go so far as to purchase in one's home county, the titles that were bestowed only on those who successfully passed the imperial examination.

Their particular weakness in 'black gauze cap' was therefore rooted more deeply than purchasing a good name for business enhancement through their art patronage and general charitable deeds, which also included printing books, funding schools and the local medical profession. 'Returning to Confucian' (归儒) was a perpetually cemented yearning in their psychological substructure. To progress was to become a scholar-official; the alternative was to turn into a travelling merchant. On reflection in their old age, one merchant, though he had reached the point of having the capacity of doing whatever he liked with his wealth, was still embarrassed by his merchant status. Some merchants even took the trouble in their retirement to supervise their posterity to study Confucian classics, for only 'poetry and book' could glorify the family name. We have learned, he who became well versed in 'poetry and book' and succeeded in the imperial examination would land himself an official position. The alternative was to display the cultivated tastes of a scholar-official.

The desire of the travelling merchants to prove their supreme cultural taste had side benefits. While 'attempting to secure an audience from the son of Heaven in the upper echelon' (上交天子), the Huizhou merchants in Yangzhou and other major centres at the same time also made acquaintances with the learned and the artistic. They acquired with keenness, antiques, paintings and calligraphies and they built 'courtyards of books' (elegant garden houses) to provide residences for writers and artists. Ma Yueguan 马曰琯 (1688–1755 CE), one of the well-known salt patrons of the two Ma brothers, built the illustrious 'Minor Exquisite Mountain Residence' (小玲珑山馆), which was anything but minor. It was an artist studio, library, gallery and, above all, a garden house for 'elegant gatherings' (雅集) of the literati, the artistic and the bohemian. One of the 'Eight Eccentrics of Yangzhou' (扬州八怪) literati painter Li E 历鄂 (1692–1752 CE), when undistinguished and destitute, was taken up by the Ma brothers and provided with not only lodging, but also servant girls. Even a shrine for the artist was erected in the Ma family temple after his death. The Ma brothers contributed more than 700 volumes of rare books to the emperor's cache of lost classics in 1773. The family also ran a printing shop to reissue classics as well as publishing contemporary authors.

By the end of the Ming dynasty, generations of patronage from the merchant sojourners had cultivated even a school of painting – the

Xin'an School (*Xin'an huapai* 新安画派), named after the ancient designation of Huizhou, and the major artery of the Xin'an River that runs, from its headstream at the foot of Yellow Mountain (Huangshan 黄山), to the major metropolis Hangzhou at its lower reach. This particular genre, along with wood block printing and wood carving is known also for its austerity: the painting, contrary to any superfluity often backed by wealth, is excessively lean in the ways in which the tectonics of the mountain are structured, and so are the ink strokes used to outline them. Opposite to a rich colour palette and warmly saturated, voluptuous brush strokes that are typically associated with art patronized by the nouveau riche, the Xin'an painting is regarded as 'dry, light, remote and cold' (*ku dan you leng* 枯淡幽冷), an expression coined to describe the art of a Daoist ascetic rather than a worldly Confucian, let alone a decadent merchant. There certainly was the expectation of the painters to be perceived as the wholeness of both their *persona poetica* and their *persona pratica*. As for the merchant, the purpose was to have this supreme cultural taste immortalized in art and furniture, and of more monumental effectiveness, in the house that he built to enshrine, in addition to his Confucian filial duty, this ensemble of elegance.

The travelling merchant evidently succeeded in his ambitious gamble: the men of Xin'an since late Ming had been widely praised as 'the ones who have an innate affinity with artistic elegance and good taste' (*xin'an ren jinya* 新安人近雅). Good taste for austere elegance had always been a hallmark that distinguished the Chinese gentry from the rest of society. The great Song dynasty poet and calligrapher Su Dongpo once famously declared: 'Rather eat food without meat, than live in a place without bamboo. Without meat, you may become thin; but without bamboo, you will become vulgar. A thin man can still get fat; a vulgar man cannot be cured. 宁可食无肉. 不可居无竹. 无肉令人瘦. 无竹令人俗. 人瘦尚可肥. 人俗不可医. '[12] Su Dongpo, of course, had simply continued the long-held Chinese literary symbolism of bamboo, which, as we have learned earlier, was the favourite plant of the Tang poet Bai Juyi. If both the manner and matter of bamboo was the austere elegance par excellence, it then was no surprise that the artistic mannerism of the Xin'an School emulated that of bamboo, ranging from its drooping leaves of humility and the bent immutability of its gaunt figure in wind, which is the symbol of the grand old age of high moral order, to the actual bamboo handle of the ink brush. The supreme achievement of an artist, in the Chinese mind, was to become a bamboo before he could paint one. Differently put, the narcissist ego of the individualistic artist was hardly considered as the precursor of great art. One therefore must be as genuine as bamboo, and be true to oneself, before one can accomplish any artistic greatness.[13]

Was then the limpid elegance of a Huizhou house disingenuous given that its creator – the travelling merchant – actually lived a life of worldly blemishes elsewhere? The flamboyant Zheng Banqiao 正板桥, also belonging to the 'Eight Eccentrics of Yangzhou', though himself a beneficiary of the travelling merchants in Yangzhou, derided the not-so-ingenuous interest in the good taste of art and learning of the Huizhou merchant. A Huizhou merchant might, said Zheng Banqiao, make a cursory foray into the art of poetry, tune the rhymes here and there as if singing a folk song and come up with four lines and 28 words. The merchant would then announce to the world that he was capable of composing poems, and could write essays.[14] Zheng Banqiao's infamous price list of his own artworks, now engraved on a stone tablet as a piece of calligraphic art work itself, should be read as a satirical attack on art for investment and vanity – a complex milieu of prosperous commerce and art patronage caused largely by this unique group of travelling merchants from Huizhou.[15]

Such would be detested by any genuine scholar-official in the past. If the same moral standard were to be applied to the modern elegance of austerity, the sleek glass and steel pavilion houses designed by Mies van der Rohe and other like-minded modern luminaries would be just as phoney, for they are usually holiday houses in the wilderness so that the perfection of austerity can never be spoiled by the sordidness of day-to-day living. Austerity, in this instance, within and beyond a Huizhou house, is aesthetics rather than morality driven: the look of 'poverty' is realized with astronomical cost in craftsmanship in perfecting the shipshape finish of its construction and, the mute and yet luxurious material of marble, travertine, leather, chromium-plated steel posts, rare wood panelling and large and full floor-to-ceiling height glass panes. What the Huizhou house and a modern Miesian house share in common, is that a *persona poetica*, conceived and built into a house at a vast cost, is to deceive the owner's *persona pratica*.

# 6

# *Literary Enchantment and the Garden House*

What was the life like for a literatus or a scholar-official living in a garden house in the Yangtze region? I hope the reader was sufficiently tantalized in the earlier chapter to find out. The later Ming dynasty was an ailing empire under the threat of the aggressive nomadic Manchus from the north. For a few short months the empire was overtaken by the Li Zicheng-led peasant uprising. The political circumstances resulted in, to some extent, the Ming gentry and the merchants to indulge a more hedonistic life. The decline of the Ming began when the Prince of Yan (燕王) in Beijing conquered Nanjing and overthrew his newly enthroned nephew Emperor Jianwen in 1402. He then proclaimed himself as Emperor Yongle (1403–1424) in the Beijing palace built by the Mongol rulers. The shift of centre in polity and court administration hurt the interests of the gentry in the Yangtze region – both the established and the new, mainly from the circle of powerful eunuchs. The concentration of wealth and agricultural produce, however, remained in the south.

By 1505 when crown prince Zhu Houzhao was inaugurated as the tenth Ming Emperor Zhengde, he was fourteen years old. Despite a strict Confucian upbringing, the young emperor had little interest in ruling the empire. He could not be bothered to give morning audiences; instead he indulged himself in women, exotic animals and extravagant military expeditions. In 1519, when the philosopher general Wang Yangming 王阳明, the governor of Jiangxi, successfully crushed the Prince of Ning's rebellion, Emperor Zhengde was frustrated that the victory was not attained by troops led by the emperor himself. Hence there was a suggestion from his advisor that the prince should be released so that he could be captured again by the emperor's troops.

Incidentally, the rather erratic behaviour of the emperor was well justified by the kind of philosophy of neo-Confucianism promulgated by his philosopher general. Wang Yangming incorporated the Buddhist theory of enlightenment into Confucian learning through the unexpected path – of innate knowing of good and evil, for example. This was effectively an endorsement of intuition at the state level. Wang's thoughts, interestingly, were taken up with zeal in Japan in their dictatorial system and even by their samurai doctrine. But the Chinese gentry, especially those from the fertile land of the Yangtze region, were not to be fooled. They formed a counter milieu of self-reflection (not the first time in Chinese history as we have already seen), which on the surface may have appeared as decadent consumption of refinement and pleasure, in both manner and matter. In 1583, Jesuit Matteo Ricci (1552–1610) arrived in China and spent the remainder of his life in the country. He concluded after many years of observation and much contemplation that the Chinese empire of superior civility was ruled by philosophers: '. . . if we critically examine his actions and sayings as they are recorded in the history, we shall be forced to admit that he was the equal of the pagan philosophers and superior to most of them.'[1]

As for things of enjoyment and pleasure, the scholar gentry in late Ming produced exhaustive discourses of them. The Ming writer Wen

Zhenheng 文震亨 (1585–1645), the great grandson of the renowned painter Wen Zhengming 文徵明 (1470–1559), in 1621 (or between 1615 and 1620) wrote a book on connoisseurship, titled *Treatise on Superfluous Things* (*Changwu zhi* 长物志).[2] The 'things' ranged from teas, incense, utensils, clothing, birds, fish, calligraphy, painting, rocks, boats, carriages to verdure (including the visually and aromatically pleasing, as well as the edible), and to houses. Much of Chapter 1 and other chapters were about gardens and houses. Another Ming writer Gao Lian 高濂 (1573–1620), in his *Eight Discourses of the Art of Living* (*Zunshen bajian* 遵生八笺) in 1591, detailed the range of techniques and tips designed to cultivate mind-and-body and for daily enjoyment. At about the same time, painter and garden planner Ji Cheng 计成 (1582–1642) had his book *Craft of Gardens* (*Yuan ye* 园冶) printed in 1634. Ji Cheng advised more on the actual technicalities of garden making, but the book probably remained relatively obscure in his lifetime.[3] Objects and their consumption, however, were the vehicle for literary expression, notwithstanding the competition for social status, vanity and differentiation of taste among the well-to-do, which were in themselves a diverse group of the old and the new gentry, as well as the merchants, including those from Huizhou in particular.

## Li Yü's world

The ardent trend of 'play and admire' (*wanshang* 玩赏) among the gentry and the merchants continued well into the Qing period under the rule of the Manchus. The eccentric seventeenth-century literatus Li Yü 李渔 (1611–1680,[4] courtesy name Liweng 笠翁) was an enthusiastic follower of the late Ming trend: a versatile playwright, drama producer, essayist, erotica novelist, musician, dress designer, beauty expert, inventor, epicure, and above all, a connoisseur of pleasurable things associated with all aspects of this mortal life.[5] The writings of Li Yü present a mosaic of vivid pictures of the garden house and the life of the gentry who lived in them, especially those in the Yangtze region.

From the Tang to the Qing, the garden attached to the house had matured and become, for the scholar-official, an indispensable escapist sanctuary; for a merchant of means by the late Ming and the Qing times, it was truly a pleasure garden of ostentation. The static and enduring idea of the garden being sanctuary was not necessarily reflected by reality. Any realistic form of recluse for a salaried scholar-official or a member of the landed gentry was in reality a 'city hermit', let alone that of a merchant. Although a site amidst mountain, water and woods was the most desirable for a garden house, as advised by both Wen Zhenheng and Ji Cheng, there were sections in *Craft of Gardens* dedicated for selecting sites for gardens in the city and on the land next to, or behind, the house. A house had increasingly been referred to as garden house (*yuanzai* 園宅) since the Song dynasty.[6] Despite historical cycles of rise and decline, the fertile soils and prosperous metropolises along the lower reaches of the Yangtze River provided the ideal seats for the urban garden dwellings so they could endure for nearly a millennium. They were the further proof of the wisdom of the 'middling hermit', promulgated by the Tang poet Bai Juyi. The Ming writer and historian Wang Shizhen 王世贞 (1526–1590) in a letter to his literati friend Chen Jiru 陈继儒, uttered almost exactly the same words as Bai Juyi: 'Mountain residence is solitary, city dwelling is boisterous, but garden house strikes the golden mean.'[7]

Among the urban centres in the Yangtze region, the exquisite city of Suzhou on the south bank of the Yangtze is the place where many of the garden houses have survived to this date. Suzhou since the Tang and Song periods had been an urban centre with a high concentration of wealth, and talents who had succeeded in the imperial examination.

Ostentatious pleasure gardens of rich landowners and industrialists had always coexisted with elegant ones of the literati, especially those of the scholar-officials who dreamed of spending retirement in private joy and contemplation within the walled garden house. It is the static nature of the city morphology, along with its courtyard houses, not the change, that is striking. Frederick W. Mote has noted that a rubbing of the engraved map of Suzhou (Pingjiang *tu*) in 1229, the Southern Song period, on a stone tablet bears an urban structure which is almost identical to that of an aerial photograph of the city taken by the American Air Force in 1945. With the exception of the elimination of the walled compound of city government – the inner city, as recorded in the Ming history, the city form and its elaborate canal web remained intact after 716 years. Most of the buildings stayed in the same places and there appeared to be almost the same number of bridges.[8] This is unthinkable anywhere else in the world, for no other great cities would have endured such longevity without any major progress, or decline, as reflected in their urban structure. But it is the extraordinary stability of the Chinese *idea* of housing that was only able to cultivate a languid spirit among the well-to-do for the nuanced art and fine things to be savoured in the garden house.

Between the seventeenth and the eighteenth centuries, Suzhou, along with other urban centres in the region, such as Nanjing, Yangzhou and Hangzhou, were dissolute urban seats where the free-spirited literati and gentry thrived together with their remarkably consistent garden houses. This is not to say that no physical changes of form and matter occurred throughout Chinese history. Many gardens of the Yangtze region in the early Ming, for example, were used predominantly for growing vegetables and fruit; gardens and fine objects in late Ming, indeed, were an inseparable part of the social web of commercial circulation and consumption.[9] The persistent pursuit of the idea and the ideal of an urban sanctuary in the house garden in literature in particular, and in practice to a large extent, had nonetheless endured in the sphere of the Chinese courtyard since antiquity.

Born in Hubei province in northern China, Li Yü's family moved back to their ancestral home in Lanxi 兰溪, Zhejiang province in 1629 after the passing of his father. He spent most of his adult life in the Yangtze region at the turn of the Ming and Qing dynasties. Like most aspiring youth, the young Li Yü set out to become a scholar-official through the conventional path of imperial examination. He was successful at the age of twenty-four in getting through the first stage of the imperial examination hierarchy and to be awarded the title of *xiucai* 秀才.[10] But fate did not turn his way. Though praised by the examiner as a literary genius, he had no luck moving up the ladder in future exams. Hence he decided, with much regret and bitterness, to give up his ambition in pursuing an official position at the age of twenty-nine. By the Chinese tradition of reckoning, he was already thirty – an age when a man 'should have taken his stand' (三十而立) by Confucius' expectation. The reasons for abandoning his 'official career' (*shitu* 仕途) were complex: political uncertainty and the civil chaos at home no doubt distracted him, but having failed several times to move beyond *xiucai* proved that his innate character was not made to fit the pedantic mould of the imperial examination system.

Li Yü was destined to live a literary life without the regular salary of a scholar-official – he, in other words, had no prospect of enjoying the life of a 'middling hermit' that was much lauded by Bai Juyi, and much desired by generations of aspiring literati. Although he always managed to spend more than he earned, and was close to destitution in his old age, Li Yü by any account lived a marvellously good life: prolific in literary accomplishments, he was a celebrity in his heyday, and was known even to the illiterate; he also appeared to have lived a happy family life, and was always accompanied by a few beautiful singsong concubines on long road shows of his many drama productions. Curiously, still (and indeed to his gratitude), his wife managed not to take a dislike to his first concubine – a young widow that Li Yü acquired as his concubine in 1645.[11]

Li Yü also built a few garden houses in various places where he sojourned, such as, Mount Yi Villa (*yishan bieye* 伊山别业) in his hometown of Lanxi, where at the foot of Yi Mountain he was able to put in practice his garden house connoisseurship. Mount Yi Villa was meant to be a modest dwelling, and Li Yü once expressed in a poem the regret of not being able to build a humble house due to the lack of funds, titled 'Failed Plan for Mount Yi Villa'.[12] His other writings prove that Mount Yi Villa was eventually built; the period when he lived in it was a sheer bliss, so much so that he was devastated when he was forced to sell this property. In an essay titled 'A Deed of Sale for My Hill' (*maishan quan* 卖山券), he went so far as to dare the future owner's chance of imprinting his name on the estate: 'I have received from you the string of copper coins in payment for the physical substance of the hill, its rocks and trees. But you will have to wait before you can obtain the spirit of the place and change its name.'[13] This may seem desperate and even a little unconventional, but this attitude is entirely consistent with the Chinese belief that the literary meaning given to a place by its creator is always far superior than its physical form. What was this garden house like? Li Yü saw no need to describe it in his essay.

When he lived in Nanjing he was able to acquire a small garden house, which he remodelled with much loving care so that each room was given a character and a name of its own – this was the famous Mustard Seed Garden (*jiezi yuan* 芥子園), which he used to name his most popular painting instruction book series. Much of the writing on house and garden in *Leisure Marginalia* (*Xianqing ouji* 闲情偶寄)[14] comes from his own work in the Mustard Seed Garden, which prompted his friend Yu Tong to comment: 'Those who enter the

Mustard Seed Garden see things they have never seen before . . .'[15] In Hangzhou where he eventually settled in his old age, he built his last house, Ceng Garden (*ceng yuan* 层園), to enjoy the ideal of a mountain and woodland site, and possibly the prospect of West Lake. Much of his later writings on the pleasures of domestic living came directly from his practice: he for example invented, among all sorts of physical and psychological gimmicks to enable one to enhance the comfort of day-to-day living, such as the famous 'landscape window' and the 'fan-shaped window', to which I shall return later.

Li Yü should be admired for making a living and, even better, pursuing an idle life that normally was available only to those who either had inheritance, or managed, as a high-ranking official, to amass wealth through corruption and robbing the poor. A glimpse of Li Yü's way of life and livelihood can be gained from the way in which his unconventional modus operandi was detested by his scholar-official contemporaries. Dong Han 董含, while he could hardly hide some degree of envy, once lashed out:

Li Yü was mean, filthy, and dishonourable. He was obsequious and skilful in anticipating and meeting people's wishes. And he frequently had three or four country whores with him. Whenever he met young masters from noble or wealthy families, he would ask his girls to sing for them behind a screen or to drink with them. For the gain of fabulous profits, he discoursed the art of lovemaking and, completely without scruples, induced his listeners to follow his advice. His behaviour was so base that he was scorned by scholars. I met him once and have shunned him ever since.[16]

Li Yü made his living as an entertainer: he wrote brilliant dramas and travelled much with his troupe to sell the productions to his patrons of officials and nobles; one of China's most infamous pornographic novels – *The Carnal Prayer Mat* (*Roupu tuan* 肉蒲团) –

was attributed allegedly to Li Yü at the tender age of twenty-two.[17] But Li Yü, above all and in addition to his drama productions, was a gifted writer of vast accomplishments in poetry, fiction, literary criticism, and the most discerning connoisseur of the pleasures of an idle life. The culmination of Li Yü's pursuit of an idle life is the publication of *Leisure Marginalia*,[18] printed reputedly in 1671 at the age of sixty when, according to Confucius, his 'ear should have tuned'. But this book should belong to the age of seventy when, again based on the grand observations of Confucius, one should follow all the desires of one's heart without breaking any rules.[19] Li Yü surely broke some rules set by the Master, but he nonetheless maintained the robust Confucian common sense that any true believer of the Chinese way of life (regardless of whether one is of the 'Dragon breed') would have shared. Li Yü approached the golden mean of the middle from surprising and unexpected paths, like the mordant wit that seeps out from a straight-faced comedian, full of delight and good humour.

This book, consisting of 300 essays organized under eight sections, offers loose discourses on the following topics: Writing Plays (*ciqu bu* 词曲部); Putting on Plays (*yanxi bu* 演习部); Women and Beauty (*shengrong bu* 声容部); House and Garden (*jushi bu* 居室部); Furniture, China and the Like (*qiwan bu* 器玩部); Food and Drink (*yinzhuan bu* 饮馔部); Flowers and Trees (*zhongzhi bu* 种植部); and Health and Pleasure (*yiyang bu* 颐养部). On the surface, the themes appear rather hedonistic or even decadent, but Li Yü had high hopes of securing his immortality through this book. Instead of being overtly self-obsessive and merely peculiar, Li Yü's appetite for life and its pleasures is a precious combination of his intrinsic flamboyance and a robust and yet conscious common sense. The result, much to one's delight, is not a dull and didactic teaching of moderation, but a vital form of the middle at its best.

On advising the well-to-do how to enjoy life for one example, Li Yü first acknowledged that much of life's pleasures came from money, before he reminded us of the perils of having too much wealth, and the agony and burden associated with managing the surplus. But he was acutely realistic about the slim chance of the rich giving away some of their mammon to the poor. In an unexpected sharp turn, he suggested rather that the rich should stop making more at a certain point. Throughout the book, Li Yü no doubt, had qualified himself, with sufficient moral bent but without any apparent preaching, as the exemplar of living a *good* life. Confucius, I incline to think, would have liked to sit down to a pot of tea with Li Yü, though the pedantic followers of Confucianism detested his modus operandi with passion. In a preface to *Leisure Marginalia*, Li Yü's contemporary Yu Huai 余怀 mocked the orthodox Confucians belittling Li Yü as 'failing to discuss the values of state governance and, instead, indulging in trivial talks of moral corruption.' Li Yü, on the other hand, defended his paramount concern for the primacy of human dimension embedded in his small talk.[20]

## Internalized garden and the 'horizon' beyond

Although 'House and Garden' occupies only one of the eight sections of the book, all the leisurely thoughts and deeds discussed in the book began in the family and, needless to say, were enshrined in its garden house. In this particular section, as well as in the following one on 'Furniture, China and the Like', Li Yü took the trouble to give detailed advice on, to name a few, building design, its placement and orientation, and a full range of eaves, ceilings, windows, pathways, pavements, various kinds of walls, the study, plaques, rocks, furniture and china. The emphasis was discreetly placed on the garden rather than the house, for the Confucian part of the universe – the axial courtyard house next to the garden – had been well taken care of. Among all the principles, refinement and elegance were of ultra-importance. Li Yü therefore warned the rich against the perils of ostentation in the garden house design, for he must have been aware of, and no doubt had seen, some of the ghastly showy garden houses in Yangzhou built by the merchants. Lin Yutang, before he introduced the reader to Li Yü's art of living on house and interior, used the following lyrical depiction of such a garden. Against this backdrop, the advice from Li Yü on all sorts of pleasures in life may begin to imprint itself on the reader's imagination:

Inside the gate there is a footpath and the footpath must be winding. At the turning of the footpath there is an outdoor screen and the screen must be small. Behind the screen there is a terrace and the terrace must be level. On the banks of the terrace there are flowers and the flowers must be fresh. Beyond the flowers is a wall and the wall must be low. By the side of the wall, there is a pine tree and the pine tree must be old. At the foot of the pine tree there are rocks and the rocks must be quaint. Over the rocks there is a pavilion and the pavilion must be simple. Behind the pavilion are bamboos and the bamboos must be thin and sparse. At the end of the bamboos there is a house and the house must be secluded. By the side of the house there is road and the road must branch off. At the point where several roads come together there is a bridge and the bridge must be tantalizing to cross. At the end of the bridge there are trees and trees must be tall. In the shade of the trees there is grass and the grass must be green. Above the grass plot there is a ditch and the ditch must be slender. At the top of the ditch there is a spring and the spring must gurgle. Above the spring there is a hill and hill must be deep. Below the hill there is a hall and the hall must be square. At the corner of the hall there is vegetable garden and the vegetable garden must be big. In the vegetable garden there is a stork and the stork must dance. The stork announces that there is a guest and guest must not be vulgar. When the guest arrives there is wine and wine must not be declined. During the service of the wine, there is drunkenness and the drunken guest must not want to go home.[21]

Though Li Yü may appear quaint and novel in his inventions of various gimmicks to enhance the pleasures of domestic living, his garden house was not unprecedented; it was only the universal kind that the Chinese had been perfecting throughout history. Lin Yutang in adopting the above description of the Chinese garden, rather cleverly and rightly so, avoided the bird's-eye view so that he could meander in Li Yü's garden house where revealing and concealing in spatial sequence alternated. For the benefit of understanding, perhaps at the risk of being scorned by the likes of Li Yü and his kindred spirits of leaving too little for the imagination, let me resort to the bird's-eye view of the Chinese garden house for the moment.

The spatial anatomy of a Chinese garden is familiar to many in our time, perhaps because in many city centres around the world there are replicas of a Chinese garden, often as a gift of friendship from Chinese municipalities or provincial governments. Large gardens built away from the house in idyllic 'mountain-and-woods' locations outside urban centres did exist, for royal retreats and for the merchants to entertain the royal visits. They were, on occasions, even accessible to ordinary mortals.[22] Most public gardens, such as ancestral temple garden (*ciyuan* 祠园), graveyard garden (*muyuan* 墓园), temple garden (*siyuan* 寺园), whether located amidst 'mountain and woods', or within the dense city fabric, were all attached to the main courtyard complex, which also could be a guildhall (*huiguan* 会馆), or a library (*shuyuan* 书院). Even the government house (*yashu* 衙署) was sometimes built with such parasitic gardens.

Shortly after his inauguration in 1144, the governor of the city of Pingjiang (平江) (today's Suzhou) in the Southern Song dynasty, Wang Huan 王唤, managed to swiftly reconstruct the city on the ruins left by the devastating ravages that the Jing army caused in 1130. Behind the government courtyard complex of Ping Jiang Fuzhi 平江府治, Wang Huan built the vast garden Junpu 郡圃, featuring an expansive pond, with handsome halls and attractive pavilions dotted around the garden. Atop the inner-city wall on the north, the tall Qiyun Lou balcony (齐云楼) was built. This tall balcony was not built to follow the ancient tradition of erecting the *tai* 台 – a magnificent balcony building on a high plateau, for observing celestial heavens, practising divination, giving audience to foreign dignitaries, and also, of more importance, legitimizing the power of the state (Ling Tai 灵台 built by King Wen 文王 some 3,000 years ago was its prototype). The true agenda of Qiyun Lou, much the same as that of the notorious Zhanghua Tai 章华台 and Gusu Tai 姑苏台 built five centuries later by corrupted kings, was to, through the height, give climax to revelling banquets. Government gardens however followed the same pattern as that of a walled private garden, though a tall balcony building within was not necessarily an essential ingredient. A private garden as such rarely existed alone, and by itself. A cursory examination of the plan of the Bi residence in Suzhou, first built in the eighteenth century of the Qing Qianlong period by the scholar-official Bi Yuan 毕沅, shows the persistent pattern of the garden and the house indeed being together, for the garden often was companion to the house (Figure 6.1).

By now, the axial and symmetrical house of multiple courtyards is legible to us. It was the microcosm of the Confucian world of the family that repeatedly reminded us of one's proper position on earth under the watchful eye of Heaven; it was a decorum that the house

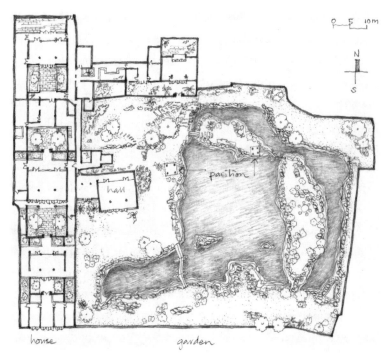

0  5  10m

N

S

house                    garden

**Figure 6.1** *Ground floor plan of house and garden, Bi residence, Suzhou.*

itself imposed on the occupier of the house. But there were discreet side doors here and there, and one could occasionally sneak out to the garden without being noticed, though the occasions and timing were determined by the very propriety of gender segregation and social hierarchy. Beyond this rather rigid structure of the courtyard house, the seemingly loose and flexible garden design, too, followed a pattern; all gardens attached to the house shared exactly the same spatial anatomy, which had been repeated over the centuries. The Chinese architect and scholar Tong Jun 童寯 once used the Chinese ideogram of the garden – 園 – to provide a crystal clear and yet quite plausible explanation of its pattern and essential elements: '口' is the enclosure of the walled compound; '土' are the plans of buildings – pavilions and halls; '口' in the middle is the pond; '亻 乂' look like rockeries, hills and verdure.[23] So, how did the garden, as much internalized as the courtyard house next to it, enable the free-spirited Chinese souls to 'expand their horizon'? The encircling wall and the walls of internal divisions are the litotes.

To experience the house garden, the bird's-eye view must now be eradicated. The art of Chinese garden, much the same as the courtyard itself, shares some essential characters with other major forms of Chinese art, including painting, calligraphy, poetry and music (though the subtlest appreciation of each demands acknowledgement of its specificity[24]). Like the garden, all of them are composed following a universal formal structure, and with a parsimonious repertoire of ingredients. In poetry, the form is highly regulated: there are fixed structures of line length (usually in three, four, five and seven characters); even in unregulated form with variable line lengths, there are specific patterns to follow; the lengths of the poem, too, usually follow a few patterns (couplets, two couplets, four couplets or multiples of four or eight) with a few exceptions; the rhythm, rhyme and tones, though more nuanced in comparison, still follow certain refined schemas and traditions. As if such formal structure does not pose nearly enough constraints, there is a limited supply of symbolic languages and their associated narratives at one's disposal: the song of the cuckoo and the traveller's homesickness; the wild geese and the absence of news from the lover afar; the east wind and spring; the west wind and the funereal feelings of autumn; mandarin ducks and love; architectural ruins and the transience of human endeavour; willow twigs and farewell; moon, wine, the abandoned woman leaning on her terraced balcony and melancholy ...[25]

In painting, the form and content are stricter: the supreme genre of 'mountain and river' (*shanshui* 山水) is a series of monotonous brushstrokes of standardized catalogue forms of trees, rocks, clouds, buildings and human figures found in painting handbooks, among them, as we recall, the popular series *Painting Catalogue of Mustard Seed Garden* published by Li Yü. When it comes to the overall artistic palette, the severest of all is calligraphy: not only the number of brushstrokes that are determined by the form of the written character, but also the sequence of brushstrokes that the calligrapher must follow, is strictly prescribed.

Without any room for invention and originality, how is the Chinese garden, like poetry, painting and calligraphy, not falling into cliché? Simon Leys, in this startling axiom, provides the pathway to the otherwise seemingly trite artistic tradition: '*By narrowing the field of its invention, an art intensifies the quality of its expression.*'[26] Such art is to be experienced – that is, to be profoundly affected bodily and mentally, and one must go beyond viewing in order to inhabit the art by *reading* it. Chinese painting (not supposed to be hung on the gallery wall), calligraphy and printed volumes of poetry are in scrolls and normally stored in cabinets. To appreciate them is to take a volume out and *read* it while unfolding and folding the scroll at the same time. The garden attached to the house, too, ought to be 'scrolled out' and at the same time 'scrolled in', so that the vignettes of the inner life in the walled garden are savoured, without the need of assistance provided by Renaissance perspectives and bird's-eye views.

To *read* such a garden, it should make perfect sense that I shall again resort to literature, given its universal recipe and the limited ingredients, the garden scenes depicted in literature can be pictured against the same garden house in Figure 6.1. This time they are the episodes from the magnificent eighteenth-century Chinese novel *Dream of the Red Chamber* (*Honglou meng* 红楼梦), by Cao Xueqin 曹雪芹. The rich and nuanced Chinese domestic life described in this book was almost entirely unfolded in the garden house, which must have been the idealized model of Li Yü's time. Incidentally, Li Yü during his sojourn in Nanjing made the acquaintance of Cao Xi曹玺, the great-grandfather of Cao Xueqin, and the superintendent of the imperial textile factory in Nanjing in 1663 and 1684.[27] Cao Xueqin must have spent his childhood and early youth in one of those large garden houses. But the family was forced to move to Beijing in his youth (at the age of fourteen by Chinese reckoning) due to political persecution by the imperial court. The unsurpassed accomplishment in the art of language and the vivid depictions of the hundreds of characters aside, *Dream of the Red Chamber* is an encyclopaedia of the *otium* of Chinese domestic life, rivalled in this respect only by Li Yü's *Leisure Marginalia*. Discussed with deep knowledge and discerning views, topics of this kind range from the garden house, food and drink, herbal medicine, textile and dress making and crafts of various kinds, through epigraphy, poetry and calligraphy to painting, which mirror chiefly what Li Yü had covered in his magnum opus. It is unknown, whether or not Cao Xueqin ever read *Leisure Marginalia*, but in *Dream of the Red Chamber*, it seemed as if Li Yü's art of living had been woven into the narratives and effortlessly staged in those garden houses.

The background of the novel are a few households under two related aristocratic families of the Ning Residence and Rong Residence. In one episode, the master of one household Jia Zheng invited some of his parasitic literary protégés (*qingke* 清客), and also his son Baoyu who was studying classics at the time, for a walk in his newly completed garden.[28] The garden, Daguan Yuan 大观园, had been prepared to receive the visit of his daughter Jia Yuanchun, who was an imperial concubine. The literati builder Shan Ziye, who was commissioned with the construction, built it according to the owners' brief but within the conventions – that is, the existing parameters of a house garden as represented by the ideogram of *yuan* 園. The sheer magnitude of Daguan Yuan, described as 'three and half *li*' in *Dream of the Red*

*Chamber,*[29] which can be easily derived as larger than ten hectares, would be completely beyond the confined sites of the surviving urban dwellings and their attached gardens in the Yangtze region. But this was not an ordinary garden house where the garden was attached to the courtyard residence. In this instance there were several exquisite courtyard clusters that were enveloped in this vast walled garden, reminiscent of those imperial gardens in northern China. All these courtyards could be readily turned into residences, which turned out to be the case later in the story. The imagined location of Daguan Yuan is open to interpretation, but it no doubt was the nostalgic vessel of Cao Xueqin's childhood and early youth. Regardless of the true location of Daguan Yuan in Cao Xueqin's mind, the size of the garden must have been the result of literary exaggeration by the author.

What then took place was a kind of competitive game where all these rather learned individuals recited classical poems, and gave them some slight twists and turns so that they could name a scene, a building, a covered walkway, water features, plants, or even a rock in the garden, thereby bestowing a meaning, which often was derived from a familiar literary narrative, and creating a spatial narrative hitherto unexpressed. The most prized rocks, we have learned, usually sourced from Lake Tai, must have been moulded by nature's hand for millions of years so that it is quaint, with features of being perforated, lean and wrinkled. It is a cosmic object in the walled garden that speaks to its communion with Heaven via the void of the courtyard. The fondness of garden rocks of the Chinese gentry began as early as in the Tang dynasty, though it became a 'stone fetish' (石癖) in the Song dynasty (see also Chapter 4). The flamboyant Mi Fu 米芾, whenever acquiring a piece of quint garden rock, would dress the rock with cloth and hat and on his knees, adopt it as his 'stone brother'; Su Dongpo (苏东坡) even founded a painting genre of 'stone and bamboo'.

The exercise is described with slight suspensions in the novel: the protégés rather deliberately started with more vulgar connotations so that the young prince Baoyu was given opportunities to boaster his learning and literary talent. But to prove himself being a strict father, Master Jia Zheng must repeatedly rebuke his son. Not that all the builder's work had been done to their satisfaction: an imitation of a rural scene, for example, was thought to be rather pretentious by Baoyu. But some subtle and clever literary naming of it would make up for its deficiencies. The naming of the garden components at this point was temporary until they were endorsed or revised by the imperial concubine when she arrived. The names were then engraved permanently in rocks and plaques hanging on the buildings in Daguan Yuan. After all these were completed, the garden was believed to have a life, and from this point onwards the garden belonged to the master's family, and in particular, the master himself – the person who had commissioned the garden. In practice, Jia Zheng, being the patriarch and the literati Confucian, paid no attention to the details of construction. The builder on the other hand had little to do with this enabling process that bestowed meanings to both the garden and its owner; the builder merely repeated, though with some of his own fancy, the century-old and universally accepted garden pattern. The garden therefore became a template, albeit standard and enclosed, for the owner to excise his literary imagination beyond any physical confinement.

The second episode from the same novel was about a particularly pleasurable thing to do in autumn when the capable granddaughter-in-law, Feng Jie, helped organize an outing in the garden for the grandmother of the Rong Residence, Lady Jia, to eat steamed crab.[30] The old lady walked across a rickety bamboo bridge to reach the pavilion; this prompted her to recall her childhood and the memory of her own garden. Later, Lady Jia and others ate crab, taking pleasure in the conviviality among the women of different generations and social ranks of this large household. They followed the proper manners for this sort of activity which dictated how one should eat crab accompanied by tea and rice wine, and how much one should eat and so on. Eating steamed crab is one of the prized culinary arts in China. Indeed, Li Yü in his *Leisure Marginalia*, concluded that the supreme delicacy is steamed crab in autumn. Like all good things in the world, Li Yü said, steamed crab is at its best when left alone: the use of ingredients will only destroy its quality, for the fresh and sweet crab meat and roe, white as jade and yellow as gold, are already second to none in colour, aroma and flavour.[31]

After enjoying the steamed crab, the grandmother was accompanied by a maid back to the house to take a siesta, while the young ones and their servants went fishing and admiring chrysanthemums. But the more literate ones – the prince Baoyu and the princesses, got together to walk to the garden hall, where the rice paper was already laid out, the ink was ground, and writing brushes were prepared, so that they could start composing poems on chrysanthemums. The poems ranged from the memory of past chrysanthemums, visiting chrysanthemums, planting chrysanthemums, arranging chrysanthemums in a vase, adorning one's hair with chrysanthemums to painting chrysanthemums, dreaming about chrysanthemums, and even appreciating withered ones and their shadows ... There seemed no limit to their literary imagination, which occurred only within the walled garden next to the courtyard house. Tong Jun thus sighed: 'After the [garden] gate is closed behind him, he wakes up from a pleasant dream.'[32]

But the literary imagination in the garden house went deeper than epicurean pleasures and admiring flowers on an outing day. After returning to the imperial court, while editing the poems and inscriptions bestowed on Daguan Yuan, the scenes of the garden sprang to the mind of the imperial concubine Jia Yuanchun: this magnificent garden house would need to be locked up after her royal visit. It would be a great pity to leave it desolate, thought Yuanchun. Why not let her gifted poet sisters live in the courtyards in this garden so that the willows and flowers would be animated by the occupation of these beauties. The imperial concubine then decided to send a royal decree to the family, which even allowed a prince – Baoyu, to live in one of the courtyards in the garden so that he could concentrate on his learning. Yuanchun, alas, neglected that the biggest distraction in Baoyu's life was his beautiful female cousins. To allow Baoyu to live among them was to surround a bee with flowers.

The choices of the courtyards selected by the princesses and Baoyu, which were only briefly mentioned in the book,[33] were laden with complex literary meanings. Though subtle and seamlessly woven into the narratives, the characters of each courtyard matched that of the occupiers. The worldly and lady-like Baochai was given the symmetrical Hengwu Yuan 蘅芜院, which was filled with pungent fragrance of *jinguihua* 金桂花 (*Osmanthus fragrans*); widowed Li Wan preferred the rustic and austere Daoxiang Cun 稻香村, where, Master Jia Zheng felt, 'all the ostentation had been completely washed away.' Baoyu wanted to be close to Daiyu and lived in the small Yihong Yuan 怡红院, which was featured by *haitang* 海棠 (begonias, or known as Chinese flowering crab apple) – a 'girl flower' that was thought to have come from the 'kingdom of women', joked his father Master Jia Zheng. Indeed, Li Yü in his *Leisure Marginalia* already compared the spring *haitang* to a married woman of voluptuous appeal, and the autumn *haitang* as a willowy virgin beauty.[34] It therefore was very fitting for the romantic prince Baoyu to be housed in this courtyard. Daiyu had chosen Xiaoxiang Guan 潇湘馆 for she preferred the serenity of the winding gallery corridor hidden behind the sparse bamboos.

Master Jia Zheng, on his first inspection of the newly built Daguan Yuan, was impressed with this particular courtyard: the building in the front yard was discreetly concealed by the bamboos; the backyard was planted with banana leaves; a spring bubbled in from a crack in the backyard wall and wound its way around the bamboos down to the front yard. Though unsaid in the book, Jia Zheng must have imagined a picture of bamboos and the moon framed by the window: 'If I could sit by the window to read on a moon lit night, I would not have wasted my life in this world,' sighed the master. But this was only a momentary wishful escape for Jia Zhen from his burden of a scholar-official in the Confucian world. This bamboo courtyard was made for Daiyu's aloof character and her ethereal beauty. Li Yü, echoing no doubt Bai Juyi and Su Dongpo, had continued the centuries-long literary tradition of singing bamboos' praises: 'Bamboos can in the blink of an eye turn the house of a vulgar mortal into that of a superior gentleman ([竹] 能令俗人之舍，不转盼而成高士之庐).'[35]

Daiyu's unwillingness to succumb to the general miscellany of life, and her fate of losing the love of her life, Baoyu, to the wordily Baochai, and dying prematurely in sickness was foreshadowed in the allegorical meaning of the bamboo courtyard. Daiyu's transcendental temperament was penetratingly painted in one of the memorable scenes in *Dream of the Red Chamber*: reading under a peach-blossom tree one morning, a shower of flower petals fell on Baoyu as a gust of wind passed. Worried that the petals might become soiled, Baoyu brushed those that had fallen on his clothes into the garden pond. While he was trying to find a way to gather those on the ground, here came Daiyu, with a flower shovel on her shoulder, a fine silk bag and a small broom in her hand, to see to the fallen flowers. But to Baoyu's surprise, Daiyu did not want to throw the petals into the pond; although the water may look clean in the walled oasis of Daguan Yuan, it would stink as it ran out to the city. She could not bear the thought that the petals would be spoiled and rot in this way. Instead, Daiyu had already prepared a flower tomb in the garden, so the fallen petals would dissolve in the earth, which to her was the cleanest treatment that flowers deserved.[36]

Bamboos on the other hand, like the slice of Heaven framed by the courtyard, became the subject of literary analogies only when they were viewed through the picture window. Li Yü, incidentally, claimed the picture window as his invention. He first fantasized fan-shaped windows for pleasure houseboats. Though he could not afford to build one, he had much joy in picturing in his mind's eye not only the beautiful moving sceneries on the banks while sitting in the boat, but also glimpses of the convivial drinking revels of singsong girls and flamboyant scholars revealed to the voyeuristic spectators on the banks. It was the latter, not the view from the boat, I am inclined to believe, that was close to Li Yü's heart. What the fan-shaped window frame did was to *internalize* an image so that its meaning, rather than the image per se, became the subject of literary imagination, which too often was a familiar connotation refreshed anew with a sharp turn. When Li Yü 'discovered' the landscape window, it was consistent with the idea of 'borrowing a view' which he believed was the most intriguing secret of creating a window. While staring at a miniature hill landscape through his studio window, Li Yü thought why not have the window mounted with cut pieces of paper around the window frame. In this way, the window was no longer a window, but a picture; the hill was no longer a hill, but a hill in a painting, except that this painting was animated by seasonal changes. This, Li Yü said, was a 'mounted picture window' (尺幅窗), as well as an 'accidental painting' (无心画).[37]

This was not a Palladian window of the Renaissance, which projected out like an optical apparatus. Indeed the Renaissance was the time when the rules of perspective were rediscovered by the great master Brunelleschi, and optical lenses and glass panes were used to depict illusions of vista and depth on a two-dimensional canvas. Man was no longer content to stay put in the house, for he found the vista and horizon afar too irresistible, and it could not possibly be internalized. But Li Yü's 'mounted picture window' was to use the picture mounting to tame the view, like a wild beast, so that nature could be brought in and domesticated. The window of *internalization* is in the same spirit of the confinement of a courtyard. To prove this point, let us look at another seemingly idiosyncratic invention of Li Yü's, which, in essence, was a miniature courtyard.

The Chinese alcove bed was like an enclosed room within a large room. Li Yü, following his hopelessly romantic temperament, must give it a twist. In addition to the shelves and drawers for all sorts of useful things, such as shoes, linens and books, Li Yü added a small hidden shelf to hold flowers and perfumed dried fruit. His theory was this: the fragrance of flowers was enjoyed during the day in the writing studio, but it too should be enjoyed at night for the fragrance would linger not only around one's mouth and nose, it also went into one's dreams. In order to create the illusion of sleeping under a flower tree, the flower shelf must be wrapped by embroidered silk, so it may look like either an irregular garden rock, or colourful clouds. Even if there were no flowers in the season, incense or quince, for example, should suffice. With this 'flower enabled bed' (床令生花), 'my body is no longer a body, but a butterfly flitting about and sleeping and eating among flowers, and the man is no longer a man but a fairy, walking about and sitting and lying in a paradise. I have thus once in my sleep felt in a half-awake state the fragrance of plum flowers so that my throat and teeth and cheeks were permeated with this subtle fragrance, as if it came out from my chest. And I felt my body so light that I almost thought I was not living in a human world. After waking up I told my wife, "Who are we to enjoy this happiness? Are we not thus 'curtailing' the entire lot of happiness allowed to us?"'[38]

Li Yü was not original in creating atmospheric ambience with scent. As early as in the Tang dynasty, the emperors, the aristocrats and the well-to-do scholar-officials used aloeswood and sandalwood for the interior that would emit pleasant aromas; incense and aromatics were also burned to the same effect.[39] This ecstatic paradisal dream of Li Yü's, however, was only possible where neither the mortal world nor the flowers could be seen. That the efficacy of the flower bed as an escapist haven lay precisely in its courtyard-like internalization is nothing but a sweet irony. Any aesthetic or pictorial appreciation (whether in Renaissance perspective or bird's-eye view) of the Chinese garden, which was as enclosed and internalized as the courtyard house next to it or contained within, always falls short, for the Chinese garden house, essentially, is more *visceral* (often in literary manners) than *visual*.

# Courtyard and decorum

But the pleasures of the garden should never surpass the demands made on the courtyard by the Confucian world; they were under the watchful eye of the grand matriarch Lady Jia – the living symbol of the Confucian world of hierarchy. Master Jia Zheng and wife Lady Wang were, in theory, the pinnacle of the family pecking order. This perhaps is because that Jia Zheng, being diligent and learned, managed to be prompted to a higher official position despite that he, unlike his elder brother Jia She, only inherited a minor position to start with. But while the grand matriarch was still alive, they were obliged to take an ancillary position in the household. Lady Jia, on the surface, was a bit of a hedonist and a connoisseur par excellence of the art of living. She did not stake her salvation on a Buddhist reincarnation, or any chance of ascending to Heaven; indeed she took a great deal of joy in both the corporeal and the literary garden life. That ranged from all sorts of seasonal and ceremonial banquets to highbrow cultural entertainments, including 'watching' opera (the Chinese seem to place the same emphasis on both acting and music), reciting poems, looking at paintings, listening to music, admiring the moon and snow, sampling fine teas and tasting wines, figuring out riddles, making jokes, taking outings in gardens and magnificent scenery, commenting on interior furniture and china, and even dress design and fashion. For all these pleasurable activities, she took the lead. On a day of clear night sky and full moon, Lady Jia suggested that such a beautiful night should not go past without music. But she ordered only remote flute sound, for too much music would dilute this exquisite ambience. The melody, Lady Jia insisted, must be slow; only in this way, could the moon be bright and the breeze gentle, and the sky remote and the earth pure; all the worldly frustrations were then eased, and worries forgotten.[40] Lady Jia's commanding authority, however, was the most potent when it came to the courtyard. The courtyards in Daguan Yuan, for example, were chosen by the princesses and Baoyu, but the choices must be endorsed by the grand matriarch. Her position, not surprisingly, was at the outset cemented in a taken-for-granted, and yet, legible manner in the courtyard hierarchy.

After the death of her mother, Daiyu went to live with the grandmother Lady Jia in the Rong Residence. Though Daiyu had not been to this place, when reaching the inner court, given its sumptuous five-bay length and the galleries running to connect to the side buildings, it was not difficult for Daiyu to immediately identify the main hall that was occupied by the paterfamilias Jia Zheng and his wife. But the wife Lady Wang normally did not spend her leisure hours in the main hall. Instead she used the subordinate side rooms on the east. This was a delicate and yet deliberate gesture: the grand matriarch Lady Jia had her courtyards on the west, in parallel to that of the son Jia Zheng and Lady Wang's. Although the two courtyard complexes had their longitudinal axes in parallel, Lady Jia occupied the main hall on the axis, not the side rooms. On her arrival, Daiyu was observant of all the novel things that she had never seen in her life, but her curiosity was not aroused by this peculiar positioning of Master Jia Zheng and Lady Wang in relation to the grand matriarch Lady Jia. It seems that the filial piety shown by the son Jia Zheng and the unquestioned authority of the grand matriarch in the Confucian cosmos was meant to be enacted only through the occupation of the courtyard house.[41]

The overall progression of the courts, the hall and the inner rooms in a Chinese courtyard had remained unchanged since Confucius made the conscious and analogous use of their original meanings. This, in *Dream of the Red Chamber*, was most vividly animated, again, through Daiyu's arrival at the courtyard complex. Sitting in her sedan chair, Daiyu saw the buzz and prosperity of the big metropolis. Suddenly on the north side of the street, an imposing three-bay gate, guarded by a pair of gigantic stone lions, was before her. There were more than a score of well-dressed male servants lounging about at the entrance, but only one of the side doors was open. A plaque engraved with 'The Emperor-Endorsed Residence of Ning' told Daiyu that she was now very close to her grandparents' place. Proceeding a little further to the west, Daiyu reached the same imposing entrance of the Rong residence. Her sedan chair was carried in through the side door at the western corner and proceed to a distance of an 'arrow's flight'. The bearers now stopped and withdrew. While maidservants alighted from their carriages to come to Daiyu, four well-dressed teenage boys took over her sedan chair. The maidservants followed the sedan on foot until they reached the next entrance – the gate of hanging flowers (垂花门), which was the threshold of the main inner court.[42] Now the young boy bearers paused and withdrew.

Daiyu stepped out, holding the hand of her maidservant, walked across this threshold to the inner court. Fronted by the main hall and its gallery verandas on both sides, they walked around the framed marble screen and the three-bay hall to reach the next court of the main chamber. Adorned with splendidly painted beams and ceilings, there were five bays in this hall. On the verandas of the side chambers there were hanging cages of parrots, thrushes and other pet birds. Greeted by a few colourfully dressed young maids sitting on the chamber platform, Daiyu was about to meet her grandma Lady Jia for the first time. But Daiyu did not really feel at home until she was led into her aunt Lady Wang's most inner chamber, and was repeatedly encouraged to sit on the *kang* 炕 bed next to her:

> Seeing her niece enter, she [Lady Wang] motioned her to sit opposite her on the *kang*, but Daiyu felt sure that this must be her uncle Zheng's place. So, having observed a row of three chairs near the *kang* with covers of flower-sprigged brocade which looked as though they were in fairly constant use, she sat upon one of those instead. Only after much further pressing from her aunt would she get up on the *kang*, and even then she would only sit beside her and not in the position of honour opposite.[43]

While in the courtyard house, Daiyu in this instance, like any well brought up young lady in an aristocratic family, behaved with strict Confucian propriety. But in the garden, as seen from the above glimpses, not only her elusive temperament but also her literary personality was fully let out. The garden therefore was the spiritual (and at times visceral, especially for the less literate) *interior* against the formal and social *exterior* of the courtyard house. What lay in *the middle* was their harmonious coexistence, characterizing the Chinese world.

# 7

# *The Golden Mean Finely Tuned*

The Manchu rule of China made no difference to this consistent Chinese way of living in the courtyard. Even more so than the Mongol rulers, the Manchu not only left the landed gentry alone, they managed to incorporate them into their administration to help run the new empire. Prior to the fall of the Ming and even in the early days of the Qing, clan pride and national sentiment confronted the foreign reign: not only the last Ming emperor who hanged himself on the hill behind the imperial palace, but also officials in high positions and imperial concubines, as well as scholars and land owners, committed suicide in large numbers. It is still a puzzling fact that a nomadic people of just more than a million in population, and with rudimentary administration, were able to take over the Ming empire without much fuss. The explanation certainly should not come down to the single historical incident, or rather the popular belief: that general Wu Sangui was no longer loyal to the Ming court and had already intended to defect to the peasant rebel Li Zicheng. But on hearing that his beloved concubine Chen Yuanyuan was abducted by Li Zicheng, the outraged general opened the gates of the Great Wall at Shanhai Pass to let in the Manchu army. Many of the gentry class, in fact, had for quite some time given up hope in the Ming court; they were acutely aware that the new Manchu reign could turn out to be a better one. Soon, the landowners and the learned elite succumbed to age-old Chinese reason and realism. Since the Manchu rulers did not take away land from the gentry in the fertile region of China, the elite offered collaboration in return for certain rights and protection.

The Manchu, too, were torn. On the one hand they did all they could to inflict insult and humiliation on the Chinese – forcing them to wear queues (braided as pigtails) and Manchurian clothing was one example. Like the Mongols, the Manchu gave themselves all the privileges of a ruling class – the Manchu did not need to sit the imperial examination to be selected as government official, and the Chinese had to work in parallel with their superior Manchu counterparts. On the other hand, they secretively admired Chinese culture. By the time of Emperor Kangxi's rule from 1661 to 1722, some twenty years after the fall of the Ming, the Manchu's conquest of China was complete. The emperor was far sighted: he showed great respect for the learned Chinese elite by placing them in the administration and he sent Manchu troops to protect the wealthy landowners from the assault of rebels. The administration, to the satisfaction of the Chinese gentry, was efficient and free from the influence of the corrupted eunuchs as seen in the late Ming era. Meanwhile Emperor Kangxi, being the first Manchu ruler born on Chinese soil, had a genuine interest in Chinese culture. He ordered ambitious encyclopaedic volumes of a wide variety of subjects to be written, ranging from geography, Tang poetry, science and technology to a dictionary to be compiled by Chinese scholars, partially to win them over from their loyalty to the old regime, and partially to help educate the emperor himself. In later years, some Qing emperors even lost their Manchu language capacity. By the time of Emperor Qianlong (ruling from 1735 to 1796), the emperor, though himself a prolific essayist and poet in Chinese, as well as a connoisseur and a most enthusiastic collector of Chinese paintings and antiques, had to take the trouble to restore the Manchu language as a national priority.

A Qing courtyard of note was Emperor Kangxi's Southern Study (*nan shufang* 南书房), located at the south-east corner of the imperial palace. It was established by the emperor in 1677 as his study (and it was in use until 1898). This courtyard of numerous rooms was manned by the expansively learned Chinese scholars to accompany the emperor to read Chinese literature and history; the scholars also served as the emperor's tutors, literary critics and decree writers. The courtyard once again in Chinese history served well both the foreign rulers and the Chinese. The Western Zhou courtyard house, reconstructed based on the ruins at Fengchu, which we examined earlier in the book, can safely be seen as the prototype of the Chinese courtyard, for it had remained as a pattern, largely unchanged. But it was a relatively crude and straightforward realization of the same idea when compared to a Ming and Qing quadrangle house in Beijing, which by now had been well worked into a finely tuned equilibrium for all its embodied meanings to be fully disseminated.

## The anatomy of a Beijing quadrangle

A prototypical Ming and Qing Beijing quadrangle, known as *siheyuan* (四合院) of three sequential courtyards was still based on the symmetry of the north to south axis. The entry gate, however, was often rather discreetly situated close to the south-east corner (Figure 7.1, see also Figure 1.4). This was the most desired and indeed ideal situation. But the configurations of a vast number of Beijing quadrangles must suit different not-so-ideal locational circumstances. The gate, for example, could be placed at the north-west corner if the quadrangle had to follow the east–west longitudinal axis. The kind of

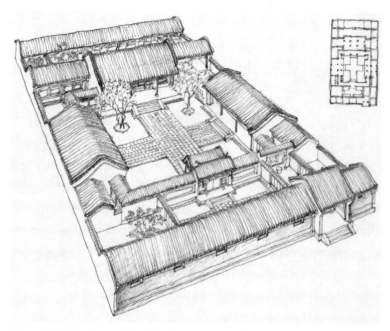

**Figure 7.1** *Bird's eye view of a three-courtyard Beijing quadrangle and the plan diagram.*

freestanding screen of antiquity outside the gate – *ping* 屏, though occasionally still in the laneway, had largely retreated into the house as a 'reflective screen' (*zhaobi* 照壁), or a 'mirror screen' (*yingbi* 影壁), which we have seen in the Song painting Lady Wenji's Return to Han. The screen inside the dwelling was the opposite wall facing the entry in the first courtyard. *Zhaobi*, either freestanding or built as part of the courtyard encircling walls, now came with a three-phase composition: the tiled roof-like capping, the finely carved brick pattern in the middle, or sometimes a marble-inlaid abstract landscape picture. The two parts then sit on a base (Figure 7.2). The freestanding screen outside the entry gate worked most effectively when the two ends were tilted towards the gate, for it helped mark a defined entry zone before the house. The true purpose of having a screen, the same

**Figure 7.2** *A zhaobi screen in the Beijing quadrangle.*

as in antiquity, now resided inside; it blocked the view into the inner world of the courtyard house. Also, as the popular belief went, whilst letting the ancestor spirit pass through the wall to the house, the evil ghost would be scared away when he saw his own image mirrored by the screen.

Turning left to the west, one entered a narrow front courtyard. The building fronting the street (*daozuo* 倒座) housed guests, a home school and male servants. Flanking the front courtyard was the main gate placed right on the central axis – this was the more adorned and elaborate 'gate of hanging flowers (*chuihua men* 垂花门)', which we have encountered in *Dream of the Red Chambers*. Behind the second layer of demarcation, one passed the threshold to the largest courtyard – the core of the Beijing quadrangle. On the north side was the main hall (*zhengfang* 正房), reserved for the elderly parents; buildings on the east and west (*dongxi xiangfang* 东西厢房), a little further down the family hierarchy, lived the married sons and their family. Covered verandas, along with the encircling walls, connected these buildings to form the very central stage of Chinese family life, much the same as in Confucius' time. Attached to the two sides of the central hall were the subordinate buildings and yards (*erfang* 耳房), in both scale and use, comprising kitchen, storage and lavatory. The very last courtyard behind the main hall was book-ended by a lower building of the entire courtyard width (*hou zhaofang* 后罩房), where the female members of the family and maidservants were accommodated.

The naming of various rooms and buildings in a Beijing quadrangle did not appear exactly the same as in Chinese antiquity, but the nature of its taxonomy followed the same principle – the names, either straightforward or analogous, described the importance of their positions and, sometimes, implied their appearance. The equivalent of the hall (*tang* 堂) was *zhengfang* (正房), which literally was 'the room right in the middle'; *dongxi xiangfang* – 'the eastern and western wing rooms' – again described the building positions; *erfang* – 'the ear rooms' of the *zhengfang*, was an anthropomorphic depiction; both *daozuo fang* 倒座房 – 'the reversed room' – and *hou zhaofang* 后罩房 – 'the wrapping room at the rear' indicated not only their respect but also less significant positions in the quadrangle compound. Lastly, *chaoshou youlang* 抄手游廊 – 'the running veranda of folded arms' – yet again a vivid anthropomorphic analogy, was a covered open gallery of approximately 1.3 metres width that wrapped around inside the main courtyard, and connected the 'hanging flower gate' and all the buildings together. This open gallery needless to say protected people from rain and sun when walking from one building to the other. But neither its name nor its form suggested that this indeed should be the main purpose of its existence. The comfortable seats provided throughout its entire length, and the fine tracery beneath the roof and under the seats yield to purposeless and useless leisure (Figure 7.3): it invited one to loaf about in the gallery to read, to converse, or to sit there doing practically nothing but watch the clouds go by ... The uses of other rooms and buildings in each zone of the overall hierarchy, though more designated, the actual occupation of the rooms was relatively flexible. They were after all buildings and rooms of different characters, or to use an anthropomorphic analogy, different parts of a living organism. There were, as we have seen, also the 'gate of hanging flowers' and the 'mirror screen'.

Figure 7.3 *The open gallery veranda in the Beijing quadrangle.*

All these names, to the modern mind, indeed are rather peculiar, for the Chinese up until the mid-twentieth century never thought it necessary to conceive and hence name the rooms and buildings in their courtyard according to the ways in which they were used, such as bedroom, living room, dining room and the like. The gradual development in Europe, from a loose and interconnected matrix of various rooms in a house to that of an elaborate web, with designated uses connected by corridors culminated in the internal layout of nineteenth-century housing in England. The efficacy of a connecting passageway, ironically, has enabled a paramount segregation and privacy. This is a level of self-consciousness, or even egotism, between which the difference is only a fine line, which the Chinese never sought in their courtyard houses. Those ordinary mortals living in a Beijing quadrangle could not have been made to see the point of a specific room solely designated to gift wrapping in the sumptuous home of a Hollywood movie star in our time.

## Life and ambience in the Hutong

A Beijing quadrangle was the elemental thread used to weave the larger urban fabric. With the exception of the corners, a quadrangle naturally shared the south to north side walls with the neighbouring courtyards (Figure 7.4). It was mostly fortified and windowless to the streets and lanes. The streets, since the founding of Yuan Dadu 元大都 (Khanbaliq – the Kahn's city, 1264–1368 CE), were well established with the network of wide streets (*dajie* 大街, approximately 37.2 metres in width), and narrow streets (*xiaojie* 小街, of approximately half the width of 18.6 metres). Apart from the streets, the lanes (*hutong* 胡同, were again approximately half the dimension of narrow streets with a width of 9.3 metres) were the main arteries

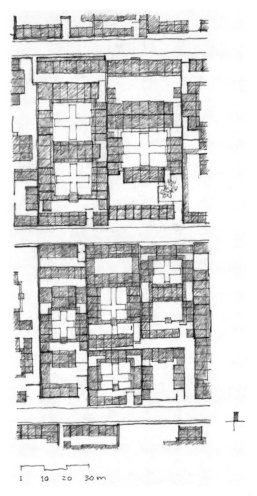

**Figure 7.4** *The figure and ground plan of a fragment of urban fabric in Beijing knitted by courtyards of various sizes.*

of the Beijing quadrangles. The unique name *hutong*, disputably regarded by scholars as either the vernacular pronunciation of lane (巷) of the Yuan, or the transliteration of the Mongolian words of either city or well,[1] has over time become the synonym for the Beijing quadrangle.

Only the *daozuo*, fronting the *hutong* and facing south, has small clerestory windows elegantly carved out towards the timber eaves brackets. Heaven above framed by this fortified Beijing quadrangle and its interior life, which we shall probe into shortly, was in essence much the same as that of any of its courtyard predecessors in Chinese history. The quiet ambience of the *hutong* was only occasionally broken by the musical cries of the street hawker, and the noises of a rowdy wedding or funeral. But the contrast between the charged theatre of family life in the quadrangle and the indolent *hutong* outside gave a finely tuned sense of content and idleness associated only with the Beijing quadrangle. This was not unlike the *otium* lauded by the learned and the well-to-do in Western antiquity, which did not seem to get lost in the mists of time.

Humanist scholar Yi-Fu Tuan is much drawn to this contrast found only in a Beijing quadrangle: 'The notion of inside and outside is familiar to all, but imagine how sensibly real these categories become when a guest – after a convivial party – leaves the lantern-lit courtyard and steps through the moon gate to the dark wind-swept lane outside.'[2] This undoubtedly is a nostalgic reimagining, but its persistence lies against the background of our time. Tuan, rather expectedly, returns to it in his old age:

I read recently an article on the architecture of the future, which boasts that buildings will not be static and will actually change shape and size in relation to the seasons (shrinking to save energy in winter) and, who knows, possibly even with one's mood. Sounds crazy to me, for we need buildings to stay the same in order to calm our fear of change and unpredictability. Suppose this madness can be applied to nature so that the hill in my neighbourhood will obligingly loom like a mountain when my mood calls for something large? Renaissance architects couldn't have guessed that one day their Vitruvian ideal of man as measure could lead to the extremity of making man so much the measure, so much in command, that the external world, having totally merged with human fantasy, simply melts away. Long before that day comes, people will surely dream of the good old days of the *hutong* and the shaded courtyard, sitting in which one could, on a hot and lazy afternoon, hear the sound of birds and the chant of peddlers drifting over the wall. I speak this way because I turned 76 on December 5.[3]

A *hutong* was not a street where the lines of shops contributed to the buzz of street life, like that of the Roman Pompeii. Different kinds of street peddlers and trades, instead, brought life to the quiet *hutong* at different times of the day. The goods they sold varied in different seasons. The market, sometimes in a temple courtyard, was an area where all sorts of shops congregated. Writers of Beiping – the name of Beijing from 1928, when the Republican Government established Nanjing as its capital city, through to 1949 – recalled vividly the quiet *hutong* animated by these mobile shops that brought life and conveniences to the doorstep of each courtyard.[4] Vegetable carts brought in cucumber, radish and green beansprouts. There were ripe cherries in May, large apricots in June, lotus seeds in July and cooked corn on the cob in August. There were also trades of various kinds, ranging from barbers and blacksmiths to craftsmen, who made lively characters from familiar dramas out of flour dough. There were also mobile snack kiosks where a delicious soup of deep-fried meat and vegetable balls and various spices could be instantly served. With a few pennies a young kid would buy a little spoon, a little bowl filled with sugar soup and a Monkey King, all made of melted sugar by the lollipop man. The child then would devour them to his heart's content. There were antique collectors, beggars and puppeteers accompanied by mini circuses of mice and birds. They chanted, sang and beat drums to break the dull air of *hutong* and drew some life out from the enigmatic inner courts to the public display. The most revealing event for a household was either a wedding or funeral. Not only the young and the house maids, but also other members of the family, would come out from their discreetly fenced courtyards to participate in this endlessly entertaining exercise to make the guesswork on the social status and wealth of the family on public display. Was the bride behind the veil beautiful? Did the son and daughter-in-law, with much of their grief on dramatic public display, fulfil their filial duties before the old man passed away?

Life in the *hutong* passed languidly and yet in a charged suspension – it was like an obscure prelude of a play that enticed one's urge to imagine the mystery concealed by the high walls. The Sri Lankan architect Geoffrey Bawa (1919–2003), rather forthrightly and with a great deal of success, introduced and reinvented courtyards houses in his hometown, Colombo. Bawa visited China in his youth. He remembered those high yellow walls, but he did not venture into any of the courtyards behind these walls.[5] As it transpired, Bawa's courtyard behind the high walls has more to do with sensual pleasure than the rites, sociality, benevolence and decorum of the Confucian world, to which I shall return in Chapter 10.

What was hidden behind the high walls in the *hutong* followed the same courtyard pattern of antiquity. The *hutong* comprised an endlessly extendable matrix woven from a single quadrangle to a sequential line-up of more than four courtyards on the longitudinal axis. The extension on the sides, too, was matter-of-fact, and was driven by necessity as well as vanity. A courtyard extended on one side with a long and narrow yard bound by an equally long and narrow building, which was often used as a kitchen, storage and rooms of miscellaneous purposes. There were no rules for combining and dividing the courtyard matrix. Two single-courtyard quadrangles lined up on the same north to south axis, could be connected and in the meantime each of them remained intact and worked as separate houses when needed. When one family amassed sufficient wealth, the adjacent neighbouring courtyards would be acquired and a multiple and grandiose 'spanning courtyard' (*kuayuan* 跨院) was then created. Conversely a family on decline would divide, without much fuss, and sell some courtyards. All was made possible due to the infinite possibilities from the extraordinary simplicity of the courtyard. Given such simplicity and its introvertive uniformity, wealth nonetheless was not easily decipherable from the bland walls encircling the exterior of a Beijing quadrangle, and the usually discreet and subdued entry.

The house of Natong 那桐, the grand secretary and councillor of the late Qing court (大学士军机大臣) lived in a house of seven 'spanning courtyards' that occupied nearly half of the famous Jinyu *hutong* 金鱼胡同 in Beijing. Among the seven courtyards, one of them was a garden. A separate garden next to the courtyard, much like those in the Yangtze region from the same period, was rare and belonged to only the elite. The exquisite ones, found either next to the house, or in the back or front yards, though much influenced by those ones from the south,[6] could nonetheless match their art. From the Yuan through to the mid-Qing, there were hundreds of them built amidst the vast sea of grey courtyards in Beijing.[7]

For most courtyard houses, grape vines, trees like the pagoda, elm, jujube, ginkgo, peach and the Chinese toona, potted plants of flowering crab apple and lilac, lake rocks and goldfish containers, appeared nonchalantly dotted in the fields and building nooks beyond the paved central cross-shaped pathway in the main courtyard. Like the Eden, the Chinese had similar ideas: the plants in a Beijing quadrangle were not only pleasing to the eye and other senses, but also good for food. Even when the garden of productivity waned in the Yangtze region from the middle of the sixteenth century, the art of horticulture in those garden houses was more visceral than pure visual 'aesthetics', for the synthesis of appearance, aroma, touch, sound and, above all, their symbolic connotations, never quite disintegrated in the Chinese mind.[8] In early spring when the chill was still in the air, flower vases of peach blossoms, freshly picked from the tree in the courtyard, gave a tantalizing lure of life's vitality after the long winter. By April, when the world was the most paradisal in the Chinese mind ('人间四月天'), the subtle fragrance of white and purple lilac now slowly filled the entire courtyard. Young leaves of toona were hooked down from the branches to fall on the ground; they made a delicious accompaniment to scrambled eggs and tender tofu. Of course, there was also the season to harvest the sweetest dates and grapes. The sound of wind and rain drops falling on tree leaves and flowers were acutely felt in the confined courtyard throughout summer. Then the sky was remote and the air was lucid in Beijing's autumn, but the melancholic chrysanthemums, though saturated in splendid colours, foreshadowed the imminent snowfalls, which made the courtyard a barren white landscape in great contrast to the warm and cosy fire in the room.

The Chinese writer Lao She 老舍 (1899–1966) in his novel *Four Generations Under One Roof* (*Sishi tongtang* 四世同堂,)[9] described a very ordinary *hutong*, named Xiao Yangjuan 小羊圈, at the dawn of the Japanese occupation of Beijing. Families living in Xiao Yangjuan were a mix of different ranks in society, though most of them were poor working people. An old saying may give a hint of Beijing's historical demography: rich east and noble west; poor south and humble north (东富西贵，南贫北贱). This was only plausible to a certain extent. Since the Ming dynasty, the warehouses used to store the goods shipped from the Yangtze region via the Grand Canal were erected in the eastern part of the city; the merchants naturally built their quadrangles in that area. Officials and aristocrats lived mostly in the west of the city, while courtyards were small in the south and beyond the city wall where the poor and the migrants congregated. Peddlers and craftsmen, the lowly professions in the Chinese mind, were in the north of the city. This was at best a stereotypical picture of Beijing's demographic map. Exceptions abounded in old Beijing. Much like that in ancient Rome, the poor and the well-to-do, the noble and the lowly, rubbed shoulders in the same neighbourhood.

In Xiao Yangjuan *hutong*, behind the 'mirror screens' recessed in the courtyard gates, there was a microcosm of Beijing in the early twentieth century. Among the half dozen courtyard houses surrounding the core of this *hutong*, the Qis had four generations living in one of the courtyards. The courtyard did not even constitute a typical Beijing quadrangle; it was long in an east and west direction, but short north and south, so the courtyard was long and narrow. Although he was almost illiterate, Old Qi lived an honourable working life and bought this courtyard by himself. His only son now ran a steady small business. Two grandsons were university educated; the third, the youngest, was still studying at the university. The elder grandson Ruixuan, who was a high school teacher, had dutifully married the woman of the parents' choice, and had produced the heirs – the fourth generation. In both means and matter, in Xiao Yangjuan this largest family was in the middle. Looking at this house, his son, grandchildren and great grandchildren, and the flowers and shrubs that he had cultivated, Old Qi, having lived in this courtyard for nearly half a century, was content. Better still he held a reasonably high moral ground to enable him to set in his mind the social pecking order of his neighbouring houses.

Old Qi held high regard for the first quadrangle from the west – No. 1, with a south facing gate. This was where the Qian family resided. Mr Qian was the same age as Old Qi's son; his two sons even went to the same school as Old Qi's elder grandson. To the eyes of other people, the Qians were a little peculiar; they were exceedingly courteous to everyone, and yet they kept a certain distance from people. It was as if they respected everyone, but they seemed to take no one too seriously. They wore clothes some twenty years behind the fashion. Their women never stepped out of the door; they only kept the gate narrowly ajar when they bought things from street peddlers. Their men came and went like the men in other courtyards, yet they were cautious and aloof. Mr Qian, when a little tight after a drink or two, would walk to the door to admire the flowers in the pagoda tree, and smile at the children playing in the *hutong*. When all the neighbours were drawn out to the *hutong* by the noisy weddings, funerals and circuses, the Qians kept their door tightly shut. Did they make a good living? What were the joys and follies in their life? No one seemed to know.

But Old Qi and his elder grandson were the only two in Xiao Yangjuan who were admitted to the inner courtyard of the Qians. Old Qi of course knew a thing or two about the Qians. In fact there were no real secrets, but Old Qi nonetheless felt obliged to keep them to himself. The Qians had a modest courtyard, which was filled with flowers lovingly attended to by Mr Qian. Old Qi had some of his flowers from the Qians. Mr Qian did not really do anything: he was a poet and a discerning connoisseur of old paintings, calligraphies and books. His poems were only for himself to chant and enjoy, and never shown to other people. The Qians in fact were poor; sometimes they were destitute and occasionally even starved. Even so, like father like son, the married elder son never wanted to do more than a few hours of teaching each week in a local high school. Every time Old Qi brought a bottle of rice wine to the Qians, Mr Qian always ordered his son to return the gift in abundance. Old Qi went to the Qian courtyard, but Mr Qian never called in to see him. When Old Qi chatted on the hurly-burly in his own household, Mr Qian listened but took nothing in;

conversely when Mr Qian talked about poetry, painting and calligraphy, Old Qi had no idea. But when it came to gardening, they had some common ground. Old Qi admired Mr Qian's learning and fine human qualities. Compared with his brothers, the pretentious Ruifeng and the hot-blooded Ruiquan, Old Qi's elder grandson, Ruixuan was a restrained gentleman. He escaped from family trivialities by quietly sneaking into Qian's courtyard to converse with Mr and Junior Qian.

In addition to the Qians, Old Qi also liked No.2 courtyard in Xiao Yangjuan, which was right opposite to the Qians. The owner of this courtyard was Li Siye. Tall but slightly hunched as a result of working in his youth as a remover by carrying precious heavy furniture on his back, Li Siye was a very kind and altruistic man. He was most professional in this trade, but never asked for even slightly more remuneration than he deserved. Quite the opposite, he only charged a modest sum, enough to pay for his meals when working for the poor. But beyond his work, he did much to serve the neighbourhood: warning people to store sufficient food well before any imminent bandit invasion, and shouting under the pagoda tree in the *hutong* to inform people that peace now had returned to Beijing. The short-sighted and snow-white-haired Mrs Li nagged only Li Siye, for she was always concerned that he had not done enough to help others. She was the big mama for all the children in this *hutong*, and for adults she and Li Siye could be counted on when help was sought. Li's house was a tiny and chaotic 'miscellaneous courtyard' (*daza yuan* 大杂院), meaning in addition to the Lis, who owned this courtyard, there were two more families who rented and lived in the same place. Despite their humble abode, Old Qi held high respect for the Lis, for when it came to the magnanimous and endless empathy for other people, Old Qi knew that he was no match for the Lis.

Li's next door No. 4 and Old Qi's immediate neighbour No. 6 were all 'miscellaneous courtyards'. There lived in No. 4, barber Sun Qi and his wife, old widow Ma and her grandson and, the wife-beating rickshaw boy Xiao Cui. In No. 6, people's jobs were not as lowly: Christian John Ding lived in the north hall; the tent builder, Master Liu and his wife, lived in the side chamber of the north hall. Master Liu was also a martial arts coach and lion dancer. The couple Mr and Mrs Xiao Wen, lived in the east building. On the surface they were amateur Peking opera singers who religiously honed their voices daily at certain times, but they charged people under the table for coming to their shows.

Between the Qians and the Qis was No. 3 – the most stately quadrangle in Xiao Yangjuan. This courtyard for Old Qi, however, was the 'nail in his eye' (more severe than 'the thorn in the flesh' for the Chinese). How could he not be a little envious of No. 3? One, there was a freestanding 'mirror screen' outside No. 3, with a large red character of *fu* (福 good fortune) painted on it. This was the only such screen in Xiao Yangjuan; two, the gate of No. 3 was a gate house with ornamented roof ridge (*qingshui ji* 清水脊) – the symbol of high status of the family in the past Qing era. The Qis, on the contrary, only had a door, which was a hole in the wall – though with decorated brickwork (*huaqiangzi* 花墙子); three, No. 3 was a neat ship-shape single quadrangle (*sihe fang* 四合房) with brick-paved courtyard; and four, they could even afford to hire Master Liu to erect, out of bamboo sheets, a summer gazebo in the courtyard.

But it was the way of living of the paterfamilias of No. 3, Guan Xiaohe, that was to the utter distaste of Old Qi. Mr Guan had two wives; the younger one once was a quite popular actress. Mr Guan was in his fifties, the same age as Old Qi's son. But Mr Guan was well preserved: he looked like someone in the early thirties. Despite his short body frame, his well-manicured hair and sartorial refinement gave him the appearance of 'a shiny little crystal ball' (in Lao She's own words). They had a chef, a well-mannered servant, and an old maid who wore silk shoes. They mingled with the top end of town; entertained guests with *mahjong* playing and home performances. Mr Guan was courteous and humble before the neighbours of higher social status, but he bossed around others in the *hutong*.

The enigmatic and idiosyncratic lives behind the 'mirror screens' in the vast sea of *hutong* had been brought to a halt after the fall of Beijing to the Japanese. To cut Lao She's long story short, the character of each courtyard in Xiao Yangjuan foreshadowed their destinies: both those who resisted Japanese occupation – the Qians and others – and those who sought protection and favour from the occupiers – the Guans and Old Qi's second grandson. The latter, for different reasons, all ended up in jail and lost their lives. Lives in Beijing's quadrangles after the Japanese occupation were never the same again, to which I will return when we examine the Chinese life after the courtyard.

# The city as a large quadrangle

The larger urban fabric of Beijing was thus superbly supported by the simple quadrangle in its various combinations; the wholeness, the completeness, and the concreteness of the social hierarchy were in return mirrored in the city form. Despite the fact that it was built by the Mongol rulers, the morphology of Yuan Dadu, with its core spatial anatomy still remaining to this date, followed the ancient rules established in the *Record of Trades* for the King's City, which we examined earlier. Starting in 1264 the inception of the Mongol rule of China, to the official inauguration of the Yuan epoch in 1271, and the rectification of its name as Dadu 大都 in 1272, the cosmic city itself as a vast courtyard was completed in 1293. The planning and design of the city was led by Liu Bingzhong 刘秉忠, a Chinese, assisted by his Central Asian apprentice Iktiyar al-Din (also known as Amir al-Din, but in Chinese as Yeheidieerding 也黑迭儿丁), and his Chinese student the brilliant hydraulic engineer and astronomer Guo Shoujing 郭守敬.

Historic record has it that in 1264, Yuan Shizu Kublai Khan 元世祖 忽必烈, the fifth Khan, visited Daning Palace on Jade Island in Lake Taiye, to the north-east of the previous Jurchen 女真 led Jin capital, Zhongdu. Enchanted by the place, perhaps due to his nomadic root and the habit of 'always searching for fertile wetlands to settle', the emperor ordered his capital to be built around the artificial lake. The founding principle of the city structure, no doubt promulgated by Liu Bingzhong, was that of the King's City – that is, the Ancestral Temple was on the east, and the Altars of Soil and Grain were on the west; the Hall of Audience was on the south at the front, and the markets were behind on the north (左祖右社，前朝后市). This was the core of any Chinese city in accord with *The Rites of Zhou*, much lauded by Confucius. But the huge area of water, enlarged by Guo Shoujing from the Jin reservoir, Lake Taiye and ingeniously channelled to the existing river and canal system to form a surface-water ecology, was unprecedented in China's urban history of imperial cities (Figure 7.5). These arrangements not only guaranteed water supply (and for that matter the purity of it for the inner imperial city due to the design of separate sources for two different lakes) but also showed that the simple courtyard pattern at urban scale could be treated much the same as a house with a garden. For the first time in Chinese urban history, a vast and elaborate water garden was used to inject much vitality into urban life, like a fairy tale enriched with more layers of meaning when it is transplanted into a different culture.

Let us return to the urban form of Yuan Dadu. Bounded by the encircling walls, the city was very close to a square – an east to west width of 6,650 metres, and a south to north length of 7,400 metres. Within the outer city and towards the south was the imperial city, and

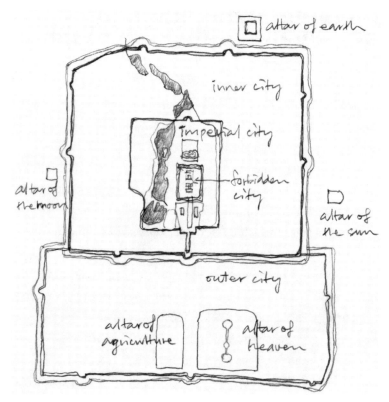

altar of earth

inner city

Imperial city

forbidden city

altar of the moon

altar of the sun

outer city

altar of agriculture

altar of heaven

**Figure 7.5** *Diagram of the Ming and Qing Beijing, showing three courtyards – forbidden city (imperial palace), imperial city and inner city, and one within the other.*

on its east was the imperial palace placed right on the south–north city axis. Differently put, Yuan Dadu, like any imperial city in China's long urban history, was three quadrangles contained one within the other. One lake, the Mongols preferred to call it 'sea' (海), was in the imperial city, but the other one was behind the imperial city, stretching out to be connected to the river. These 'seas' had been reshaped in the Ming dynasty into 'the southern sea, the central sea, the northern sea and the rear sea' (南海，中海，北海，后海). They have survived to this date, with 'the central-southern sea' (Zhongnaihai 中南海) still enclosed behind the high walls for the exclusive use and enjoyment of the senior communist party officials and the administration of the headquarters of the Communist Party of China. Within the well-established Yuan grid of wide street, narrow street and *hutong* were the infill of courtyard houses. There are, however, very few traces of the Yuan house in today's Beijing.

Both the Ming and Qing sumptuary laws determined that only the imperial city and the imperial palace could be covered with glazed golden tiles. On the top of Jingshan 景山, the hill immediately behind the imperial palace, which was formed atop a small mound by the soil excavated from the lakes and moat, the emperor enjoyed the privilege of inspecting his magnificent palace crowned with shiny golden tiles against the expansive sea of grey courtyard houses. Due to the advance brick firing techniques in the Ming dynasty, the city walls and gates as well as houses, had been built predominately with bricks. For the common mortal, the spectacle, from above, of the golden jewel of the imperial city and palace set off by the background of grey courtyards in Beijing, would occur only occasionally in one's imagination. The prospect of gazing towards the horizon from a higher vantage point, however, would not have had much allure to him, for he was chiefly content with his slice of the sky framed by his own courtyard. Being acutely aware that he was constantly under the watchful eye of Heaven, he would rather mind only his own business, and happily leave the responsibility of answering Heaven to 'the son of Heaven' – the emperor. This is not to say that his cityscape was dull as he walked about it; the horizontal city was adorned, with much legibility and rhythm, by vertical structures of bell and drum towers, city gates and white Tibetan pagodas built by the Mongols. All offered him familiarity, and a great deal of solace that his world had remained unchanged, and would remain so for a long time to come.

# Distinctive character versus uniformity

Behind the uniform high walls, windowless buildings, and the 'mirror screens' inside courtyard gates, which showed only a small degree of variety in official rank and social status allowed by the sumptuary laws, the vast city fabric of quadrangles was far from homogenous. All effortlessly housed by courtyards, there were libraries, guildhalls, theatres, temples and markets during the Ming dynasty. The houses themselves gained distinctive characters not through the novelty of their external forms and styles, but because of the interior life associated with the residents who occupied them.

Novelty and monumentality, on the contrary, were exactly what the English aristocrats set out to pursue so that they could cement the marks of their ranks and vanity in stones. Innovation, nonetheless, occurred as a side effect. I shall describe the English approach at some length, against which the distinctive Beijing quadrangle can be better understood. The Countess of Shrewsbury, known as the formidable Bess of Hardwick, initially tried her hand on building the first Chatsworth House during her second marriage to Sir William Cavendish, Treasurer of the King's Chamber. In 1553, by the time Bess started building Chatsworth House, the influence of Italian Renaissance architecture would have been felt in England. Grander than a Tudor estate, the original Chatsworth had a quadrangle of 50 metres by 60 metres. The front entry on the west was embellished by four towers, reminiscent of the English castle; the hall on the east side of the quadrangle was still medieval in its look, though its use, unlike the social mixing of the lord and the lowly class in the hall of past manors, would have been exclusively reserved for the nobilities.

Bess was not satisfied by Chatsworth. After four judicious marriages and armed with her accumulated wealth, in her sixties she returned to her birth place of Hardwick Hall to build, next to the old hall,

Hardwick New Hall, which was to become her true mark of sheer novelty. Legend has it that Bess was already contemplating building Hardwick New Hall a few weeks before her fourth husband, Lord Shrewsbury, died in 1590. The most distinctive feature – though perhaps aided by the surveyor and master stonemason, Robert Smythson's initial plans, the extravagant use of glass windows, more so than the Wollaton Hall built by Smythson – would have been Bess' signature. This was where the famous rhyme – 'Hardwick Hall, more glass than wall' – originated. Bess perhaps was more allured by the vision afar, projected from within a building as promised by the Italian Renaissance, which undoubtedly was new to the Elizabethans.

Despite the innovation, the persistent English desire to retreat into the interior managed to find its way in another English invention – the long gallery of Elizabethan architecture. In the case of Hardwick, it is its magnificent 51-metre long gallery that married the views of the outside world and the internalized activities of reading, looking at paintings and conversing into one room. By the time John Vanbrugh convinced the 3rd Earl of Carlisle that he was the right architect to build his Castle Howard in 1699, Inigo Jones had already made the work of the Italian master Andrea Palladio known in England. It remains a mystery as to how Vanbrugh, who was a dramatist and had not built anything, was able to convince Carlisle to take him up as his architect after the dismissal of the original architect William Talman. Incidentally he was the architect of Chatsworth House, with a reputation of having a bad temper. The camaraderie between Vanbrugh and Carlisle established through the mystic Kit-Cat Club notwithstanding, Vanbrugh offered more novelty than Talman could have done: the former, like the Venetian master, crowned Castle Howard with a dome, which for the first time in England imposed the language of sacred architecture on domestic use. Again the quintessential English galleries were implanted inside. Castle Howard, by 1709, from the outside at least, looked like a Palladian villa in the English countryside. Vanbrugh went on to tackle the more grandiose Blenheim Palace, entrusted by the First Duke of Marlborough. The Duchess of Marlborough, the strong-willed Sarah Churchill and Queen Anne's confidante, however, wanted Sir Christopher Wren to be her architect, which foreshadowed Blenheim Palace as an ill-fated commission for Vanbrugh, which ended his career as an architect of novel, stately houses. Similar examples abounded throughout European history.

For the Chinese aristocrats and the corrupted court officials in Qing Beijing, rank and vanity were shown through simple multiplication of courtyards, occasionally helped to some extent by the refinement of craftsmanship and the subtle distinctiveness in their garden making. The quadrangles bestowed on princes and princelings frequently featured three parallel courtyards, which, judging from the outside, showed little majestic gesture and the same windowless high walls occasionally punctuated by gate houses. The Residence of Prince Fu (孚王府), one of the largest among its kind, had its courtyards strung on the central north to south axis dedicated to ceremonies and rituals; the courtyards on the parallel western axis were the residence whilst the courtyards on the east accommodated only amenities and entertainments (Figure 7.6). The courtyards were originally built for Prince Yi, Yunxiang 允祥 the 13th son of Emperor Kangxi. Peerage was bestowed on him, along with the quadrangle complex, by his brother Emperor Yongzheng, who was very close to Prince Yi. By the sixth generation of the lineage, Prince Yi, Zai Yuan 载垣, was captured by the Dowager Cixi after her successful coup in 1861, the year of the death of Emperor Xianfeng 咸丰. Zai Yuan was given white silk rope to hang himself, and the quadrangle complex was confiscated by the court, which was then given to the 9th son of Emperor Daoguang 道光 – Prince Fu 孚群王奕譓, hence the current name of the

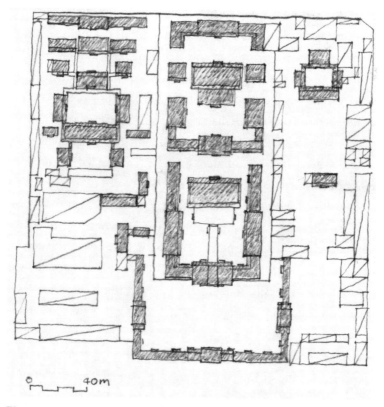

**Figure 7.6a** *Diagram of the plan of Prince Fu's residence, showing three parallel courtyards and the existing structures in shade.*

quadrangle. During its more than 180 years history as the royal prince residence and despite the change of ownership, the essential configuration of this quadrangle complex had remained unchanged.

The same story applied to other stately Qing quadrangles. The now fully restored Residence of Prince Gong 恭王府 has a colourful history. It was built by the corrupt official He Shen 和珅. Between 1769 and 1786, in less than twenty years, He Shen amassed vast wealth and built a quadrangle complex that would rival the best of princely residences. As might be expected, his quadrangle became the envy of

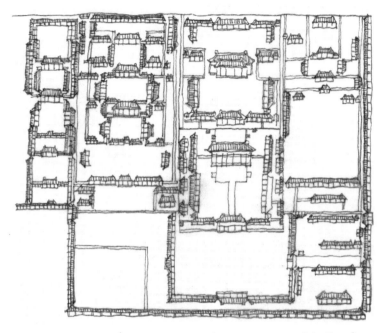

**Figure 7.6b** *The same courtyard complex as it appeared in* Jingcheng quantu 京城全图 *(The Complete Map of the Capital) of the Qianlong period (1750), showing remarkable details of building layouts in diagrammatic elevations.*

the nobilities, and in particular Yonglin 永璘, the 17th son of Emperor Qianlong 乾隆. The opportunity to repossess He Shen's courtyard came after the coronation of Yonglin's brother Emperor Jiaqing 嘉庆 in 1799: He Shen was found guilty of twenty major crimes, and the emperor granted him the gift of hanging himself. His entire property was confiscated by the court and subsequently given to Yonglin along with the title Prince Qingjun 庆郡. The ownership changed hands a few times in the next fifty years until it was given to the powerful Yixin 奕訢 – Prince Gong – in 1852, hence its current name. This is still a quadrangle of three parallel courtyards; the ceremonial one in the middle and the residences on the east and the west side. The vast courtyard on the north, which has the width of three parallel courtyards, contains the garden, the theatre, and also a vegetable garden, which allegedly was once regarded as the prototype of Daguan Yuan in *Dream of the Red Chamber*. Indeed, some of the not-so-vast quadrangle houses in Qing Beijing gained their distinction through the garden in one of the parallel courtyards. Among the five parallel courtyards in the residence of the late Qing Grand Secretary Wenyu 文煜宅, the middle one of Keyuan garden 可园 was well known in Beijing as one of the gardens that followed the fine tradition of the garden house in the Yangtze region. Another smaller quadrangle built by the Qing official Linqing 麟庆 was predominately known in Beijing for its garden, Banmu Yuan 半亩园, allegedly planned by Li Yü when the house was first built.

Writers and scholars congregated in Beijing in the early part of the twentieth century. They often occupied modest and medium-sized quadrangles. Neither the Qing aristocrats nor the eccentric writers and artists could count on reaching immortality through any distinctive physical features of their houses. But the lingering souls of the past movers and shakers, strangely, made the places of their past transient sojourns no less fascinating than those novel stately houses built by the European nobilities and cultural personalities. Writer Lu Xun purchased a modest courtyard after falling out with his brothers, with whom he once shared a large dwelling. This was not even a regular single courtyard quadrangle, and he only spent two years in this house. The place, however, has become the pilgrimage destination of not only aspiring writers but also many from the educated populace. It is the small backyard of scarcely manicured plants and weeds which is reminiscent of the 'one-hundred herbs garden' (百草园), lovingly depicted in one of his most widely read essays that can be recited by any attentive primary school pupil in China. Indeed, some of his seminal works were written in this modest quadrangle.

Lao She grew up in poverty. By the time he could afford to buy a house in 1951, he too acquired a not-so-regular quadrangle. Lao She lived in this courtyard for sixteen years and wrote many of the works in his socialist era. The central courtyard was characterized by two persimmon trees planted by Lao She, and it had been named by the writer himself as 'Petty Courtyard of Red Persimmon' (丹柿小院). But any visitor today would be tempted to speculate as to which courtyard in Xiao Yangjuan described in *Four Generations Under One Roof*, was modelled based on his own quadrangle. Mei Lanfang, China's most celebrated Peking opera singer who gained his fame by playing exquisite female roles, once had a large quadrangle complex. During the Japanese occupation of Beijing, Mei famously grew a beard and refused to perform for the occupiers. As a consequence, he fell into financial difficulties and was forced to sell the complex. From 1950 to 1961, the last decade of his life, Mei lived in a small quadrangle, which, though chosen by himself, was awarded to Mei by the new government. This was a typical Beijing quadrangle with all the essential ingredients that we have examined thus far. But this courtyard today is filled with a special aura of Mei's spirit mainly because we know most of the trees and flowers in the central court had been planted by Mei himself; this was his favourite place to exercise his sword and play with his grandchildren.[10]

The Beijing quadrangle, and the Chinese courtyard in general, acquired a distinctiveness and a charged ambience exclusively through its association with the way in which it was lived in, be the occupation of it literary or actual. To the modern mind, that the universal courtyard could gain distinctive cultural and regional characters may seem puzzling, but a mathematical understanding of this problem offers crystallization – that is, the relationship between the concepts of pattern and type. According to Edmund Leach, the British preacher of French Structuralism, the emphasis on type is like 'butterfly collecting'.[11] One can be in the race of gathering myriads of types in the search for a new butterfly. But after all they are the same as a butterfly, which in itself is, mathematically, a pattern. Let me attempt to justify the courtyard as a pattern. Take, for example, a print of a square courtyard on a piece of thin rubber sheet, and then stretch and even twist the sheet. The shape and dimension of the square courtyard no doubt will be changed. With every turn and twist, there will be a different kind of courtyard: they are, in other words, different types of the same courtyard house. But the courtyard pattern itself remains mathematically the same one.

The most atypical twentieth-century American architect, Louis Kahn, understood this only too well: Form (with a capital F), proclaimed Kahn, must be held, whilst Design (with a capital D) is circumstantial. Kahn used the example of a spoon to illustrate: the Form of a spoon, the idea – comprising a bowl and a handle, must be held. The Design of a spoon – silver or wood handle, round or oval-shaped bowl – is largely determined by the availability of materials, economy, taste or fashion, hence is circumstantial. Although Kahn was a superb architect with a rich material palette, he was more interested in developing a concentric pattern in plan configuration that would enshrine what Kahn saw as the two essential activities of human life – meeting and learning, which, in a broad sense, represent a collective, group life and the development of self and individual. Such a pattern can be either a library or a parliament house. Kahn, I should like to think, understood intuitively one of the primary meanings embedded, and indeed embodied, in the universal courtyard, that is, its robust capacity to house both the group and the individual. Kahn's courtyards often are roofed, but the celestial skylight that Kahn ably let in makes his buildings anomalies in our secular world.

The Chinese courtyard, it might be concluded at this point, was a generic 'butterfly' pattern, and the Beijing quadrangle was a particularly beautiful type belonging to the same pattern. This is one of the riskier generalizations that the author has thus far embarked on, but Leach again offered some degree of justification: 'Generalization is inductive; it consists in perceiving possible general laws in the circumstances of special cases; it is guesswork, a gamble, you may be wrong or you may be right, but if you happen to be right you have learnt something altogether new.'[12]

If the Beijing quadrangle itself was one pattern that fitted all, from which richness and variety were derived to suit the simple life of common folks, and the social status and vanity of aristocrats and merchants, as well as the idiosyncrasies of scholars and artists, this was also the same courtyard pattern as that of the past and in other regions – a legible microcosm of the Confucian world of family, institution and state. The Beijing quadrangle, however, did not have a tower in it, as seen in the Han clay house models, to which the gentry might occasionally escape from the Confucian world. Most of them did not even have a separate garden, as depicted in Tang poems and seen in the Yangtze region from the Ming onwards, as a substitute for the loss of the tower (if it ever existed in the Han). The men of the Beijing quadrangle did not leave their homes to become travelling merchants as seen in the Ming Huizhou; on the contrary they happily cohabited in the same house with not only their women and children, but also the elder and younger generations. 'Four generations under one roof' hence was the norm, and even the ideal. Even the same degree of segregation from the outside world was peculiar, for life in a *hutong* was nowhere near the bustle of a street lined with shops and peddlers as portrayed in a Song painting.

I have attempted to show, armed with this robust vehicle of the courtyard house, that the Chinese had never quite changed their worldview since they fashioned it some 2,500 years ago, but rather always rounded it in one way or another. What then made the Beijing quadrangle more in tune with the Chinese middle way? First and foremost, the Beijing quadrangle was more expansive. This was not merely the measure of the actual scale, but more an attitude bent further towards the earthly life. Unlike the courtyards in the Yangtze region, there were rarely any multi-storey buildings (*lou* 楼) in the Beijing quadrangle. For both the prominent and the lowly, the courtyard, either expansive or modest, was a more secular social template where the Chinese were going about their day to day life. Both the royal prince and the rickshaw puller were chiefly content with their life on earth. To most of the common mortals living in Beijing quadrangles, a separate garden as an escapist haven was not necessary for he was quite happy to combine his leisure garden, the place for the miscellany of everyday activities, and family ceremonies and rituals into the one quadrangle. Indeed, Beijing was characterized by expansiveness: from the physical scale of the imperial palace, the imperial city, the courtyard houses that constituted the entire city fabric, even to the temperament of the place and its people. Lin Yutang lovingly portrayed the charming character of the common folk in Beijing as magnanimous. The background of Lin's admiration for Beijing was based on a diagnosis of the quite different temperaments of Shanghai and Beijing in the early twentieth century, which appears still to be eerily true in our time despite almost a century's change and turmoil in both cities. In an essay titled 'A Hymn to Shanghai', Lin began with these lines:

> Shanghai is terrible, very terrible. Shanghai is terrible in her strange mixture of Eastern and Western vulgarity, in her superficial refinements, in her naked and unmasked worship of Mammon, in her emptiness, commonness, and her bad taste. She is terrible in her denaturalized women, dehumanized coolies, devitalized newspapers, decapitalized banks, and denationalized creatures. She is terrible in her joys and follies, and in her tears, bitterness, and

degradation, terrible in her immutable stone edifices that rear their heads high on the Bund and in the abject huts of creatures subsisting on their discoveries from refuse cans. . .[13]

In the 'alleyway houses' (*lilong* 里弄), built by both foreign and local developers as speculative urban housing in colonial Shanghai, the traces of courtyards still existed. But the very Chinese idea of a courtyard was begun to give respect to a matter-of-fact *raison d'être* of light and air, and also the very core of a modern metropolis – commerce. I shall return to the Shanghai alleyway house when I examine Chinese life post-courtyard.

Lin, in another essay written in the same period, described Beijing as 'a grand old personality', who was 'generous, magnanimous, big-hearted, and cosmopolitan [. . .] Modern young misses in high-heeled shoes brush shoulders with Manchu ladies on wooden soles, and Peking doesn't care. Old painters with white, magnificent long beards live across the yard from young college students in their "public hostelries," and Peking doesn't care. Packards and Buicks compete with rickshaws and mule carts and caravans, and Peking doesn't care.'

Lin singled out three things that made Beijing the ideal city to live in: its architecture, its mode of living, and its common people. It seems to me that Lin ranked mode of living more important than architecture, for it made Beijing a charming place. And yet he said:

> The greatest charm of Peking is, however, the common people, not the saints and professors, but the rickshaw coolies. Paying about a dollar for a trip by rickshaw from the West City to the Summer Palace, a distance of five miles, you might think that you are getting cheap labour; that is correct, but you are not getting disgruntled labour. You are mystified by the good cheer of the coolies as they babble all the way among themselves and crack jokes and laugh at other people's misfortunes.[14]

I have wondered what Lin would say about Beijing's taxi drivers these days, who have been urged by the government to make sure they have brushed their teeth before work, and know how to say 'Welcome to Beijing' in English. Lin would not have said anything different, I imagine, for you still hear the taxi drivers tell you their sad stories with what Lin called 'humour, refinement, and fatalistic good cheer' (if the taxi driver happens to be a local, which is becoming increasingly rare). Such was the temperament of Beijing. The amazement about past Beijing, I am inclined to believe, lay in its mode of living, and traces of it still exist. This may elucidate the puzzle of some of the most hostile-looking leftover urban junctions in modern Beijing – the place beneath an elevated freeway for example, which are happily occupied by people who gracefully practice their *taiji* or ballroom dancing. That would be inconceivable in Chicago, for the purposefully designed and provided public space is seen as the precursor of a civic life.

Within the expansive quadrangle, the social demarcation, demanded by the Confucian world, had been tuned to reach a level of supreme artifice out of extraordinary simplicity. A pleasure garden as an escapist haven was thus a little extraneous in most circumstances. Like a clever maze, its tricks designed to be deceiving are simple and yet effective. It began at the gate, which as we already know was not centred on the axis of the overall symmetry but at the south-east corner. The front door often was left ajar, but the inner life of the courtyard was concealed behind the 'mirror screen' wall. The freestanding 'reflective screen' before the centred gate of a courtyard house in the Yangtze river region, though marking an entry zone, did not prevent one from peeking into the courtyard if the door was open. This was the same as seen in Chinese antiquity. The development, or rather the perfection, of the 'mirror screen' in a Beijing quadrangle was the result of efficacy out of simplicity, which was in accord with the highest order of things Chinese. In Chinese art, the ultimate pursuit was that 'the great image has no form' (大象无形); in one's mode of living, 'true splendour comes down to blandness' (绚烂之极归于平淡).

The same efficacy and the same simplicity continued throughout the quadrangle: after turning into the first narrow courtyard on the left, as we have already experienced, servants and guests may enter the central quadrangle through the splendid 'hanging flower gate' on the axis, but they were put up in the 'reversed room' fronting the *hutong* and facing the 'hanging flower gate' – a message, politely and yet categorically delivered by architecture, about the hierarchy of social demarcation in the quadrangle. The 'wrapping room at the rear' and the 'spanning courtyard' on the side work to the similar effect to separate the unmarried daughters, maids, and the miscellany of cooking, washing and answering nature's call from the central universe of the quadrangle.

Not that the Beijing quadrangle was the elegant living par excellence: it was not a monument of one's filial duty and a showcase of good taste as seen in the Ming and Qing Huizhou courtyards, nor was it the pleasure garden house indulged by romantic mortals such as Li Yü, or the stupendous courtyard built by a decadent Ming dynasty travelling merchant in Yangzhou while away from his home in Huizhou. Whilst endlessly pursuing the quintessential natural moment 'when the lotus flower blooms out of water' (芙蓉出水), the Chinese have always reserved their weakness for 'saturated colours and gild' (错彩镂金). But these two seemingly uncompromising extremes effortlessly coexisted in a Beijing quadrangle: timber beams and columns were covered, literally with 'saturated colours and gild' using thick enamel paint. When it came to the themes and patterns of polychrome decorative painting on buildings, the Qing sumptuary laws permitted the imperial palace to have dragons and the nobilities to have flower petals, but the gentry and lowly class could only have landscape, people, birds and flowers. The woodwork in a modest quadrangle, however, was painted predominately in red and green while timber and brick tracery, and stone carving, often were elaborate and even tediously detailed.

But all these indulgencies were kept in check by the paramount power and simplicity of the courtyard configuration. In summer when the vitality of life was at its peak, the common mortal in the Beijing quadrangle went about his life with 'bamboo sheet gazebo, fish pond, pomegranate tree, the master of the house, his fat dog and his chubby daughter' (天棚鱼缸石榴树，先生肥狗胖丫头). But he was acutely aware that Heaven's solemnity returned to his quadrangle when the little indulgencies in his mortal life were covered in snow in winter. The Chinese had worked long enough to get to this point in a Beijing quadrangle, as the twentieth-century Swiss painter Paul Klee hence would have concluded: the Chinese have stopped looking at their courtyard, and the courtyard has started looking back. Indeed the Beijing quadrangle was the very embodiment of the Chinese character at his best: he may be a rickshaw coolie, a great scholar as the middling hermit – considered the ideal mode of living by the Tang poet Bai Juyi, but he, as Lin Yutang painted for us, nonetheless was a reasonable and happy-go-lucky mortal. The eagerness for success deeply built in the modern mortal's psyche was unknown to him. He knew, however, that expansive and magnanimous Heaven, from time to time, kept his wicked humour, fatalistic good cheer, eccentricities, and even bad taste, in good check.

# 8

# *Living like 'the Chinese'*

The non-Chinese ethnic groups, called minority nationalities in today's China, have always had entangled love and hate relations with the Han, the majority and dominant population. Perhaps because they live in a land where 'Heaven is high and the emperor is far away' (天高皇帝远), some, like the Tai linguistic groups in southern China such as the Dai and the Dong, have managed to maintain a way of living, which, on the surface at least, is distinctively different from that of the Han. The Dai and the Dong do not live in courtyard houses at all. Instead they are housed in freestanding pile-built timber and bamboo houses elevated on stilts – a common feature found throughout South-East Asia and many parts of the Pacific Islands. Neither climatic reasoning nor technological rationale offers a plausible explanation. Though Chinese influences for centuries have been felt deeply on almost all aspects of their agrarian cultures (including architecture), an elusive animistic religious belief and their tribal social structure are the true reasons behind the often nuclear family-centred freestanding house that does not have to answer to Heaven, or any singular god.

Nested in mountain river valleys, a Dong hamlet is reached by elaborately covered 'wind and rain' bridges. Profiled by a magnificent drum tower and an opera stage in most villages, the freestanding pile-built houses serve as the background for a picturesque silhouette that rivals any idyllic-looking European medieval townscape. The Chinese appearance of their buildings, and the visible signs of the Chinese-influenced building techniques are deceiving, for the social structure and the way of living supported by such a built world is in essence non-Chinese.[1] Like a camouflaged creature, the real agenda is to hide the difference and go unnoticed. The microcosm of the Chinese courtyard – its Confucian world of family structure and its ambivalent relations to Heaven are nowhere to be seen in the Dong world. Indeed, it is never too far-fetched to compare the physical structure of a Dong hamlet to that of an affluent inner-city suburb in the Western world, populated by a like-minded demography and compatible incomes.

Some other distinctive and ethnic minority groups, such as the Hakka in Fujian province and the Bai and the Naxi in Yunnan province, on the contrary, have built a diverse, and sometimes even opulent, array of courtyard houses. Are these subtle or overt displays of Chineseness in their courtyard houses a genuine emulation out of admiration, or rather a deceiving technique, albeit not fully conscious, for survival and co-existence? They are both.[2]

# The 'guest' Chinese and their Chinese courtyards

The Hakka have built courtyard houses of monumental scale, with rammed earth, baked bricks, tiles and timber, and in a multitude of round, square and rectangular shapes (Figure 8.1). Known as *tulou* 土楼 (earthen building), the name, however, does not do justice to its rich material palette and diverse forms. They are not courtyard complexes that accommodate four generations under one roof; rather they are 'fortress ramparts'[3] with each complex housing an entire clan.

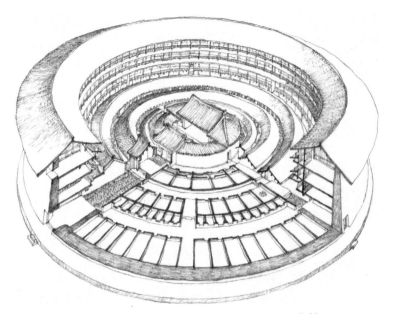

**Figure 8.1** *The cutaway bird's eye view of Chengqi Lou* 承启楼 *in Yongding county, Fujian province.*

The fortified and defensive castle-like appearance and the monumental scale of collective living, to the modern eye, gives the impression of something distinctively non-Chinese, and even exotic. Clan-based collective living, as it appears in any of the Hakka courtyard fortresses, might be sufficient a reason to assume so, for the Chinese had, by the lifetime of Confucius, long given up tribal society in favour of the family as the primary building block for society – the Confucian world from the cosmic city and the imperial court to the household, had been enshrined exclusively by the courtyard.

The Hakka, examined from this angle, much like the Dai and the Dong, do not appear like the Chinese. Despite their distinctiveness, the Hakka, in general, have been regarded as a branch of the Han. But their ethnicity has been a topic of debate in anthropology and ethnography. The migration history of Hakka, however, does not seem to help draw any categorical conclusions from the standpoint of ethnicity, which is notoriously difficult to define. Any definition of ethnicity and culture, including the majority Han, is throughout a long history inevitably some sort of 'social construct'. Language sometimes offers a strong hold. The Hakka dialect, which is aligned with Cantonese and those of the Yangtze region – the *wu* dialect (*wuyu* 吴语), for example, belongs to the Sino-Tibetan family, but it is inconclusive among linguists as to whether or not the Hakka dialect itself constitutes a distinctive language. Like many of the minority groups in China, the Hakka have not developed their written language. It is commonly believed that its pronunciation has retained some characters of classic Chinese, dating mainly from the Tang and Song periods. The name Hakka – meaning 'guest families' (客家) in Chinese – is a commonly held belief among the Hakka themselves that they are the descendants of the ancient Chinese who migrated from northern China to the remote and mountainous regions in today's Fujian, Guangdong and Jiangxi provinces.

This, too, is no unique sentiment among the minority groups: the Dong, to some extent, hold a similar belief, and the Dong linguists have detected some traces of classic Chinese in the Dong language despite the fact that it is part of the Tai linguistic family. To the Dong, the attempts to align themselves more with the Han, are complex and yet understandable. On the one hand this is one way of showing their superiority among the minority groups in the region, on the other hand it is a combination of survival tactic and genuine admiration for Han culture.[4] For the Hakka, this is not so clean-cut on the surface. The several scenarios of the charted migration history of the Hakka have been gleaned from scattered sources, and their authenticity to this date is still impossible for the historians to verify.

The Hakka migration, if it ever happened, is generally perceived by historians as part of the several waves of north-to-south migration in

Chinese history. The first was the 'Yongjia Upheaval' (永嘉之乱). In 290 CE, after the death of the emperor Wudi of the Jing 晋武帝, the fight for the crown among the princes instigated a war of sixteen years. The minority groups in the north, in the meantime, took the advantage and expanded their territories well into the Han domain. The tribal chief Liu Yuan 刘渊 of the southern Xiongnu, the ironically self-proclaimed Han descendant, established in 304 CE the 'Kingdom of Han' in the name of 'the great Han revival'. In 316 CE the son of Liu Yuan took over Luoyang and Chang'an, and captured the emperor Mindi of the Jing 晋愍帝. Along with the Xiongnu, other northern minority groups like the Jie 羯, the Zhi 氐, the Qiang 羌 and the Xianbei 鲜卑, invaded northern China. This was the period known also as 'The Unrest of China under Five Foreign Races' (五胡乱中华). The brutal killing of the Han by non-Han ruling groups caused massive migration to the Yangtze region. It is generally believed by the Hakka that their ancestors were part of this southern movement, and continued their journey further south.

The second wave happened by the middle of the Tang dynasty, against the background of the so-called 'An-Shi Rebellion' (安史之乱) from 755 CE through to 762. The uprisings led by the general An Lushan 安禄山, and later the general Shi Siming 史思明 resulted in eight years of chaos and immense suffering due to open looting and killing. The migration from the middle and lower reaches of the Yellow River caused a chain reaction, with the earlier settlers from the first wave of migration in the Yangtze region venturing into the southern frontiers. The Hakka ancestors could well be part of this move. Some historians believe that the real Hakka migration to the location they occupy today occurred after the end of the Northern Song dynasty, and was regarded by the Han as the 'Humiliation of Jingkang' (靖康之难). The northern nomads, Jurchen of the Jin, sacked the capital Bianjing (today's Kaifeng) in 1127 CE and abducted the emperor Qinzong 宋钦宗 and his father the emperor emeritus Huizong 宋徽宗. This was the beginning of weeks of looting, killing and raping. Before he conceded to appease the Jin and the permanent retreat to the south, Zhao Gou 赵构, the ninth son of Huizong and the future first emperor of the Southern Song, still staged formidable resistance against the Jin army by taking back the city of Luoyang. The fear of a comeback of the Song troops prompted Emperor Taizong of the Jin to order the captivity of more than 14,000 people, including the entire imperial entourage to march north to the Jin capital Shangjing. Many died *en route*; Empress Zhu committed suicide to avoid the humiliation of having to serve Jin aristocrats.[5] The sufferings of Song subjects were further compounded by the collapse of the Yellow River banks in 1048 CE. The Hakka, among others under the pressure of mass migration from the north, went further into the virgin lands of the Lingnan and Wuyi mountains. Given the integrity of the Hakka dialect, it is more plausible that there was one major migration rather than several, for it would be almost impossible to maintain such a level of linguistic consistency over several waves of southern migration crossing the centuries.[6]

All the migration myths thus far support the Hakka assertion that they are indeed 'guest families' – the descendants of ancient Chinese, but they built the 'fortress ramparts' rather than the Chinese courtyard. Legend has it that in the Ming dynasty there lived in the Yongding 永定 area a sister and a brother of the Xu family, who were poor and subsisted on cutting hay and raising cattle for others. When Sister Xu turned sixteen, she was spotted by the court at the imperial concubine selection. Soon after her admission to the imperial court, Concubine Xu quickly won the emperor's favour and was elevated to the highest rank of the imperial concubines. But Concubine Xu missed her brother day and night. She begged the emperor to allow her brother to come to live in the court, which His Majesty permitted with a royal decree. But this brother-in-law of the emperor was used to his untamed life of singing to his heart's content while raising cattle in the field. Whilst he was robed in silk and feasted on delicacies, he was much bothered by the elaborate rituals and etiquettes of the court life.

Brother Xu wanted to return home, and the emperor failed to persuade him to stay. When parting, His Majesty asked what his brother-in-law would wish to have. 'My abode at home is low and shabby,' complained Brother Xu, 'and there are no tall and majestic courtyards in Yongding.' The emperor on hearing this plea was sympathetic. He ordered the Yongding county government to build his brother-in-law the multi-storey courtyard which matched that of the county government. But Brother Xu felt lonely in the stately home and asked His Majesty to permit all his relatives to come to live with him in the same house. The emperor once again obliged. This, unexpectedly, became exemplary. The locals all started building multi-storey 'fortress ramparts' to house the families from the same clan.[7]

The migration myths and the legend of Brother Xu would support two quite different rationales behind the fortress-like multi-storey courtyards houses built by the Hakka. The first was a true defensive fortification to protect the Hakka from ambush by the indigenous settlers and bandits, whilst the latter was driven by the economy of a stately-looking house devoted to communal living. The physical configuration of the Hakka house seems to support both explanations. Hakka houses come in various shapes and sizes ranging from circular, square to rectangular, but the *parti* of all these diverse forms is a consistent one (Figure 8.2). This pattern can be most clearly deciphered from the round 'fortress ramparts' of two rings.

Zhencheng Lou in Yongding county is one such round rampart with a diameter of 52 metres (Figure 8.3). The four-level defensive outer wall is made of thick rammed earth with only small fenestrations for the two top storeys. Structurally supported with eight internal

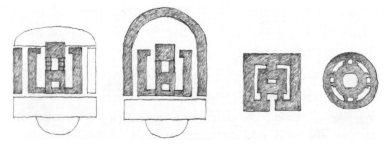

**Figure 8.2** *Diagrams of four plan types of Hakka house, showing diverse forms based on one consistent courtyard pattern.*

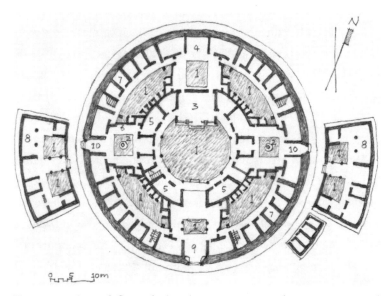

**Figure 8.3** *Ground floor of Zhencheng Lou in Yongding county. Legend: 1. Courtyard/Voids; 2. Void with a well; 3. Hall; 4. Ancestral hall; 5. Reception hall; 6. Bath; 7. Kitchen; 8. Barn, mill and storage; 9. Main entry; 10. Side door.*

brick piers, the four levels of evenly divided rooms are made entirely of timber beams, posts, planks and panels. The eight sections in plan, connected by an open veranda on upper levels, are popularly attributed to the Chinese 'Eight Trigrams' (八卦), although those who live there may not know this in any conscious way. The two-level inner ring however is made of fine bricks. Both rings are covered with tile roofs. The single gate and the fortified rammed earth wall do provide effective self-defence, but there are two 'ear' buildings placed beyond the outer ring, used as the barn, mill and storage. This seems to defeat the purpose of fortification, for the food supply can easily fall into the hands of the enemies. A fortified fortress rampart with buildings attached to it may be an odd case, but the true meaning, in this instance, may not lie in its fortification. The local belief of these two 'ear' buildings symbolizing the flaps of a traditional official's hat, too, could be discounted as a fabricated tale to please the tourists,[8] it nonetheless reveals a desired Chineseness in the deep psyche of the Hakka. What is not far-fetched, however, is the Chinese courtyard *parti* as cemented in its plan and spatial configuration.

In the ground plan, beginning at the gate portico is the central axis. Passing through an atrium-like small skywell between the outer ring and the inner ring, one reaches the round courtyard and the sky framed by the inner ring. Behind it lies the ceremonial and ritual hall with its own pyramidal roof. The hall is extended, with another skywell between the two rings in the middle, to the end of the outer ring – this is where the ancestor's shrine is housed, hence the ancestor hall. The ceremonial hall on the axis is elevated above the paved central courtyard and it has three bays. The hall, and the inner ring building divided as subordinate halls, all face and are open to the central court without definitive enclosures. This is eerily familiar: Confucius could have hosted the respected blind musician Mian in the hall (*tang* 堂) of this Hakka rampart, as he could have done in the Fengchu ruin site and the courtyard *parti* of the gentry in the Spring and Autumn period derived by the Qing scholar Zhang Huiyan, and indeed in any courtyard that we have visited so far.

Beyond this central axis there are rooms for fulfilling basic needs: facing the four linear courts are a pigsty and chicken coops attached to the inner ring, and kitchens in the outer ring. Perpendicular to the central spine is the subordinate axis with two side doors leading to the two 'ear' buildings. In the two small skywells on this axis there are wells and bathrooms around them. On the first level, there are storage and miscellaneous rooms in both the inner ring and the outer ring, where there are no external windows. The two top levels in the outer ring are the living and sleeping rooms for individual families. These, to reference the Chinese courtyard *parti*, are really the *shi* 室, that is, rooms or chambers. The only difference between a Hakka rampart and a Chinese courtyard is that the communal living of the individual families in the former, are relatively egalitarian, whereas the four generations under one roof in the latter are hierarchical. But when it comes to the central axis, both the Hakka rampart and the Chinese courtyard are Confucian, in essence.

The circular Hakka house is one particular type of the same courtyard pattern, as a 'butterfly' (referring to the discussion of pattern versus type in Chapter 7), to which the Beijing quadrangle also belongs. There are many different kinds of circular 'butterflies' – from single ring and double-ring with a variety of configurations of the inner ring, even to multiple rings. Let us try again the same exercise of theoretically turning the circle into a semi-circle, or a semi-circle combined with a square and rectangle, even to simply square and rectangular shapes. As it turns out, there are Hakka houses built in all of these forms and shapes. One thing, as seen thus far in all Chinese courtyards, real or literary, is consistently tenacious – that is, the progression along the central axis that is gradually turned upwards to Heaven. But this is not quite the singular *axis mundi* of a heavenly trajectory. The Chinese liked to vacillate around the middle between Heaven's watchful eye above the courtyard and their indulgent earthly life now and then in the courtyard. The ceremonial life in the hall thus was used to tweak this delicate balance as the Chinese saw fit between the burden of needs on earth and the lofty spirit that must soar on occasions. The secret of this golden mean, too often, lay in their faith in Heaven's magnanimous forgiveness, and in their own fatalistic cheer, wicked sense of humour, as well as their lack of absolute conviction about reason whilst remaining quite reasonable overall. The Hakka are no exception.

If Hakka's fortress rampart is effectively a Chinese courtyard, why then do the Hakka build vast compounds of egalitarian and communal living, which appear rather un-Chinese? The medieval explanation based on the migration myths and the necessity of fortification is overstated if not plainly dubious in some cases. The pair of 'ear' buildings attached to Zhencheng Lou certainly is curiously non-defensive. Besides, unlike real fortresses, Hakka *tulou* are rarely found commanding high ground.[9] Among the diverse 'butterflies' of Hakka ramparts, some of them are not even fortified – *weilong wu* 围拢屋 (encircling ridge house, or 围龙屋 encircling dragon house) is either a semi-circle combined with a rectangular front, or simply square and rectangular in shape, both of which have multiple gates. *Banyuan lou* 半圆楼 (half-circle house) is completely open with multiple entry points (Figure 8.4). Variations of these types include, *bagua lou* 八卦楼 (eight-trigram house), *santang wu* 三堂屋 (three-hall house) and *daifu di* 大夫弟 (gentry house), which are semi or completely open. None of the above lack the core axis of the Chinese courtyard of framed Heaven and the elevated hall.

The consolidated fortress and its communal living must come down to the symbolism of a stately mansion and the economic advantages of collective living. The legendary tale of Brother Xu's mansion bestowed by the emperor, tells more of the true insight of the collective imagination of the Hakka than the reason for the necessary fortification – being 'guest families' permanently sojourned in the remote land. In most circumstances, families belonging to the same clan (hence sharing the same surname) would live in one *tulou*. The circular form therefore is

**Figure 8.4** *Plan diagram of a half-circle house, showing an unfortified complex with multiple entry points and with ancestral hall in the centre before a crescent pond.*

undoubtedly the most favourable one, for it is the economical optimum par excellence of minimum material and maximum floor area. Nearly two-thirds of the existing Hakka houses were built after 1900.[10] Zhencheng Lou, for example, was erected in 1921. The ironic change of fortune of the Hakka house occurred in the heydays of the socialist era when the impoverished economy and 'people's commune' – the period of collective living and production regulated by the central government – saw their perfect match. Between 1950 and 1970, one-third of the current Hakka houses mushroomed,[11] and the Confucian axis retreated to obscurity during this period. The locals recall fondly the communal spirit in that period: people helped each other build the compounds when no one had any money.[12]

## Chinese form and exotic meaning

The Bai, the Naxi, and to some extent the Hani and the Yi, to name a few out of twenty-four ethnic minority groups living in south-west Yunnan province, have always built courtyard houses that look very much like those of the Chinese. Among them the Bai have had a long and amicable relationship with Han Chinese. By the eighth century when the Kingdom of Nanzhao was established, many in the upper echelon were Bai chiefs who were well versed in Chinese. By the tenth century when the Bai established their own Kingdom of Dali (937–1254 CE), the Han in central China and the Bai in the frontiers had developed close economic and cultural ties. From the Yuan through to the Qing periods and onwards, most of the Bai would have learned Chinese, and their agrarian economy, craftsmanship and merchandising would have been largely the same as that of the Chinese.

It is debatable whether or not the Bai had been whole-heartedly turned into Confucians. They, however, like the Chinese, had embraced Buddhism with zeal. Until the founding of the Yuan dynasty in the early thirteenth century, the Bai had more than four hundred years of devotion to Buddhism. In an elegantly composed essay, titled 'The Travelogue of Dali' (大理行记), the official, Guo Songnian 郭松年, gave a vivid description of such fervour of the Bai in the early years under the rule of Yuan: whether poor or rich, almost always there was a Buddhist shrine in every household; whether old or young, in their hands they all held strings of Buddhist beads. There were several fasting seasons during the year, and the locals never touched alcohol and meat until each period ended. The hills were dotted with temples, which were too numerous to account for.[13] Guo Songnian, in the same essay, made a curious remark: prior to the reign of the Yuan when Dali was an independent kingdom, Buddhist monks, who could marry and raise a family, also read Confucian classics. These monks also happened to be candidates of the kingdom's own imperial examination. What Guo Songnian did not say in this essay was the unique feature of the Dali model: in addition to Confucian classics as found in the Chinese system, Buddhist classics were an essential part of the examination. Guo Songnian, however, observed in the same essay that Buddhist devotees of his time were more orthodox, and applied Buddhist doctrines more sternly. The temples as a result became a place devoid of any desire for fame and fortune.

It may, in the first instance, appear puzzling that it was the Mongol emperor of the Yuan Kublai Khan who ordered his Dali governor to instigate state Confucianism in the first six years of the Mongol reign. The governor promulgated the 'Confucian ethics', prompted Confucian studies, built Confucian temples and government schools, and allowed his adopted subjects of Dali a career path through the state imperial examination. Like any state Confucianism of the past and the future, the distortion (always for the purpose of blind legitimization of totalitarian rule) of Confucius' thought on societal stratification and obedient decorum, would not be recognized by Confucius himself. In state Confucianism, very little of the Master's truth-seeking free spirit and common decency remained. The intensified Buddhist enthusiasm as observed by Guo Songnian, was likely a local reaction to the state-imposed worldview, and it could have been a show of revulsion against the politically motivated state Confucianism. Indeed, a few of the kings of Dali since the Yuan dynasty, have been singled out in history because they relinquished their power in order to revert back to being Buddhist devotees. A prominent Confucian (*juru* 巨儒) of the Ming dynasty Li Yuanyang 李元阳, for example, renounced his official position at the age of forty to become a reclusive pupil of Buddhism in the hills of the Buddhist mecca of Mountain Jizu 鸡足山 near Dali.

But the Bai up to this date have largely maintained their animistic beliefs whilst promoting a Primary God 本主 as their protector for a village or a region. Some of the Bai gods have specific capacities to expel clouds or protect a river. Many wise rulers and heroes of the past, however, have been elevated to the status of a Primary God. Have the Bai more or less turned into Chinese through this long process of acculturation? An examination of their courtyard house may provide a clue.

There are two prototypes of Bai courtyards – 'three rooms and one screen' (三坊一照壁) and 'a quadrangle of five courts' (四合五天井) (Figure 8.5). The first is a courtyard bordered by rooms on three sides with a screen wall sealing it on the fourth side, the same name as the Chinese *zhaobi* 照壁. The second is a courtyard encircled by rooms on four sides. For both prototypes, in addition to the central court, there is a small court, known as 'leaking corner skywell' (漏角天井), at the junction of each corner, hence three courts for the first prototype and five courts for the latter. Based on these two prototypes, other variations suitable for different sites and family circumstances are derived.

Unlike the Chinese courtyard, a Bai house is orientated on an east–west axis. The main building and its central hall therefore face east, with the entry gate to the house often situated at the north-eastern corner. The conventional wisdom has it that such orientation – with the back of the main hall facing west – avoids the fierce westerly, with which the Bai region of Dali 大理 and Jianchuan 剑川 is infamously characterized. The topography of Dali and Jianchuan belongs to the distinctively broad north–south mountain range, known as the Hengduan Mountains (横断山脉), in south-west China. Towns and villages in these two areas are in narrow alignment between the mountain range on the west and the lake on the east. Situated on the gentle slopes of the eastern side of the mountain range, the adaptation of only one aspect of the Chinese *fengshui* posture – that is, a house, backed by the mountain, ought to face water, seems a little half-hearted if not disingenuous. Despite the considerably different climatic zones and vastly complex geography of the country, the Han almost always placed their courtyards on the Chinese cardinal disposition of a north–south axis, with only a slight degree of variation to acknowledge local circumstances. A complete disregard of this cosmic positioning in having their courtyard placed on an east–west axis, and consequently with the hall and main rooms facing east, hardly qualifies the Bai courtyard in Dali as a Chinese one.

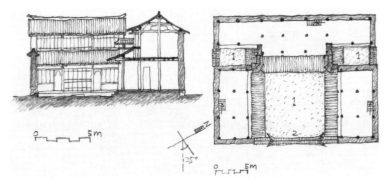

**Figure 8.5a.** *The cross section and the upper level plan of a 'three rooms and one screen' Bai courtyard.*

On the surface, the bay in the middle of the main building, facing west, and often called *mingjian* 明间 (bright room) by the Bai, is the equivalent of *tang* in the Chinese courtyard. The width of *mingjian* on the ground, not nearly as ceremonial as that of the Chinese *tang*, is about the same as, or often narrower than, the two side bedrooms. Like the Chinese *tang*, this is where the guests are received. Unlike the Chinese *tang*, *mingjian* is not dedicated to the ancestors but rather the shrines of gods. Even more curious is that there is the central staircase positioned at the back of *mingjian* in the Dali region. The spacious upstairs room – occupying the entire length of the building without internal division – is where the more celebrated Buddhist shrine is often housed. A revisit to the Ming and Qing two-storey Chinese courtyard in the Huizhou region is revealing here. The upstairs *mingjian*, right on top of the ground level *tang*, though not occupying the entire length of the building, is devoted solely to the family ancestor. The staircase in a two-storey Chinese house, it should be noted, is on the side, therefore does not cause any disruption to the Confucian world cemented in a courtyard. The Bai may not be half-hearted converts of the Chinese, but they nonetheless are in two or even three minds about their beliefs: the Primary God of theirs, the borrowed Buddha and the

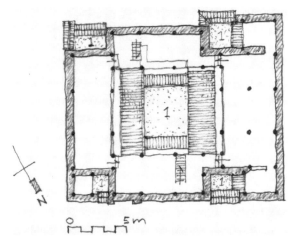

**Figure 8.5b.** *The upper level plan of a 'quadrangle of five courts' Bai courtyard. Legend: 1. Courtyard/void; 2.* Zhaobi *(screen).*

Confucian demand for ancestor tribute (which may well coincide with their ancestry commemoration) are all being looked after.

Where then, is the ancestor in a Bai courtyard? The screen wall *zhaobi* in a Bai house does not serve the purpose of blocking the view into the house or of repelling the evil spirit, nor does it work as a barrier to raise the level of awe and solemnity before the guest is admitted to the inner court of a noble family as seen in Chinese antiquity. A Bai *zhaobi* is the inside wall facing the courtyard. The modern explanation is that the whitewashed wall is to reflect daylight into the hall and the bedrooms on the other side of the court. Since the *zhaobi* wall is lower than the two-storey building, it may allow a view to the lake from the upstairs rooms. More adorned than the Chinese *zhaobi* – the wall is not only crowned with a tiled roof, it is also framed by exquisite local marble inlay, quarried locally and known as Dali stone (大理石), which happens to be the Chinese name for marble in general. In addition to 'fortune' (福), the Bai use both sides of *zhaobi* to write more mottos on them: *qinhe jiasheng* 琴鹤家声 and *bairen jiafeng* 百忍家风 are two examples. The first depicts the Zhao family ancestor as an incorruptible official of supreme taste, for he went about doing his business and daily life accompanied by a stringed instrument and a crane. The latter tells of the large Zhang family ancestors of several generations co-inhabiting harmoniously under one roof which had helped cultivate the family doctrine of tolerance.[14] The Bai no doubt are the earnest student of the Chinese. The reincarnation of *zhaobi* in their houses show, however, their light-hearted good nature when it comes to making tributes to the ancestors. The fatal tweak of the courtyard orientation, the showy use of *zhaobi*, and the amenity-leaning courtyard itself – used for drying crops and lovingly attended potted plants (more akin to the Roman peristyle than the atrium of gods and ancestor worship) – make the Bai courtyard less a Confucian world and more of a court of its own with a distinctive character.

But the delight of the ancient town of Lijiang built by the talented Naxi (also known as Nakhi or Nashi), which no other Chinese or Bai townscape in the region can equal, is the pleasure garden bounded by their courtyard. That the crystal-clear stream from the nearby Mountain Xiangshan is channelled to the town to fill its web of canals to every single house and even to their inner courtyards, simply adds to the sheer enchantment (Figure 8.6). The Naxi, now inhabiting the foothills of the Himalayans in north-western Yunnan and south-eastern Sichuan, were a nomadic people allegedly springing from the Tibetans and the ancient Qiang. The southern migration not only turned the Naxi into sedentary and agrarian people, but also put them in contact with the Han. The acculturation between the Naxi and the Han has been a long time in the making, and is now entangled with much complexity. The Naxi contact with central China can be dated back to the eighth century CE – the Tang Kaiyuan 唐开元 period. Much of their building technics and skills have been borrowed from the Tibetans and the Bai. But their courtyard configurations chiefly

**Figure 8.6** *A section perspective of the town of Lijiang, showing the street canal channelled into a courtyard house for water supply.*

come from the Bai and the Chinese, with 'three rooms and one screen' and 'quadrangle of five courts' as two of the dominant patterns.

The Naxi, however, are too staunch and unyielding to take pedantically their learnings from the Chinese and the Bai. The lingering nomadic tribal spirit in their blood, and the remnants of matriarchy and animism in their society, too, make them less apt a pupil of Confucius. In addition to their own Dongba – an animistic belief –, they have, to varying degrees, adopted Lamaism, Buddhism and Daoism. The most non-Han, and indeed the most resilient, character of the Naxi is their pursuit of free love. A more extreme case, thanks to ever-increasing tourist enthusiasm, is the 'walking marriage' custom still being practiced among the Mosuo, who are believed to be an ethnic cousin of the Naxi.[15] Considered as a matrilineal society, hence naturally matriarchal, a coming-of-age Mosuo woman is free to choose her sexual partner. With her permission, the 'husband' visits the woman at night and leaves her house before dawn. The children of such consummation are raised by the woman's family, with the woman's brother, the maternal uncle, serving as the father figure. The biological father of the children continues to live with his own family. A Mosuo woman in her lifetime may maintain such romantic assignation with one partner. She, however, is free to terminate it and move on to a different man. It is not unusual for a Mosuo woman, and a Mosuo man, to have multiple 'marriage' partners in a lifetime, but societal conventions unusually prevent this from occurring at the same time.

The concept of marriage as understood by the Han and other societies remains tenuous among the Mosuo. In a Mosuo courtyard house, one private room among those encircling the central court is set aside and named as the 'flowering room' for the coming-of-age daughter, though there is no particular size or spatial disposition assigned to it. A nicer room, though still undistinguishable, is reserved for the visiting monks. The salient feature in a Mosuo courtyard is the matriarch suite, which is the largest in the house, with its own miscellaneous rooms around it, and its own entry from outside the courtyard compound. The central room in the suite, non-axial in relation to other rooms in the courtyard, has the matriarch's bed, female and male pillars, fire basin, and shrines of gods and ancestor. This is where the family congregate, but a Mosuo house is not a Confucius courtyard.

Marriage, on the contrary, is largely cemented and practiced in Naxi society. The right to choose one's life partner has been a persistent belief despite parents feeling an obligation to decide for their children. Though often expressed in strikingly different ways to that of the Mosuo, the spirit of free love lingers on. Naxi legend has it that the founder of Dongba cohabited with a hundred women during his lifetime. A Naxi proverb says that a man plants his seeds wherever he goes. Chinese influence only began to take root among the Naxi in the Yuan dynasty, but both Yuan and Ming emperors nevertheless decided to let the indigenous settlers in the frontier keep their old way of living, and they ruled by following the local customs (不改其旧，顺俗施政).

In the Ming dynasty, the local nobles and chiefs were supported by the Chinese court, but the Chinese cultural influence was deliberately contained within the elite group. The Qing rulers, however, saw matters differently. In 1697, the 66th-generation descendant of Confucius, Kong Xingxun 孔兴询, was appointed by the Qing court to Tongpan 通判 of Lijiang. This was a position especially designed for the remote frontier towns, and had equal status to that of the local governor. It was designed to keep an eye on the work of the governor and to balance power. When reaching Lijiang, Kong Xingxun pronounced that for any change to happen to the indigenous population, rites and music must be used. In order to have rites and music established, Confucian temples ought to do the job.[16] Confucius would have endorsed the former, but not the latter.

By 1723, the Qing court instigated the official policy of 'turning native customs into the mainstream' (改土归流), and 'using Chinese culture to change the barbarians' (以夏变夷). State Confucianism, once again, was the most effective apparatus for assimilating the Naxi. By the late nineteenth century, on the surface, no matriarchal remains could be detected in Naxi. The opposite was nearly true: women were prohibited from going to the temple to burn incense, not allowed to participate in Heaven-worship ritual, banned from merchandising, sleeping in the main hall of the house, and sharing a meal with her father-in-law. The parents could at their discretion, marry off their daughter to whomever they so chose. The latter was the main cause of the tragic trend of young women and men 'dying for love' that was rampant from the eighteenth century through to the 1950s. This twin-suicide committed by young couples for free love, rather disturbingly, is aestheticized by Dongba literature and scripture with the promise of an afterlife of eternal ecstasy in the pure snow of Mountain Yulong.

Such solemn and stirring sublimity is alien to the Confucian world. Nonetheless it is behind the exuberant and pictorial Naxi courtyards.

The *zhaobi* in their courtyard bears no Chinese words to boast the glory of their ancestors. They are either adorned with marble patterns, or simply whitewashed walls framed by elaborate brick inlays. In the latter case, they serve as the background for an eclectic collection of potted plants and flowers. The number of the courtyards, their sizes and orientations vary a great deal to suit the circumstances of the

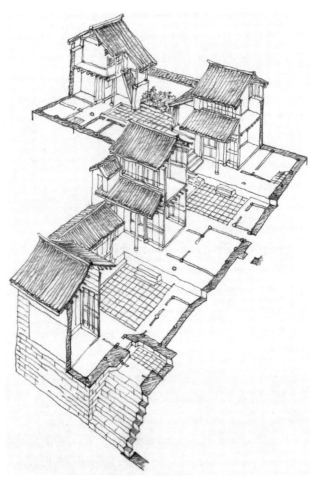

**Figure 8.7** *A cutaway bird's eye view of No. 87 in Xinhua Street, Lijiang, showing multiple courtyards arranged to suit the contour of a sloping site.*

family status, its means, needs and the actual site on which the house is built (Figure 8.7). Often there are two or more courtyards, with one paved to match the hall and the main building, while the others are filled with plants and vegetable pads. The hall, of course, has shrines of various kinds, but is used as a bedroom when circumstances justify it. Much of the activity of receiving guests, dining and doing house chores occur in the generous veranda, called *shazi* 厦子, before the hall and the main building. The stone paving in the main courtyard and in their streets, reminiscent of the intricate flowery patterns seen in the Chinese Ming and Qing garden houses, are, however, executed with passion and panache. The Naxi had used colourful river stones which had become brilliantly shiny after centuries of stamping from human feet. More reminiscent of Pompeii and resembling less of Huizhou or Suzhou, any sign of Confucian rite and decorum is not even faintly detectable in those lively and robust Naxi courtyards. If the Naxi indeed had adopted the courtyard from the Chinese via the Bai, they have kept the form but changed its meaning to suit not only their land but also their temperament.

*Part Three*

# Earth

## The Emancipation of Desire and the Loss of Courtyard

# 9

# *The Irresistible Metropolis*

The vast urban tapestry knitted together by quadrangles in Beijing continued well into the twentieth century, but the story of the courtyard in Shanghai was quite a different one. The reason for Lin Yutang's distaste for Shanghai may lie precisely in the loss of courtyards when this small walled frontier town of 2 kilometres in diameter at the lower reach of the Yangtze, was transformed into a modern metropolis. The two Opium Wars, from 1839 to 1842 and from 1856 to 1860 respectively, not only humiliated the once prosperous and grand empire of the Qing court, they also forced China to open several of its coastal port cities to the British, the French and other Western powers. But Shanghai, like an eccentric child among his more conventional siblings, has always been an anomaly. The Yangtze region had been populated with towns and early cities since the Spring and Autumn period, and the name Shanghai – meaning 'on the sea' – appeared much later in the Tang dynasty, as a river port.

Unlike China's imperial cities, Shanghai, since its inception until the middle of the Ming dynasty, was not walled. Instead it had always been a market town (*zhen* 镇), which had its official designation at the end of the Southern Song dynasty in 1276 CE. A market town, usually not walled in the lower reaches of the Yangtze, was always at the periphery in the Chinese cosmos. Shanghai unsurprisingly was not founded based on the Chinese cosmic model. Judging from the schematic Chinese cartographic maps from the Yuan to the Ming dynasties, the persistent urban pattern of Shanghai – a matrix of transverse canals connecting to the Huangpu River – continued until the town was walled in 1553 (Figure 9.1), and well into the twentieth century until the city wall was demolished between 1911 and 1914. This was the aftermath of the Revolution of 1911 led by Dr Sun Yat-sen which overthrew the Qing court.

The city wall encircling Shanghai was erected to ward off the frequent assaults of Japanese pirates (though some of them were Chinese bandits and hooligans), known as Wokou 倭寇. It was 4,500 metres long, and 7.2 metres in height. The moat outside the city wall was approximately 4,900 metres long and 19.8 metres wide with a depth of 5.6 metres.

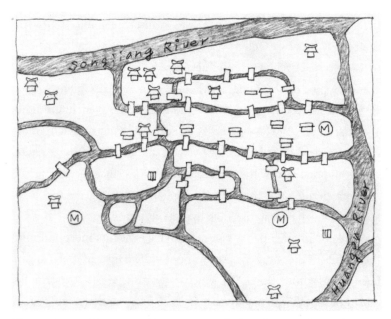

**Figure 9.1a.** *Schematic Chinese map of Shanghai in the early Yuan dynasty (late thirteenth century).*

It might have had the appearance of a Chinese town, but any salient connection with the cosmic King's City was nowhere to be detected. The shape of the city wall was oval rather than square; there was no nine-square grid but a traverse canal and street matrix; and three of its six gates faced the Huangpu River, which signalled the town's dependence on the port even after the city had been enclosed by the wall. The Qing painter Cao Shiting 曹史亭, relying on early works, repeated the depiction of the prosperous scene of Shanghai's Shiliu Pu port (十六铺) in the late nineteenth century. Merchants, we have learned, belonged to the lowest rank of the four major classes in China, so merchandizing was never encouraged by Confucian doctrine. Shanghai was destined to be an atypical Chinese town.

Not unlike the hamlets and towns built by ethnic minority groups in China's frontiers, Shanghai, too, was a place where 'Heaven is high

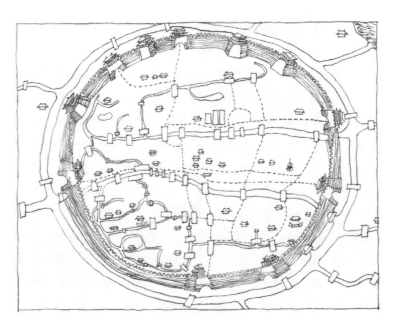

**Figure 9.1b.** *Schematic Chinese map of Shanghai in the Ming dynasty (early seventeenth century) when the city was walled.*

and the emperor is far away'. Such fringe status was both geographical and symbolic, but it was the latter that defined Shanghai's position in the Chinese cosmos, resulting in a character and a temperament that demanded a different kind of urban form, and eventually its fitting housing configuration after Shanghai was 'sacked' by the British. Some scholars of Shanghai's urban history hold the view that Confucian rites were either lost or token in Shanghai well before its port was opened to the British and other Western powers in the middle of nineteenth century.[1]

One example of its non-Confucian character was that Shanghai, for a long time in Chinese history, was an outpost for free-spirited literati and failed scholar-officials. This was the edge of the empire (and the universe since China had been the Middle Kingdom), beyond which the non-conformists and eccentrics could not possibly venture further. It should be no surprise that the Chinese Communist Party was founded in Shanghai by a group of young revolutionaries in July 1921. The location of its first meeting was in a girl's school in the French concession. It was next to a densely populated *Lilong* 里弄 – the archetypal 'alleyway neighbourhood' that, in a few stages of rapid development, mushroomed in Shanghai from the 1860s through to the 1920s to become the primary housing pattern of its urban fabric. Like a beehive happily infested by the busy bees, this was indeed a deep and porous receptacle of the joys and follies of the 'Shanghai petty urbanites' (上海小市民), an expression coined by one of Shanghai's favourite literary daughters and the exceedingly talented writer Eileen Chang 张爱玲 (Zhang Ailing). Chang, a native of Shanghai born in 1920, was a child protégé, and wrote much on her indulgence in the pleasures of bourgeois life in her beloved city. She spent her first five dollars of royalty on a lipstick, earned from publishing a cartoon drawing in an English newspaper![2] Shanghai could hardly be recognized as a Chinese city. But Chang laid bare her affection for the intoxicating city and its residents: 'Shanghai people are distilled from traditional Chinese people under the pressure of modern life; they are the product of a deformed mix of old and new culture. The result may not be healthy, but in it there is also a curious wisdom.'[3]

# Modern city born of refugee crisis

This 'deformed mix of old and new culture' was first and foremost cemented in *Lilong*, an instant formation of the city fabric entirely caused by chance. The prosperity of the new Shanghai beyond the old Shanghai town began, rather unexpectedly, not through trade as the British and the French had hoped for, but from an ad hoc real estate boom as the result of a refugee crisis, to which I shall return later. The British sailed into the Huangpu River on 19 June 1842; they entered Shanghai without meeting any resistance. The major ports north of Guangzhou fell, and the emperor sued for peace when the British marched into Nanjing. In August, the Treaty of Nanjing was signed to grant the British, among other things, the cession of Hong Kong and the opening of the five so-called treaty ports of Guangzhou, Xiamen, Fuzhou, Ningbo and Shanghai for residence and trade. Accompanying these rights was the establishment of foreign consulates at the treaty ports. On 14 November 1843, the first appointed British consul of Shanghai, George Balfour declared that the official inauguration of the Shanghai treaty port would be on the 17th of the same month. It was Balfour who argued before the British parliament that Shanghai was 'destined to become the great emporium for the China trade'.[4] By the end of 1843, in merely two months, there were twenty-five foreigners registered as residents in Shanghai. In the following year, the Americans and the French followed suit.

In the early months, Balfour did set up the British consular office within the walls of the old Shanghai town. The large courtyard complex of 52 rooms, rented from the Gu residence, instantly became the focal point of local curiosity: Shanghai residents – men, women and children, flocked to the British consulate to observe with much interest the foreigners' strange daily customs of eating, shaving, washing, reading and even sleeping . . .[5] But the foreign merchants quickly complained about the difficulties in obtaining leases for accommodation and the circumstantially inflated rents. Balfour, perhaps always wanting to establish a foreigner-only settlement in Shanghai, used this excuse of rental problem to make a request to the Qing court for a piece of land to build their merchant guildhall (known in Chinese as *huiguang* 会馆). This request was timely, for it incidentally suited the Qing court, who never agreed to allow foreigners to choose land freely to build their merchant guild halls as desired by the British negotiator Henry Pottinger.[6] To the mind of the Qing court, there was trouble brewing in permitting the current situation of mixed Chinese and foreigners to continue. It would be of tremendous benefit for all if the foreigners were to be segregated, as was the case of the so-called 'factory' designated for British and other foreign traders outside Canton (today's Guangzhou) before the Opium War. At the end of 1843, a piece of 'wasteland' to the north of walled Shanghai, bounded by the Huangpu River on the east, Lijia Zhuang 李家庄 on the north, Yangjing Bing 杨泾浜[7] on the south, and the vast barren land on the west, was granted to the British. This particular territory was in the future to become the famous Bund, which originated from the Hindi word, embankment (Figure 9.2).

Balfour could not have imagined in his wildest dreams the prosperous modern metropolis to come. His master plan for this British-only settlement was neither visionary nor aspirational. It was a rudimentary division of land blocks driven by sheer pragmatism –

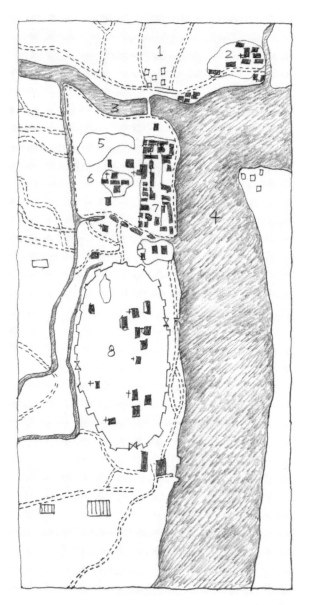

**Figure 9.2** *The schematic map of foreign settlements in Shanghai in 1853. Legend: 1. Hongkou; 2. American Settlement; 3. Suzhou Creek; 4. Huangpu River; 5. Race Course; 6. British Settlement; 7. French Settlement; 8. The Walled Shanghai Town.*

east–west roads leading towards the Huangpu River bank, which has lasted, to this day, as the enduring urban structure of the Bund within the boundaries of Suzhou Creek (also known as the Wusong River) to the north and the west bank of Yangtze Creek. Such an urban grid had nothing to do with the fine grains of the courtyard matrix in old Shanghai town. It was not even a nineteenth-century European urban ideal of 'city beautiful' that was hitherto achieved through handsome neo-classical buildings, tree-lined boulevards and vistas marked by monuments. Even the naming of roads was matter of fact: from Bridge Street, Church Street, to Consulate Road and Park Lane that led to a park, which is today's Nanjing Road – the most frequented shopping street in China. Early buildings, dotted on the marsh land of graves and shanty workshops, were built fronting the Huangpu River bank with approximately 30 metres setback from it. The first foreign settlers took a lazy approach to design and build in these structures. They adopted the so-called 'Compradoric Style' for their consulates, trade offices and houses – a masonry colonial building surrounded by wide open colonnades on all sides. Such was the building type developed for the British and other European colonies in South-East Asia and its tropical climate, but when transplanted to Shanghai, its openness proved to be quite miserable for the bitterly cold winter. The British Consulate Building (built in 1873, still standing today though largely remodelled) and the French Consulate (built in 1896, now demolished) were early examples.

These buildings, sitting oddly on the muddy ground to the Chinese eye, were not built to last. The settlers slept rough. Hoping to make a quick fortune in Shanghai, they did not intend to stay put for too long. This piece of 'wasteland', one-kilometre long on the river frontage with easy waterway connection to the vast interior, turned out to be the most convenient and indeed strategic location for the British. The French, too, quickly saw the advantage. In 1856 they secured a segment known as the French Bund between the old Shanghai town and the British Bund, though it was not as grand and was only 10 metres wide. By the end of 1844, eleven merchant firms landed in this territory, including those that would become household names in Shanghai: Jardine, Matheson & Co., Gibb Livingston & Co., Holliday Wise & Co., Blenlein, Rawson & Co., Dent & Co. and Wolcott, Bate & Co. By 1846, the number, including three American firms, increased to twenty-four. There were also five retail shops, 25 private residences, a church, a hotel, a dispensary, a club house at the race track and the first cemetery. In one decade, the merchant firms, coming from major European powers of the Netherlands, Germany, Austria, Spain and Denmark, reached more than 120.[8] But the truly remarkable growth of population and prosperity occurred in the second decade of the establishment of foreign settlement when the large influx of Chinese refugees sought sojourn in the safe haven of foreign concession lands. This was the inception of Eileen Chang's 'deformed mix of new and old', and indeed the foundation of modern Shanghai.

The major cause of this refugee crisis was the Taiping Rebellion and Small Sword Society. The Christian convert Hong Xiuquan 洪秀全, who also happened to be a repeated reject of the imperial examination, gathered remarkable momentum among his own Hakka people and minority groups through the God Worshiping Society. The compelling teaching of Protestant Christianity and anti-Confucian sentiment from Hong might have further confused the inherent identity crisis of the Hakka and other minorities, who, as we have learned in the preceding chapter, had long vouched their loyalty to the Han by declaring themselves as Han's ancient descendants. But still they felt rejected by the dominant culture and polity. By 1850, Hong amassed a formidable force of poor peasants and impoverished labourers that were capable of confronting the Qing army. In 1851, Hong proclaimed himself the leader of the new imperial dynasty

Taiping Tianguo 太平天国 (Heavenly Kingdom of Great Peace), and would share his power with five other kings. In 1853, Nanjing was sacked and renamed as Tianjing (Heavenly Capital). In the meantime, from 1853 to 1855, the secretive Small Sword Society 小刀会 of self-defence, too, turned into a rebellion against the Qing court in the Shanghai region. The Small Sword Society took control of only the old Shanghai town; they deliberately sought peaceful coexistence with the foreign settlements. But soon they declared their loyalty to Taiping Tianguo and willingly submitted themselves to the rule of the great leader Hong Xiuquan.

In the early years of upheaval, British, American and French powers were ambivalent about taking sides and participating in the conflict. However, whilst maintaining neutrality on the surface, they gave much assistance to the Small Sword Society behind the scenes. Some British and Americans even fought against the Qing army, which triggered the Qing court to seek support from foreign powers to build a trench around the old Shanghai town in order to block the supply lines to the rebel-controlled town. The Americans were passive, and the British were never fully committed until they realized that those who fought for the Small Sword Society against the Qing army and its French ally were in fact deserter British and American sailors. The French, being on the frontline due to the location of their settlement, became the major force. In a bloody battle on the eve of Chinese New Year in 1855, they helped the Qing court defeat the Small Sword Society. The ringleader Liu Lichuan 刘丽川 was killed in the battle; another leader Chen Alin 陈阿林 fled to South-East Asia to start a new life as a merchant, and the others left to join the Taiping Tianguo. Five years later in the winter of 1860, the Taiping army marched towards Shanghai, but the city was spared by a severe snowstorm. By now, any Western sympathy for the Taiping Tianguo had completely waned. The Qing court and the Western powers formed a coalition of

'The Ever Victorious Army' led by the American Frederick Ward Townsend, and later the Englishman Charles George Gordon after Townsend was killed in an 1862 battle. During the years of turmoil starting from the threat of the Small Sword Society in old Shanghai town to the collapse of the Taiping Tianguo in 1864, Shanghai was never seized. More than 30 million people, however, lost their lives during the fourteen years of revolution and rebellion.

It was against this disturbing background that the Chinese refugees flocked to the foreign settlements in Shanghai to seek asylum. By 1865, the population in Shanghai's foreign concession had reached 150,000, which comprised 21.5 per cent of the entire population in Shanghai. Approximately 110,000 were Chinese.[9] Although foreign merchants were predominantly involved in trading opium, silk, cotton and tea, building houses and letting them to the Chinese refugees proved to be far more profitable than the trading they originally set out to do. An English merchant explicitly declared his business ambition to the British Consul, Rutherford Alcock (Balfour's successor). With a profit margin of 30 to 40 per cent in this property development business, he would hope to make a quick fortune and leave: '... what can it matter to me, if all Shanghai disappears afterwards, in fire or flood?'[10] This was the first time in Chinese history that the notion of profit-driven property development was explicitly displayed before the Chinese.

The segregation between the Chinese and foreigners as determined by the Land Regulations was dissolved, and the regulations themselves were subsequently revised by the Consuls of Britain, America and France without any consultation with the Qing court. By law, foreigners (*yiren* 夷人) were not allowed to own land under the 'heavenly court' of the Qing, though the slight irony here is the definition of non-foreigner – was it the ruling Manchu or the Chinese? It was only a matter of self-deceiving pride. Foreigners could purchase land under a permanent 'lease', as long as they paid a token annual land tax to the government. This ingenious idea of maintaining 'face' for the Qing court as well as the profit of foreign merchants, as it turned out, was the result of a joint effort between the then Shanghai governor Xian Ling 咸齡 and British Consul Alcock.[11]

Another set of statistics proves that property development would remain as one of the most lucrative businesses for a long time to come: from 1869 to 1927, the population in Shanghai increased nine times whilst land value increased forty times.[12] While land value fluctuated significantly in different foreign concessions and at different times, the naked desire of both foreigners and the Chinese to earn great profit through land transactions was on full display. The Americans on the north side of Suzhou Creek speculated on land without doing much development. From 1844 through to 1856, land value as a result increased four-fold. The bubble eventually burst, though with a long period of 'soft landing'. By the end of the nineteenth century, land value in the American concession dropped to less than half of its price in mid-century. The British, on the other hand, not only kept their acquired land on the south bank of Suzhou Creek, they also bought into the American concession. The development of Astor House and Hotel (renamed from the earlier Richards Hotel and Restaurant) by the Scottish merchant Peter Felix Richards was one example.[13] The influx of people into the foreign settlements also enabled an inevitable transition of economic structure from trade only to production and industry. In addition to the construction industry, reeling mills, yarn and flour factories emerged on the banks of Huangpu River and Suzhou Creek. They provided a vital driving force to turn the unskilled farmers from the hinterland into various trades – a marker of the rapid urbanization and modernization of Shanghai.

The early houses were makeshift terraces built with timber in shanty construction, which were named *li* 里 (the ancient name of

neighbourhood in general). Some 800 houses were built between
September 1853 and July 1854. By 1860, there were 8,740 such makeshift
timber terraces being erected. It should be noted that such short-lived
terrace housing was based entirely on the English model. But this sort
of construction was abolished by the governments of foreign settlement
after 1870, mainly because it was prone to fire. From then on, the mixed
construction of timber and masonry called *shiku men* 石庫門 (meaning
stone gate building) gradually replaced the early makeshift timber
terraces as the dominant residential pattern, which spread to become
the urban fabric of modern Shanghai. Like chemically accelerated
metal corrosion, the evolution from the early configuration of *shiku
men* to that of the later periods shows the incremental erosion of the
inner courtyard to a more street oriented 'terrace' house that became a
porous extension of the street and the larger metropolis.

In April 1860, just several months before Shanghai was spared
sacking by the Taiping army, the American lawyer-turned-into-sailor,
Richard Henry Dana Junior, on his around-the-world steamboat
voyage, anchored on the Wusong River while the ship discharged
opium. The crew transferred to small boats to reach Shanghai wharf.
Dana was impressed with the level, regularly laid out European part –
the Concession, and its stately solid buildings. He foresaw that Shanghai
would soon overtake Canton as a great trading port of China. Having
just visited Canton, Dana found the old Shanghai town within the
walls not as impressive: 'The streets are as narrow as those of Canton, &
here, as there, there are no horses or carriages, & only human foot-falls.
There is less wealth & style here, & the people do not seem so neat, &
the city arrangements are not so good. The temples, ancestral halls,
yamuns [*sic, yamen* – government buildings] &c. bear no comparison
with those of Canton. It is like comparing Limerick with Dublin.'[14]
While in Hong Kong and Canton, Dana spilled much ink in his journal
on how literary the Chinese were: the use of printed words everywhere,

the reading habits of shopkeepers and the preparation schools for the imperial examination.[15] But in Shanghai it was the 'utmost freedom' allowed to both the Chinese and foreigner that caught his attention.[16] Dana also recorded his knowledge of Shanghai's population: 500,000 total with one-third living in the foreign concessions.[17]

# From diminishing courtyard to porous house

Built with half-masonry and half-timber, the 'old style *shiku men*' was featured with a heavy wooden door framed by stone, and also the fire protecting high gable walls on both sides called 'horse-head wall' as seen in the Ming and Qing houses in Huizhou and other places in the Yangtze region. Although they still looked like Chinese houses, or arguably still based on courtyard houses of the lower Yangtze, they were clustered together like the English terrace house, one next to the other within the parallel urban grids of streets and lanes (Figure 9.3).

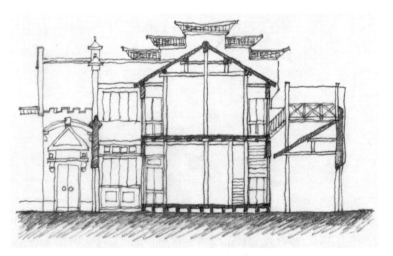

**Figure 9.3a.** *The cross section of an old style* shiku men *house.*

Better built and more costly than the earlier makeshift timber houses, the parsimony of their land use, low maintenance and high rent, however, had made the *shiku men* housing very popular in Shanghai. It then hastily spread to old Shanghai town and other places occupied only by the Chinese. The surviving examples can be seen from a neighbourhood named Xingren Li 興仁里 built in 1872,[18] which had a lane of 107.5 metres comprising 24 *shiku men* of three or five bays (Figure 9.4). The five-bay plan appears more like a Roman *domus* with its door in the middle bay opening to the front yard, which, too, is

**Figure 9.3b.** *The figure and ground plan diagram of Mianyangli – an old style* shiku men *housing complex.*

called 'skywell' as in other courtyards in the region. The backyard, called 'rear skywell', is narrow and across the entire length of the block to ensure segregation between the main living quarters and the service area of kitchen and miscellaneous rooms.

The hall on the central axis behind the front yard might still appear like a Confucian construct, but its actual meaning was tenuous at best. This was the beginning of an end, for the use of 'skywell' in this circumstance was more a matter of functional fact – that is, the necessity of light and air. The erosion of the Confucian world, as tangibly and physically manifested in the Chinese courtyard, was to accelerate rapidly driven by the profit gain in modern property development and population densification. This is explicitly shown in the evolution of *shiku men* from the old style to the gradual shrinking in size of the skywell, its final disappearance and the conversion to free-standing villas and multi-storey urban apartments.

Faint traces of the Chinese courtyard dwelling remain not only in the exterior look of the house, but also in the arrangement of rooms – the only differentiation among the rooms is between the main hall (now called reception hall 客堂), secondary chamber 次间, subsidiary chamber 稍间 and miscellaneous chamber 余间. In the smaller two-bay or three-bay *shiku men*, the distinction simply is between the main hall and various other subsidiary rooms 厢房 (see Figure 9.4). The country gentry and landowners seeking refuge in the Concession had to downsize to settle in these small houses. To subsidize the cost of skyrocketing rent, they often sublet spare rooms, which were conveniently provided by the old style *shiku men*. For foreign and local developers, with such lucrative rent and ever-increasing demand, the cost of construction and development could be recouped in less than a decade. However, skywells continued to shrink in size, and rear bed chambers were added both on the ground and upper levels. By the turn of the twentieth century, light and ventilation could hardly be

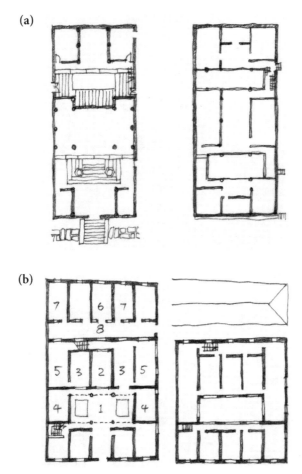

**Figure 9.4** *A comparison of* (a) *the ground and the first floors of a courtyard house in the Yangtze region and* (b) *that of a five-bay old style* shiku men *house in Xingren Li* lilong *complex. Note also that, contrary to any traditional Chinese courtyard, the* shiku men *house is open via windows to both the front street and the back lane. Legend: 1. 'Skywell' Court; 2. Reception Hall; 3. Secondary Chamber; 4. Subsidiary Room; 5. Subsidiary Chamber; 6. Kitchen; 7. Miscellaneous Chamber; 8. Rear 'Skywell' Court.*

sufficed by the narrow sky-wells. As a result, the rear portion of the dwelling and the front stone gate had to be lowered to let more light and air in.

In the second decade of the twentieth century, the new style *shiku men* was better built using more loadbearing brick walls, reinforced concrete columns and floor slabs. Along with the increasing use of masonry and machine-made roof tiles, eclectic and neo-classical Western ornamentation began to adorn the stone gates, gable walls and windows. Imported patterned floor tiles, modern flush toilets and bathrooms, too, appeared in well-to-do households.[19] The structure itself reached three floors, but the depth of new *shiku men* was reduced to 12 metres, which made the use of backyard redundant. As for the 'skywell' fronting the house, by now it provided no frame of the sky above, but merely an entry court. The rooms on upper levels, often used as bedrooms, could be enclosed for privacy, while the ground level rooms, without relying on the use of a corridor, were interconnected to accommodate a wide range of mixed daily activities (Figure 9.5).

The country gentry and landowners had their first taste of modern urban life during their sojourns in these *shiku men* houses. The house was small, confined, dark and poorly ventilated. The Confucian world of paterfamilias, though tenuously held by the hall and the symmetry of the old *shiku men*, began to be disturbed by the distraction and allure of the larger 'interior' of the city – the extension of the confined *shiku men* to the lanes and streets led to the world of delicious and exotic food, intoxicating drinks, shops selling fine things, sleazy opium dens and brothels, splendid dancing halls holding elegant balls, racetracks and casinos. All were irresistible. The porosity between the house and street saw the birth of a modern metropolis, and the city as the replacement of the internalized Confucian world of family – the courtyard. Though still sojourners in the emerging metropolis, while

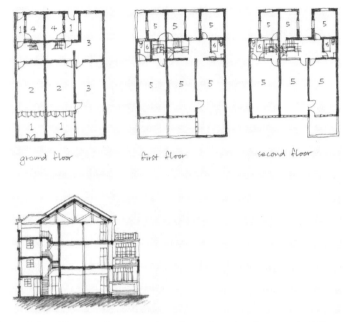

**Figure 9.5a.** *Plans and cross section of two three-level new style* shiku men *houses, each of which are one and two bays respectively; Legend: 1. 'Skywell' void; 2. Reception Hall; 3. Subsidiary Room; 4. Kitchen; 5. Bedroom; 6. Bathroom (with modern sanitary ware).*

contemplating a return to the hinterland when peace was restored at home, the Chinese residents in the foreign concessions were still attracted to the commercial opportunities presented to them as a result of population concentration and the mixture of foreigners and Chinese from different places.

One such lucrative business was to work between the foreign property developers and Chinese landowners, builders and tenants – as the so-called comprador. Among them there was the shrewd Cheng Jinxuan 程谨轩, known as 'the king of Chinese real estate' in the late nineteenth century. Cheng tasted the fruit of this profitable business when he helped the American business broker Edwin M. Smith to

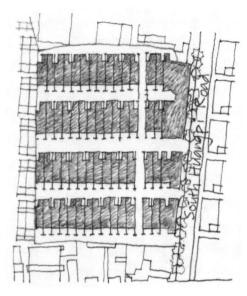

**Figure 9.5b.** *The figure and ground plan diagram of Meilanfang – a new style* shiku men *housing complex.*

build the early makeshift timber houses. But the symbiotic and mutually beneficial relationship between the foreign developer and the Chinese comprador can be seen from a brilliant deal that Cheng made with the famous Sassoons. By then, the Sassoons had already managed to reinvent their identity, via Bombay to Shanghai, from Oriental merchants of displaced Baghdad Jews to Westerners belonging to the club of English gentlemen. Cheng proposed to the Sassoons that he would rebuild their appallingly deteriorated houses at his own cost on the condition that the Sassoons would accept the current rent for the next twenty-five years before they could regain the ownership of their property. The Sassoons happily signed the deal. As it turned out, Cheng, reused the salvaged building materials from the demolished houses, rebuilt them with remarkable economy, and managed to charge a rent twice as high as the Sassoons imposed. In merely two years, Cheng recovered his construction cost. With such exponential profit, Cheng continued to rebuild more of Sassoons' houses. Another Baghdadi refugee, Silas Aaron Hardoon, formerly employed by the Sassoons, became in the early twentieth century another 'king of real estate'.[20] The irresistible appeal of successful business and the lavish life of the Shanghai nouveaux riches trickled down into the streets and laneways of *lilong* and the halls of *shiku men* houses.

When the modern urban economy penetrated into the *lilong* neighbourhoods in Shanghai, the effect was quite different from the urban transformations that occurred in the Tang and Song dynasties. The 'medieval urban revolution', coined by some scholars, in the Song capital Bianliang did not result in the collapse of the inner courtyard of the Confucian world and the escapist gardens attached to them.[21] We have already seen that the integrity of the enclosed courtyard houses was camouflaged behind the outer layer of shops and the bustling street life as depicted in the Song painting Qingming Festival on the River. In *lilong*, however, commercial activities permeated into houses from the street, and neighbours mingled and mixed in the lanes. The *shiku men* dwellings, unlike a true Chinese courtyard, became part of the larger interior, that is, the city, as if they were the furniture in a room. Its *raison d'être* depends on its complete exposure to the interior. The street and the laneway were raucous with activities, and windows and balconies on upper levels were made open to the street. The concentration of certain trades, and the courtesan houses of pleasure, in particular, gave distinctive features to different *lilong*. Wining and dining, or 'watching' (as the Chinese do) an opera, in a large handsome hall of a courtesan house in a reversed way turned the inside of a house into an integral part of this increasingly intoxicated city. The Shanghai writer Wang Anyi has portrayed this as a 'spirit that belongs to everyday life', which is 'neither large-hearted nor high minded'.[22]

Such 'street-smart' character is the result of a gradual loss of the inner world, which, in the Chinese sense, is the efficacy of the courtyard throughout the pre-modern history of several millennia. When a dwelling, the first time in Chinese history, had become a commodity produced by profit-driven business and according to the modern doctrine of land economy, the 'modernity' of this rather 'deformed mixture of new and old', Chinese and Western, and its consequential 'curious wisdom', again in the words of Eileen Chang, emerged in the urban life of Shanghai. There is nothing mysterious about the evolution of the *shiku men* housing from the old style to that of the new – parsimony of land use and profit maximization were the ultimate goals. Reducing the size of the dwelling and increasing density, naturally, was the most effective approach. By 1949, the so-called new style constituted half of the housing stock in Shanghai. A new style *shiku men* dwelling occupied approximately one-fourth of the land of the old one, and its width was reduced to one bay of 4 metres. The increasingly confined interior was compensated by more windows and terraces open to alleyway and street.

In *The Song of Everlasting Sorrow* (长恨歌), Wang Anyi at the outset frames her female protagonist Wang Qiyao 王琦瑶 in the first chapter against the background of *longtang* 弄堂 (alleyway), *liuyan* 流言 (gossip and rumour), *guige* 闺阁 (young lady's bedchamber), and *gezi* 鸽子 (pigeons). On *longtang*, Wang asserts:

> But regardless of the type of *longtang*, this atmosphere penetrates everywhere. You could say that it is the *genius loci* of Shanghai's alleys. If the *longtang* of Shanghai could speak, they would undoubtedly speak in rumours. They are the thoughts of Shanghai's *longtang*, disseminating themselves through day and night. If the *longtang* of Shanghai could dream, that dream would be gossip.[23] [...] In places like the *longtang*, it travels from back

door to back door, and in the blink of an eye the whole world knows all. Gossip is like the silent electrical waves crisscrossing in the air above the city, like formless clouds that enshroud the whole city, slowly brewing into a shower, intermixing right and wrong. The rain comes down not in a torrent but as a hazy spring-time drizzle. Although not violent, it drenches the air with an inescapable humidity. Never underestimate these rumours: soft and fine as these raindrops may be, you will never struggle free of them.[24]

Such is the feminine aura of Shanghai that is both adored and loathed by her own daughter of the house Wang Anyi. It is no surprise that in Wang Anyi's *The Song of Everlasting Sorrow*, only the young lady's bedchamber in a *shiku men* house has been given a close examination, for it is the efficacy of an architectural apparatus that has helped constitute her female character, who is 'mostly modern, seductive, coquettish, and heavily made-up', and of course 'shrewd'. The confined bedchamber, which is called *tingzi jian* 亭子间 (pavilion room), is typically added atop the kitchen at the rear of the house (see the first and the second floor plans in Figure 9.5a.). With a depth and the minimum ceiling height of approximately 2.4 metres, *tingzi jian* is accessed from the landing of the staircase in the reception hall. The same staircase continues to reach the main bedchamber. *Tingzi jian*, serving as the buffer zone between *longtang* and the house, therefore looks into the *longtang*, where domestic life congregates – food preparation, laundry and all sorts of house chores, as well as relaxation and children's play. It also looks straight into the reception hall and the main bedchamber of the house on the other side of *longtang*. The flowery curtains of the young lady's *tingzi jian* were always drawn. But even so, the immediate distraction of worldly calculation and subsistence of this modern commercial metropolis could hardly be fenced off from the confined room: Western priests were out there attempting to persuade them to follow the Lord; the showgirl next door had just found herself a husband; and the middle-aged couple sitting in the hall were planning to start a new business . . .

The young daughter of Shanghai had neither the room nor the time to indulge her innocent childhood and adolescence. She must learn very quickly, if she had no other choices, to become quintessentially parsimonious, which defined the character of a Shanghai woman, or even a gold digger, which was treated with both distain and envy by those still holding onto the rapidly declining Confucian world of morality. If the confinement of *tingzi jian*, and the house itself, had any effect on the young woman of Shanghai, it was not a restoration of peace belonging to the inner landscape of the mind. Quite the contrary, it had made the young woman eager to go out to immerse herself in this glittering world of mammon, jazz, cinema, ballroom, gambling, opium, and the other sins offered by this vast metropolis. Of course there was much pleasure to be found, even for a 'petty urbanite', in this new interior called the city. When the young woman left her *tingzi jian* to an appointed apartment in a handsome tall art deco building, as Eileen Chang affectionately recalled in her essay 'The Joy of Apartment Living' (公寓生活记趣), she could not fall asleep without the accompany of the traffic noise of tram cars, and the chants of street hawkers were the music to her ears. Eileen Chang loved both the taste of Western sweets and the pungent smell of the Chinese 'stinky tofu'. The fine things – clothes and cosmetics – that she indulged in as a bourgeois consumer were all readily available at arm's reach of a quick elevator ride.[25]

The densification of housing as represented by the new style of *shiku men* was the result of both cultural and economic transformations in the making of a modern metropolis. Although the early *lilong* housing was built to provide safe havens for the country gentry and merchants driven out by the upheavals in the hinterland, accompanying them also were the poor and their dependents. Economic pressure and low-income restricted sizes of these families; life in dense *lilong* neighbourhood made the multi-generation cohabitation of the Confucian world increasingly untenable. This was the beginning of the modern nuclear family structure in China. Some new-style *lilong* catered for the well-to-do with modern sanitary wares, indoor heating and increased width of lanes for cars. In the heyday of *lilong*, the complete chain of modern property development from land acquisition, design, construction to sale and lease was well established. From blossom to decline, Shanghai's urbanity, not surprisingly, was mirrored concretely in the deterioration and overcrowding in *lilong* neighbourhood and *shiku men* houses. In the 1920s, professionals and trades were in high demand; the college educated and the well remunerated settled in the new *shiku men* housing and lived a comfortable bourgeois life. Indeed, the period from 1930 to 1945 in Shanghai was marked by some scholars as 'the flowering of a new urban culture in China'.[26]

But the Sino-Japanese War broke out in 1937, and the bloody war dragged on for eight years, which was followed by three years of civil war and the fall of the Nationalist Government to the communist takeover in 1949. The decline of social and economic infrastructure in Shanghai was compounded with exponential population growth. The new waves of refugees during the Sino-Japanese War added 780,000 to the foreign concessions with the total population increasing by 2.08 million in Shanghai during the three-year-long civil war.[27] The scarcity of housing, food and fuel made the thrilling urban life and bourgeois comfort a thing of the past. Through sub-lease and endless sub-divisions within a *shiku men* house, the *lilong* had become an urban mayhem. In the late 1930s, one new style of *shiku men* housed the following cohabitation:

Front reception hall: a police man, his wife and two teenage
daughters

Sub-divided reception hall: a *lilong* primary school teacher couple
and three children

First floor bedchamber: two showgirls and one prostitute

First floor mezzanine: a cobbler and his wife

Second floor bedchamber: a thirty something mistress and her
maid

Kitchen: the sub-landlord and his wife

Roof terrace: a newspaper proof-reader

Second floor *tingzi jian*: a couple (the husband was a loafer)

First floor *tingzi jian*: four waiters working in a western restaurant

Second floor mezzanine: a primary school teacher[28]

When *lilong* neighbourhoods and *shiku men* houses became the
bustling and rowdy mixed-use urban receptacles of commercial
activities and living, the well-to-do moved out to the quieter and
segregated areas of Western-style terraced houses and free-standing
villas. In these Western houses, rooms were differentiated according
to their uses – living room, dining room, bedroom, bathroom, food
preparation and servants' rooms. The use of a corridor combined with
a staircase helped to reduce the permeability of interconnected rooms
to create more privacy, as seen in the development of English houses
from the eighteenth to nineteenth century. The Chinese bourgeoisie
in Shanghai and other coastal cities no longer had the need to answer
to Heaven. The Confucian world and its courtyard appeared to have
been lost, at least for now.

# 10

# *The Assault of Modernity*

In February 1950, driven by a tenacious desire to revitalize China's pre-modern architecture, and indeed mixed with high optimism generated by the new Communist government, American Beaux-Arts-trained Liang Sicheng and his UK-educated colleague Chen Zhanxiang proposed housing the new government administration outside the city wall of Ming-Qing Beijing on its west, thereby saving the integrity of the imperial city.[1] This, however, was not an unprecedented idea. As early as the late 1920s, the debate already occurred about whether Beijing should be expanded radially. Those who advocated building a new town to the west of the old city centre were likely influenced by the capital planning of Nanjing in 1929. The American architect Henry Murphy proposed building a new administrative centre for the Nationalist Government to the east, outside the Ming dynasty city core of Nanjing. When Beijing was sacked by the Japanese in 1937, the occupiers wasted no time in planning their administrative centre and the enclaves for the Japanese population, in the western suburb of Beijing. By 1943, the Japanese planned new town saw the preparation of basic infrastructure, parks, sports facilities and the erection of more than 500 buildings, including a nursery and a hospital. After Japan surrendered in 1946, the Construction Bureau of Beijing nonetheless continued the same line of thinking in planning – that is, to build the new town to the west beyond the old city centre.

The Liang-Chen scheme, which proposed placing the new administration in between the new town built by the Japanese and Beijing's old city core, was a counter proposal to the radiating plan advocated by the powerful former Soviet Union planning experts entrusted by Chairman Mao Zedong and his administration at the time. The idea was rejected: it would cost too much and take too long to realize when the Korean War was looming. Whether or not, in psychological substructure, Mao would like to have the opportunity to live within the Forbidden City like past emperors. We will never know. During the first five-year plan of nation building from 1953 to 1957, large-scale government buildings were constructed within the ancient city fabric. The trend culminated in the late 1950s when Tiananmen Square was enlarged to become the world's largest, and when 'the great 10 buildings' were erected to commemorate the tenth anniversary of the new republic.

As a last resort, Liang Sicheng hoped that the least the new government should do was to save the magnificent city wall (dated back to 1264 when the Mongols began to build their imperial capital) by turning it into a civic park for the leisure life of the citizens of the new era. Indulged by his hopeless romanticism, Liang Sicheng fantasized in giving the new republic capital a splendid 'green necklace' of 39.75 kilometres, for the city wall that enclosed imperial Beijing would be greened by lawns and plants. This would be the world's only city-ring-park in the sky. It was not merely a civic place, but also would, like the tower found in Han dynasty clay models and *mingqi* of courtyards, allow the residents of the new Beijing to break away from the confined courtyards to 'climb high and inspect the horizon'

(Figure 10.1). This, if materialized, would be the magnificent restoration at a civic scale of a Chinese idea that might have existed only in imagination. It would be the collective garden for the sea of courtyards in Beijing that lacked the attached gardens of the escapist haven found in the Yangtze region.

Legend has it that, in the early days of the new republic, Chairman Mao once stood on Tiananmen – the Gate of Heavenly Peace. While facing a sea of red flags below in the square, Mao reared his head to inspect the horizon: he envisioned a forest of gigantic industrial chimneys with black smoke bellowing into the sky. Mao saw this as the future of Beijing. Liang Sicheng was devastated! The government went ahead to tear down the entire city wall to give way to roads – the symbol of progress, and indeed modernity. Liang Sicheng's final destiny, dying in impoverishment and regret, was not merely caused by the Chinese Cultural Revolution at the time, but was also the result

**Figure 10.1** *Liang Sicheng's proposal to turn Beijing's city wall into a city-ring-park in the sky.*

of a desired image of modernity. Like the actual taste of a meal disguised by its flowery presentation in a posh restaurant, such spectacle of modernity has made its intended idea, and also the truth, trivialized. Following the model of modernity provided by the former Soviet Union, the path to a city of building objects was well prepared when Tiananmen Square was created, and when Beijing's city wall came down in a pile of broken bricks. From this point onwards, the future growth of Beijing has become a 'pancake', that is, ever increasing ring roads radiating from the same core. Along with the demolition of the city wall, large tracts of courtyards also had to be torn down to build mammoth government and institutional buildings and multi-storey apartment buildings.

Amidst the conflicting voices of conservation and demolition, intellectuals, too, were divided. Writer Lu Xun, who in the early twentieth century wrote fondly about his courtyard in Beijing, praised on the other hand, the mentality of creating the new by smashing the old in his widely read essay titled 'On the Collapse of Leifeng Tower' (论雷锋塔的倒掉), in which the tower is the symbol of the past and an evil guardian of a tradition that suppresses free love. Lu Xun rejoiced in the release of the free-spirited legendary Lady White Snake who was allegedly captured beneath the tower. Liang's colleague and close friend Zhu Ziqing 朱自清, a prominent writer and public intellectual in his own right, even wrote a newspaper essay to publicly denounce Liang's conservation proposal. Although Zhu did not single out the Beijing quadrangle in particular, he expressed his aversion to the confinement of the old built world and his frustration with the revisionist approach. Instead, Zhu advocated the 'progressive' approach of starting anew from scratch. His thesis, though, was based on a simplistic moral and economic reasoning – that is, feeding and clothing the impoverished populace must take the priority over the conservation of the old city structure. Liang in his rejoinder certainly was not shy to point out the flaws of this crude moral high ground by emphasizing the economic benefits of providing employment to people and the long-term gain of conservation rather than demolition. Although in the end Zhu privately conceded in his diary that Liang had a point,[2] this incident was not singular but a recurrent debate among both the elite literati and the general populace. In essence it reveals the uncertainty in the Chinese mind as to whether or not the Chinese world of courtyard had become superfluous.

# Quadrangle without the Confucian world

It should be no surprise to wake up in today's Beijing, after three decades of economic stagnation and political turmoil, followed up by four decades of economic development at breakneck pace, to confront a city centre, which looks much like a gigantic sculpture garden, packed with flaunting building objects in a beauty pageantry. Even the current Chinese president Xi Jinping, has not resisted the temptation to express his aversion: he has called for a resistance to 'weird architecture'. Faint traces of Li Yutang's Beijing, framed and nourished by the extensive web of quadrangles, can still be seen in the surviving *hutong* in central Beijing, too often in slum conditions or cosmetically made up to satisfy tourist curiosities. In those *hutongs*, multiple families occupy one quadrangle with makeshift alterations and additions. The gradual erosion of the Confucian world has turned the Beijing quadrangle into the so-called *da zayuan* 大杂院 – big miscellaneous courtyard (Figure 10.2). Increasingly, in between here and there, some quadrangles have been restored and modernized by those who have the means and are nostalgic for the life of a pre-modern Beijing quadrangle of its enclosed oasis amidst the hassle of urban life (though not so much the Confucian doctrines). Boutique hotels and

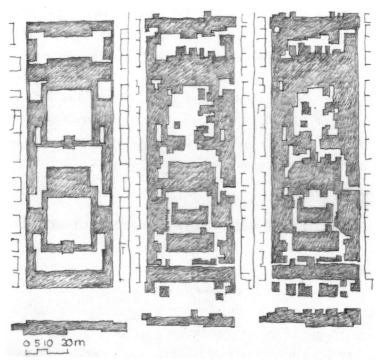

**Figure 10.2** *The figure and ground diagrams of a Beijing quadrangle, from left to right respectively, in the 1950s, 1970s and 1980s, showing the gradual transformation of a single-family courtyard house to a 'big miscellaneous courtyard' with multiple occupants.*

fancy restaurants too have found their exclusive status in these reinvented quadrangle buildings.

But the debate between conservation and demolition still rings the same tone as that of the early 1950s. When major demolition of large tract *hutong* occurs, often executed to give way to developments of mammoth scale, such as the 2008 Beijing Olympic projects, progressive writers like Liu Xinwu 刘心武, Li Guowen 李国文, Chen Jiangong 陈建功 and Wang Shuo 王朔, though lamenting the overcrowding and the lack of basic sanitation in the existing quadrangles, expressed their eagerness to break away from the confinement of the courtyard to pursue the expansiveness and freedom of space. In the words of Li Guowen, 'Tight enclosure is the most salient characteristic of the quadrangle. [...] If the Chinese do not in their spirit walk out of this sort of tightly enclosed quadrangle, it is difficult, I am afraid, to have major development and achievement.'[3] It is however no surprise to find the opposite voice from Shu Yi 舒乙, the son of Lao She, and from other writers such as Xiao Gan 萧乾 and Feng Jicai 冯骥才. Prominent architects, including Liang's protégé Wu Liangyong 吴良镛, one of the country's most revered professors of architecture, and the American Chinese architect I. M. Pei, petitioned for the protection and conservation of the old city fabric, including the remaining tracts of *hutong* and quadrangles.[4] Much of the debate has been focused on the climatically adaptive properties and other amenities of the Beijing quadrangle. The inbuilt meaning of the Confucian world and the reunion, though sometimes at arm's length, of Heaven and Earth, as it appears, has been largely lost in the mists of time.

Nowhere else reveals more patently a modern misinterpretation of Beijing quadrangle than the famed and yet up-until-now still the singular case of 'new quadrangle' designed by the conservationist Wu Liangyong himself – the Ju'er Hutong 菊儿胡同.[5] In the late 1980s, the prevalent problem of Beijing's overcrowded *da zayuan* – that is, structurally unsound, flood prone and leaking roofs (*wei ji lou* 危积漏) – reached a hazardous level in the Ju'er Hutong neighbourhood. Since most residents who lived there at the time, like the rest of the country, rented at a modest sum from the state-run institutions called *danwei* 单位 (work unit), they started a petition to ask the municipal government to address this problem of unbearably poor living conditions in this area. The petition, it seemed, initially fell on the deaf ears of the authorities, but unexpectedly caught the attention of Wu Liangyong, who, when approached by the then Beijing Housing Office, thought this could be a pilot project to put his theory of 'organic renewal' into practice. Armed with this theory, Wu thought it should be possible to come up with a kind of social housing that not only would meet the demands and comfort level of modern life, but also fit well into the existing historic city fabric. The gist of his 'organic renewal' theory, Wu explained, is like a skilful tailor's work – the patching work involved in repairing a piece of torn cloth, if done well, can be seamless and even beautiful.

Wu therefore instructed his post-graduate students at Beijing's Tsinghua University to undertake a fieldwork assessment of the existing courtyards in Ju'er Hutong. Three types of housing were identified: solidly built multi-storey housing of the 1970s would be kept; historic courtyards of reasonable quality would be preserved and refurbished; dangerous and shanty buildings would be demolished to give way to new housing, which happened to be No. 41 compound and seven other courtyards surrounding this compound. To come up with a new housing design, Wu had to understand the economic and urban design conundrum – that is, the necessary plot ratio to accommodate the existing population, or achieving an even higher living density whilst the scale and the bulk of the new building must fit in with the existing historic urban fabric. But the architectural challenge identified for this undertaking was a curious one: Wu wanted to recreate the kind of gregarious sociality as found in the existing *da zayuan* occupied by multiple families. The very meaning of a Chinese courtyard being a Confucian world of one single clan of three to four generations, as it seemed, was at the outset neglected all together.

The result of Phase 1 was a three-storey stacked apartment building surrounding four courtyard voids – Wu's New Beijing Quadrangle (Figure 10.3). The building, again curiously, was given somehow the look of the Ming and Qing Huizhou courtyard house, with walls clad with white tiles, partially pitched roofs and 'horsehead' gable walls crowned with black tiles. Two large trees were preserved and served

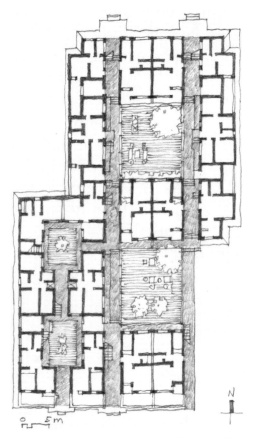

**Figure 10.3** *The ground floor plan of Ju'er Hutong Phase 1, with the passageways shaded.*

to define the two major courts, which were called *jinyuan* 进院 (sequential courts). The two smaller ones in parallel, were called *kuayuan* 跨院 (subsidiary courts), which all come from traditional courtyards. Three major longitudinal passageways that connected individual apartments, too, were given the name *beilong* 备弄, used in multiple courtyards found in Suzhou. The cross passageways that linked the parallel buildings were called *jiadao* 夹道, which come from the aristocratic quadrangles in Beijing. Despite the use of courtyard nomenclature to name these passageways, they served, first and foremost, to separate, and then, connect the individual apartments in his complex, just like the corridor in a nineteenth-century English house. Wu, however, also made these passageways open to the courtyards so that they would help animate social intercourse, much like the *youlang* 游廊 (the running veranda) in a southern Chinese courtyard. Wu and his students envisaged that, through these open passageways, visual and physical connection between the individual apartments and the families would enable the courts to become an outdoor common living room. But no courtyard in the Chinese house ever worked as a common living room devoid of cultural and societal connotations. The residents, to Wu's dismay, did not allow the ivy to adorn the open passages. Rather they quickly sealed them with glass so that they could prevent the fierce draught from coming into the rooms in the bitterly cold winter; in addition they gained some useable room to compensate for the small apartments.

Since the completion of Phase 1 in 1990 and Phase 2 in 1994, Ju'er Hutong new quadrangle has won numerous national and international laurels, including the World Habitat Award from the United Nations in 1993. Wu and his team were lauded by the award citation for having invented a new housing model of not only the inherited traits of the Beijing quadrangle, but also the level of density matching the plot ratio of high-rise residential development. It was also optimistically predicated that this new housing model would be repeated and grow to have exponential impact on collective housing throughout China.[6] But Ju'er Hutong, after Phase 2, has remained a singular case in China.

Some twenty years later, on reflection, old residents and observers conclude that the neighbouring and community relations in Ju'er Hutong, when compared with the multi-family occupied *da zayuan*, are not nearly as warm and intimate.[7] In fact there is not much difference from that of the high-rise residential neighbourhoods.

Some residents, however, show no nostalgia for the uncomfortably gregarious life in a *da zayuan*. Indeed, they feel that the privacy of the individual apartments in the complex, much the same as that of any high-rise residential building, is necessary, whilst the enclosure of the common courtyards does facilitate a friendly ambience, for the neighbours encounter each other more often. Unexpectedly, Ju'er Hutong has been a popular choice among the expatriate communities in Beijing. In 2011, out of the 210 households in the entire new quadrangle complex in Ju'er Hutong, seventy of them are expatriate families, for this neighbourhood provides just the right dose of social interaction that is desired by those who come from places where very little community life exists.

Surprisingly though, the pre-modern *hutong* neighbourhood has not been used as a benchmark for Ju'er Hutong, and no question has been raised as to why *dao zayuan* should have been in anyway, factored into the invention of the new quadrangle. Lao She's Xiao Yangjuan, an ordinary *hutong* neighbourhood in the early twentieth century, as described previously, may serve as a useful background against which Ju'er Hutong is understood: the privacy of each apartment is not the same as that in various courtyard houses, humble or elaborate, found in Xiao Yangjuan, for each of them was its own Confucian world centred on a family clan (with one exception of a multiple-family occupancy). Neighbourly relations in Ju'er Hutong are engineered encounters rather than a consciously sought and constructed web of social intricacy as seen in Xiao Yangjuan. It may be bewildering for the modern architect as to why a common living room conceived by the architect for Ju'er Hutong does not facilitate nearly the amount of social interaction as found in Xiao Yangjuan, which does not really have a physical public room as such, except the *hutong* itself – the alleyway. Social intercourse in Xiao Yangjuan, in a uniquely Chinese way, was a charged social sphere animated not by any physical definition of a public place but rather by the curiosity aroused from the tantalizingly revealed glimpses of inner life of each family behind the courtyard walls and screens – that is, *tout court*, the necessity of enclosure of Chinese courtyard, and the city. Sociality in Chinese houses and cities was thus not dependent on the provision of designated public places in a civic sense. The very meaning of a Chinese courtyard as a Confucian microcosm, and their workings in a social cluster such as the *hutong* in Beijing, was not part of the conceptual apparatus used by Wu when he and his team designed their new quadrangle.

More to Wu and his colleagues' surprise, perhaps, is that their new quadrangle, though it greatly improved the living conditions of the residents whilst sensibly preserving and renewing the urban fabric, was short-lived due to the economic reality facing modern collective housing. Ju'er Hutong was the pilot project when China underwent the transition from the state provision of housing of modest rent to private ownership. An innovative financing model was tested: those residents who were willing to return to the new development only paid a fractional cost, approximately one-tenth of the market price; their *danwei* (work unit) contributed to make up the gap, and the municipal government offered tax incentives. The households that did not wish to return were given decent rental apartments elsewhere. The remainder of the apartments were then listed to be sold at market price. Also there were those who were willing to exchange their Ju'er Hutong rights for the better apartments others were living in. For the new households in Ju'er Hutong, the government offered low interest mortgages, perhaps the first ever housing loan in China after 1949. In the initial stage, only thirteen households out of forty-four signed up with this 'public and private partnership'.

Although this was a promising and indeed honourable financial model for collective housing, it occurred in China at the time of financial stagnation in 1989 when the inflation rate was at a historic high of 18.5 per cent. This low point of China's economic reform no doubt contributed to the short-lived and singular case of the Ju'er Hutong experiment. A decade later when the state provision of housing was officially ended in 1998, the market forces of speculative housing development were unstoppable. The early economic conundrum resolved by Wu to fit the multi-storey courtyard housing into a historic urban fabric could no longer stack up against the market. Ju'er Hutong Phase 1 had a development plot ratio (useable floor area of housing against the land size) of 1.32, and 1.56 for Phase 2, but the expectation of commercial residential development was to have a plot ratio of between 2 to 6 for high-rise residential development. In today's Beijing, given the central location of Ju'er Hutong, the small-size apartments seem to belie the high development potential, but as a solution for mass housing for average and low-income households, this particular Ju'er Hutong model cannot possibly be sustained by the market. The majority of housing developments in Beijing, and elsewhere in China, have adopted the modernist version of rows of multi-storey and increasingly high-rise residential buildings. With the benefit of open space, light and air, the modernist housing model has physically changed and hugely expanded the urban fabric of Beijing. The disappearance of large tracts of Beijing quadrangle aside, the questions is whether or not a new Beijing has emerged as the result of the physical transformation of its residential pattern and urban form.

## The lingering courtyard

The 2005 Chinese movie *You and Me* (*Women lia* 我们俩) tells the story of the unfinished legacy of the Beijing quadrangle. The young female undergraduate rented a room from the old landlady in her shabby courtyard dwelling. The plot started off rather inauspiciously as the old lady refused to give an inch in the rent negotiation; the desperate young student succumbed to it. The story then unfolded with much conflict between the two largely due to the inconveniences of living in a courtyard dwelling – the lack of telephone cables, modern sanitation, and, above all, privacy, which was much desired by the young woman because of the inevitable path-crossing in a courtyard house in the absence of corridors and terminal rooms (accessible from the corridor via a single door). The young woman had to go past the old lady's room to reach the kitchen. Whilst enjoying the winter sun in front of her south-facing hall, the landlady could see right into the girl's room at the south-eastern corner. But much to the surprise of both characters, over the seasonal change an affectionate relationship slowly grew between the two, thanks to the architecture of courtyard house that facilitated more intimate encounters.

The girl began to enjoy their routine chatting times, and they became more dependent on each other. Between the two of them, they hung and filled the central court with red lanterns for the Chinese New Year, and instantly charged the hollow court with convivial warmth of the festival season. But the girl eventually moved out to live with her boyfriend in an apartment with better living conditions and convenient transport. The young woman visited her landlady, removed from her courtyard dwelling and lying in her deathbed in the hospital, for the last time: emotion was running high in their eyes filled with tears. This story of modern life in a courtyard dwelling has only tenuous connotations of the Confucian world, but it is potent enough to show the lingering traces of the kind of Chinese life which is only played out in the courtyard enclosure. It is much more than a universal human nostalgia devoid of cultural and historical consciousness.

Among three traits, as singled out by Lin Yutang to define the charm of Beijing – its architecture, its mode of living, and its common people –, the physical template of architecture, suffice it to say, is largely gone. Would Lin Yutang have been disheartened to see a city centre that has been turned into this vast sculpture garden packed, not with the 'immutable stone edifices that rear their heads high' as seen in Shanghai's Bund in the early twentieth century, but shiny, irregular and air-conditioned glass and steel structures, like the taxonomic display of animals in a zoo. If the Chinese worldview, formed as early as the Chinese Golden Age, as asserted by this author, did not undergo any radical change for more than two millennia, is the physical collapse of its enclosed houses and cities the manifestation of a fundamental uprooting of the resolute state of the Chinese mind? The large-scale breakdown of the Chinese enclosure and its walls did not happen at certain points in pre-modern Chinese history when commerce flourished. Early examples of urban transformation can be traced back from the Tang to Song dynasties – the enclosed residential wards of the Tang city might have been weakened or even dissolved in the Song urban structure due to the prosperity of street commerce, though the integrity of the enclosed courtyard and the larger city remained intact.

The early reading of the Song painting Qingming Festival on the River shows a glimpse of the co-existence of street commerce and the enclosed courtyards behind the retail façade. Shanghai could have been an anomaly when the *lilong* emerged in the late nineteenth century to become the primary building block of the modern metropolis. Its heydays, we have seen, did not last long. The assault of modernity on the Chinese world, unexpectedly and even surprisingly, was brought in at a time when the People's Republic of China was established in the middle of the twentieth century. The demolition of Beijing's city wall, the unquestioned dominance of traffic engineering in altering the old city structure, and the ongoing wiping out of the quadrangle urban fabric in Beijing did not make Beijing an *open* city.

Whilst smashing the old occurred at mammoth scale and with whirlwind speed in Beijing and elsewhere in China, the new administration at the same time introduced to the Chinese world another form of powerful institutional enclosure – that is, the walled compound of the *danwei* (work unit), to and within which, the majority of urban population belonged (Figure 10.4).

Although for a short period of merely a few decades, Shanghai seemingly was built to function as a modern metropolis, when it came

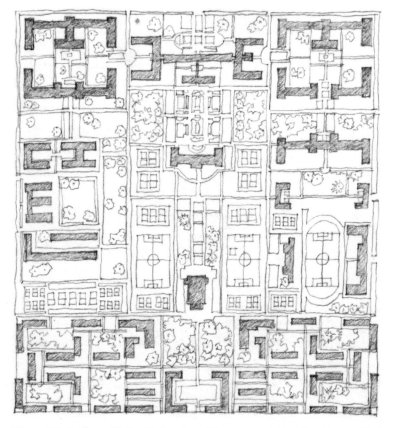

**Figure 10. 4** *Plan of Xi'an University of Communication, showing a walled* danwei *compound.*

to the introduction of *danwei*, like the rest of China, Shanghai was no exception. The housing reforms of the 1980s and the 1990s, and its associated market imperatives, have, on the surface, aggressively demolished the physical enclosure of *danwei*. But the walls are not completely gone – academics and students, for example, may live elsewhere in open high-rise residential neighbourhoods, but the campus itself is still physically walled with its visible enclosure to define the presence and prestige of its ongoing existence. The visible 'open' city form, predominantly marked by rows of multi-storey and high-rise apartments, is now increasingly challenged by the demand of gated (and inevitably walled) neighbourhoods driven, not so much by security need or elite demographic ghettos as seen in the West, but rather the persistent desire for enclosure which has not yet been consciously interpreted and let alone artfully manipulated in China's new urban morphology.

Early in the book we have learned that writer Lin Yutang took a passionate dislike to Shanghai, but was much drawn to the charm of Beijing, its mode of living and its 'grand old personality'. Like Lin, some modern writers of the city liken it to a human person; there seems to be curious and yet persistent genetics that continue to linger once the temperament of a city was formed. Despite the countless forces that make the city – the numerous 'pulls and pushes', be they economic, political or socio-cultural, great cities, after all, develop a character, the process of which is not unlike the constitution of a human character. New York, Jan Morris observed in the 1970s, may have mellowed – an old 'New World city', so to speak, but its temperament is still neurotic. To take Sydney, the city where the author used to reside, as another example, Morris painted a chilling picture of it in the early 1960s by singling out its steely looking and unsmiling women! Although it took a full five years before the last letter of complaint reached the author from down under, Morris has never had enough of Sydney. In the 1980s, Morris announced: 'This is it. It will probably get richer, it will certainly get more Asian, but aesthetically, metaphysically, my bones tell me I am already seeing the definitive Sydney, the more or less absolute Australia. A few more tower blocks here, an extra suburb there, a louder Chinatown, more futuristic ferryboats perhaps – otherwise, this is how Sydney is always going to be.'[8] Yet Morris has returned again and again, calling this strange appeal of Sydney 'Australian distractions', and her earlier essay on Sydney a 'reckless foray', though she does not want to entirely retract her judgements of thirty years ago.[9] All of this culminated in a book in 1992 simply titled *Sydney*, in which she said: '... not I think the best of the cities the British Empire created, not the most beautiful either, but the most hyperbolic, the youngest in heart, the *shiniest*.'[10]

The temperament of Beijing, I incline to conclude, lies in its persistent artifice, with or without physical form, of good living and good life. This may explain the puzzle that some of the most hostile leftover urban excrescences – the place beneath an elevated freeway for example – are happily occupied by people who gracefully practice their *taiji*, or ballroom dancing. Is then the invisible walled enclosure of a courtyard the genetics of the Chinese world despite its physical collapse under the unstoppable assault not of socialist modernity but of market forces?

# Nothingness, horizon and discreet pleasure

The growing trend of remodelling pre-modern courtyards into sleek modern homes, boutique hotels and elegant restaurants is no indication of a conscious recognition of the meaning of the Chinese microcosm condensed in the courtyard. Such a trend rather reflects the continuing influence of a modern misconception of the courtyard and the meaning of voids. Not that the modern meaning, as promulgated by the German-American architect Mies van der Rohe and his ilk, has found its resonance in modern China, it is quite simply more a continuing vogue of modern aesthetics. Mies nonetheless was more serious than the generations of enthusiastic followers of his unprecedented architecture of gleaming emptiness and void. Like moths drawn to a light bulb, they do not consider the consequences of such a fanatical act.

In his early work, Mies created voids inserted into his buildings, which were much like the courtyards. But his trademark came later when he made his buildings devoid of any traces of life's miscellany. His buildings are bare and minimal, though the surface materials are an ensemble of sumptuous marble, travertine, leather upholstery, walnut timber panels and shiny chromium-coated slender steel pillars. His void and nothingness par excellence is Farnsworth House – a weekend retreat outside of Chicago for a female doctor. Situated amidst the dense bush of a private estate, the house, elevated on slender stilts and on a platform, is sealed from inclement weather only by a thin sheet of floor-to-ceiling glass around the building (see Figure 5.5b). 'I can't put a clothes hanger in my house without considering how it effects everything from the outside,' complained Dr Farnsworth.[11] Mies, however, brushed off such demands for convenience and comfort in a house: hang your clothes on the hook behind your bathroom door is the advice given by the architect, for one only needs one dress in a weekend house. 'I would not like to live in a cubical house allotted of small rooms. I would rather live on a bench in Hyde Park,' declared the architect when he further dismissed the demands of the very notion of a house that protects our innate weakness.[12] Saint Paul would have smiled at Mies, but he went further to dismantle the very necessity of the house that is to conceal our inner fear:

While we look not at the things which are seen, but at the things which are not seen: for the things which are seen are temporal; but the things which are not seen are eternal.

For we know that if our earthly house of this tabernacle were dissolved, we have a building of God, a house not made with hands, eternal in the heavens.[13]

Such is the state of not being at home – an innate homelessness. The lustrous surfaces that clad the poverty of the 'nothingness' in Mies' buildings then seem a conundrum: are they simply a camouflage of a vacuous void?

Mies had a good collection of books on oriental philosophy, including works of Confucius and Laozi, and even once acknowledged the influence of Chinese architecture on his work.[14] Although it has been speculated that it is the Chinese courtyard – the void in the building – that had a bearing in the framed verdure in Mies' buildings (but also the Chinese post and beam structure on his bony buildings of only 'skin and skeleton'),[15] we can only assume that it was Laozi's *wuwei* 无为 ('doing nothing' is the literary translation) that might be tenuously linked to Mies' 'almost nothing.'[16] Confucius demanded participation, hence the void in the building was to be filled with rites and ceremonies, as well as life's miscellany as we have already seen. The Chinese, nonetheless, never settled on only one of the two. *Ru dao hubu* – the complementation of the Confucian worldview and the *dao* as established as early as in the Han dynasty (see the discussion in Chapter 3) – being the doctrine of Chinese life, had their most vivid materialization in a Chinese courtyard. Even the bad taste and a wicked sense of humour that filled the courtyard was put in good check when the solemnity of Heaven cast a thick layer of snow to cover everything in it.

*Wuwei* from Laozi, however, is not about doing nothing. Even the potent example of the usefulness of the emptiness – the void, as we have learned early in the book, is to fill it: we make vessels from clay; it is the void within the vessel that makes it useful. Though the void should never be filled fully to lose its potentiality, it is not to be left empty. Neither Laozi, nor Zhuangzi (who reminded us of the usefulness of the useless), let alone Confucius, preached a complete state of homelessness. Mies, too, did not give up the very protection offered by a shelter all together, but his pursuit of a *higher state of being* has become devoid of *the being*. The very conundrum of having a shelter (despite its thinness and transparency) as the void of emptiness, is the opposite of the universal idea of the courtyard. Khan, Mies' modern contemporary, and, I should like to think, the sixteenth-century master Palladio also, were both much drawn to the higher state of being. Kahn once brushed off the corporeal demand in architecture: 'Need is so many bananas; need is ham sandwich!'[17] Five hundred years earlier, Palladio, too, showed very little concern for the amenities of a household tucked away under the podium and in the mezzanine. A splendid country villa for a Veneto noble was a matrix of lofty and intimate rooms for the leisure of literary and philosophical pursuit in summer. Although both Kahn and Palladio often roofed the void in the centre, the void is the monumentalized backdrop, rather than devoid of *the being*.

Unlike Mies, the mid- and late twentieth–century modern master Jørn Utzon was not cryptic about his obsession with the Chinese courtyard. The Danish architect, renowned for his design of the hyperbolic curvature form of the Sydney Opera House, was in his lifetime much drawn to China's past – its architecture and the way of life. Utzon's warm flirtation with China was on the record: he even named his daughter Lin after his favourite Chinese author Dr Lin Yutang.[18] It, however, does seem farfetched to relate the 'vaulted sails' of the Sydney Opera House to Chinese architecture. More than half a century ago, the English architectural historian Joseph Rykwert, against the lavish praises from the competition jury report on the Opera House, set out his position with this blunt assessment: 'It seems as if it were conceived entirely in a spirit of fancy, and had little to do with imagination let alone method. Beyond the one blowsy overdramatization it has few pleasures to offer.'[19] This was chiefly true when it comes to the 'sails'. Utzon's competition-winning entry was a rather sketchy stroke of a series of free-form, interlocking thin concrete shells. The saving grace as it turned out, is the structural solution, for the organic form of the 'sails' could not be built. Utzon, after having given it much thought, rather ingeniously resorted to the geometrical fragments of a sphere to define the shapes of the 'sails'. In this way he, with the help of Arup engineers, managed to assemble the 'sails' with prefabricated concrete ribs that are strung together. This, according to Utzon, was inspired by the early twelfth-century Chinese building manual *Yingzao fashi* and its principal ideas of prefabrication and standardization, which made a strong appeal to the architect. But in the conceptualization of the Sydney Opera House design, there was also the key idea of 'platform' from Chinese architecture. Utzon attributed a feeling of 'firmness and security' – an architectural quality that he held dear – to the Chinese platform on which a house, or a temple, stands. 'Platform', or 'plateau', became his lifelong architectural fixation. But in what way is a feeling of security aroused through the use of a platform?

There was a peculiar omission in Utzon's interpretation of Chinese architecture. In his famous *parti* diagram illustrating the idea of the Sydney Opera House design, the prominent Chinese roof above a raised platform was compared to the floating cloud hovering over the ocean horizon (Figure 10.5). The walls of the building's enclosure were deemed insignificant, hence diminished by the modern master. We therefore assume that Chinese architecture, too, facilitated a command of the panoramic horizon as promised by modern

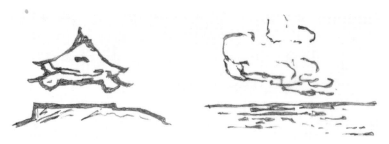

**Figure 10.5** *Utzon's sketch of the Sydney Opera House concept, showing the prominent Chinese roof above a raised platform that is likened to a cloud floating over the ocean horizon.*

**Figure 10.6** *Utzon's sketch modified by the author to conform to the reality of courtyard enclosure.*

architecture. This *parti*, which is now iconic, has been repeatedly used by architects and scholars to understand the defining character not only of the Sydney Opera House, but also the remainder of the works in Utzon's oeuvre. But what was all together neglected was that any such pre-modern Chinese building, be it a house or a temple, ought to be confined in a walled compound – that is, a courtyard, like a piece of precious jade stone sitting unlidded in its wrapping box. There was no possibility of privileging horizon as dictated by Utzon, but only the sky framed by the courtyard (Figure 10.6).

In his widely quoted essay, 'Platforms and Plateaus', published in *Zodiac* no. 10 in 1962,[20] in addition to describing the sensation of the splendid 'visual life' of the ancient Mayans when they emerged from the dense jungle to reach the top of their temple – the plateau, Utzon, curiously, was also attracted to the Chinese house, where he found 'firmness and security'. Utzon's feeling for the Chinese house, I am inclined to think, has something to do with the serenity of the Chinese 'skywell', and the Chinese courtyard in general. Though that he never elaborated on it, Utzon had a keen interest in the Chinese courtyard, which he incorporated in some of his widely published housing designs. It is therefore puzzling to say the least, why Utzon did not attribute 'security' to the encircling walls, which, together with the platform and other elements, comprised a Chinese courtyard building.

In his lifetime, Utzon built three houses for himself and his family. These houses, more so than the Sydney Opera House, reflect his persistent effort to reconcile 'platform' and 'courtyard', for they seemed to be in opposition in the mind of the architect. There appeared to be a conflict between a 'visual life' provided by the 'firmness (or rather the height)' of the platform, and a feeling of 'security', which perhaps should have been attributed to the courtyard, though the architect never made the connection as such. This conflict is a recurrent theme in all three houses built by Utzon. Let us examine one of Utzon's houses for their courtyards.

Between 1970 and 1972, Utzon built a small family villa on Spain's Mallorca Island, which was named Can Lis after his wife. In this villa, plateau and 'visual life' appear to rule. Five separate room-like components – courtyard, kitchen and dining, living, and two bedrooms contained in one building – are laid out on the cliff edge one next to the other to maximize the view (Figure 10.7). The defining walls of the courtyard, instead of framing only the sky, are corrupted with semicircular openings; a semicircular table is placed in the middle of the courtyard to accentuate the view towards the sea (now superseded by overgrown trees ...). Utzon was consistent in 'corrupting' the encircling walls of a courtyard towards the distant view and horizon. In his collective courtyard housing schemes, the Kingo for example, Utzon consciously lowered one side of the courtyard parapet wall in order to gain the district landscape view.

This viewfinder tendency has been applied to every single room in Can Lis, and it culminates in the living room. The large semicircular stone-built seat makes the room like a theatre setting. The stage is the sea and the horizon. The deep window alcoves poke out like eyes. But the cross section of this room is, oddly, cave-like: the ceiling soars high above the eye-like viewfinder windows. Such verticality, it seems, wants to internalize the room. Utzon apparently spent much time contemplating in a cave right below the Can Lis site when the design was conceived, but the cave, as he explained, gave him only the 'unit of place and view', not the sense of verticality gleaned from the Can Lis living room.[21] A small clerestory corner opening, up against the wall, gives the textured stone wall a divine wash of daylight (though it only lasts for 20 minutes during the day …). This heavenly light from above, it is said, was an afterthought. Still, there was far too much glare from the Mediterranean Sea, and the unwanted attention from architectural pilgrims. Utzon felt the urge for further retreat. Some twenty years later, he built another family villa, Can Feliz, on the same island further away from the sea. But the effort in reconciling the view and the internalized room still rings true in Can Feliz.

Although it may seem to have little to do with the courtyard, the problem of this conflict was already foreshadowed in Utzon's interpretation of the ancient Mayan temple: while the vision of the Mayans was limited in the dense jungle, the flat-top pyramid plateau, in his mind's eye, would enable the Mayans to expand their horizon.[22] But then the Mayans were not unique in this instance: for any pre-modern people, vision was limited to the place. The imagination of distance afar often was helped with building a watchtower or a raised platform, which was a necessary component of a stratified

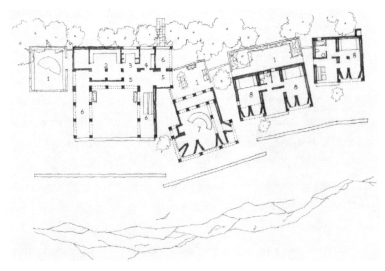

**Figure 10.7a.** *Plan of Utzon's holiday villa Can Lis. Legend: 1. Courtyard (as rooms open to the sky); 2. Dining room; 3. Kitchen; 4. Study; 5. Entry; 6. Verandah; 7. Living room; 8. Bedroom.*

cosmic model. Like many pre-modern people, there were three major planes in the Mayan cosmos: the earth, the underworld and the heaven above. The actual habit of climbing high to inspect the horizon would have been an occasional affair, for the tower or the raised platform was a sacred place. In other words, the summit of a stratified cosmos was reserved by pre-modern people for celestial connection with their gods – that is, the dialogue with heaven. Of course, it was also reserved for the rulers so that the representation of their power could be seen and felt from vast distances. Utzon's reading of this ancient architecture is a modern imagining: he saw no difference between the horizon, privileged by the dominance of vision in modern times, and the heaven above. The ancients, alas, did not, as we moderns do, demand a visual life. The consolation gained through the devotion to their gods overrode any visual pleasure.

**Figure 10.7b.** *The featured courtyard in Can Lis with openings in the encircling wall enclosure.*

In the same essay, Utzon, rather unexpectedly, provided a description of the platform at Monte Alban in Southern Mexico where the central part of the platform is kept at a lower level by building step-like edges. He then offered this reading: 'the mountain top has been converted into a completely independent thing floating in the air, separated from the earth, and from up there you see actually nothing but the sky and the passing clouds, – a new planet.'[23] Such is what one may feel in a confined Chinese courtyard! The Mexican architect, Luis Barragán, one of the modern luminaries in Utzon's time, made a fatal tweak to his famous house in Mexico City: he replaced a low parapet of wooden planks on the roof terrace, which allowed a view to the garden at the rear of the house, with a high wall, thereby ensuring the supremacy of the sky, like that seen from the summit of Monte Alban. The pedantic architect even went so far as to prune the overgrown neighbouring trees so that the purity of the framed sky was not distracted by any horizontal vista . . .[24]

Utzon, deep in his subconsciousness, was a sensitive soul: whilst much seduced by the splendid visual life and the capacious world out there, he was compelled also to pursue 'firmness and security', as felt in the Chinese courtyard. But Utzon may have already been torn apart by this irreconcilable conflict – his affection for both the Japanese house, where the outward pavilion-like buildings were connected on a raised platform, and the internalized Chinese courtyard that answered only to the heaven above is another example.

The Sri Lankan architect Geoffrey Bawa (1919–2003) built houses that look like pre-modern courtyards. Although Bawa, unlike Utzon, was not attracted by the view into the capacious world, his courtyard contains pleasure rather than facilitates a skyward zenith. Much to his frustration, Bawa during his lifetime had often been lazily pigeonholed into the category of regionalists who produced 'vernacular' buildings according to local traditions. His solo exhibition at the Royal Institute of British Architects in 1986 received polite and yet rather lukewarm reception: few in London, his beloved city and spiritual home, showed any genuine enthusiasm in his works, even though the vernacular and traditional look of post-modernism was still in vogue in the late 1980s. Bawa's buildings, much like his own persona, seem to radiate a certain aloofness that is belied by their appearance.

With an almost self-indulgent cosmopolitan upbringing, Bawa could not have settled for either traditionalist or vernacular regionalism. The fabrication of his buildings may have been 'hand-made' and labour intensive, but it is by no means according to vernacular tradition. In the House for Dr. Bartholomeusz (1961–1963), a building whose *parti* we will now examine, Bawa experimented with new ways of construction: polished coconut trunks were placed on granite bases as columns; half-round Portuguese roof tiles were laid beneath and over the corrugated cement sheeting for better waterproofing and thermal property. Bawa would continue his innovation in materials for building fabrication, but technique was never his forte. Being a gentleman architect, Bawa would not lift a finger just for the sake of fabrication, as the Bauhaus school might have preached. His conviction, if there is any, seems that his buildings ought to provide pleasure to its occupants.

Contained in a walled compound, the House for Dr Bartholomeusz consists of three pavilion buildings and three inner courtyards in an axial and linear fashion (Figure 10.8). The first pavilion was to house servants and cars, the second was to contain a dining room and kitchen, and the third was to be the living room with bedrooms on the upper floor. The three open rooms in succession – the courtyards – were pleasure gardens, though the first one could be used for the visitors to park their cars, whilst the centre piece – the pool court – served as the reception to the main pavilion; the backyard was filled with lush trees, yet one more garden of sheer pleasure. Close to completion, Dr Bartholomeusz decided to migrate to Australia, hence called off the project. Bawa, as if already in anticipation of what was to happen to this project, acted decisively to persuade his partners to take over the building as their office. The transformation from a purposefully designed house for a doctor and his family to an architectural office was effortless: the first pavilion became the gate house and storage (Bawa's vintage Rolls-Royce by then sat comfortably in the garage); the first courtyard also was used for the partners and clients to park their cars; the second pavilion was perfect for the design offices; and the pool court turned out to be just ideal as the reception foyer for the main pavilion. Here Bawa and his design partner Ulrik Plesner, a Danish architect, were housed on the ground floor while the upper floor was used as the cramped drafting offices.

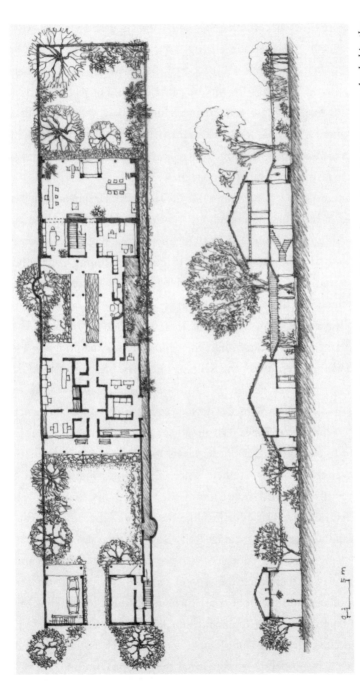

**Figure 10.8** *Plan and longitudinal section of House for Dr Bartholomeusz, with Bawa's secret escape passageway shaded in the plan.*

This office courtyard complex was to become exemplary for future clients: it showed the open airy passive design in the warm tropical climate, where the walled compound, large roofs and their deep eaves were the defining architectural elements. Beneath these roofs were the loosely organized room divisions. Like a sixteenth-century Renaissance villa in Italy, the rooms were an interconnected matrix: even the central axis was a see-through vista, except that the view was contained within the walled compound. This *parti*, inevitably, facilitated the kind of idle life that the architect himself had lived. Bawa on his numerous Italian sojourns in his youth spent months exploring the villas and their gardens in Tuscany. He once stayed in Palladio's Villa Foscari, and even contemplated purchasing a villa near Cola-di-Lazise overlooking Lake Garda so that he could settle in Italy for good. Although he did not find Corbusier any more interesting than Alberti or Vignola or Palladio, Bawa's formal architectural education at the Architectural Association in London gave him a heavy dose of modernism and the seemingly contrasting Miesians and Corbusians. In fact, he had already visited buildings by Mies van der Rohe and Frank Lloyd Wright before he went to the Architectural Association.

But Bawa's *parti* is a true hybrid: it is neither the lucid Renaissance room matrix where the vista would be extended to the cultivated landscape and the horizon beyond the interior of the building, nor a Miesian pinwheel open plan within which space flows for the sake of being free. The traditional look of this house aside, it was not a Chinese courtyard either, for the carnal and visual pleasures were, albeit subtly, hinted at rather than regulated into the gradient and hierarchy of order and rite, like that of a Chinese house. In a Chinese house, which we have seen, the pleasure garden and the house, were both walled, and were juxtaposed but separated. Bawa visited China at the age of fifteen. He remembered those high yellow walls, but he must have been rather curious about what was contained behind them: secrecy, or pleasure? An enigma![25]

Legend has it that in this new office, 'Bawa occupied a fixed desk on the cross-axis of the main ground floor room in a position that signified his seniority. This gave him an oblique view of all the comings and goings along the main axis of the pool court and enabled him to observe the waiting area without himself being seen. When unwelcome visitors appeared, Bawa would escape down the secret corridor (see Figure 10.8 the shaded area in plan). Plesner sat opposite Bawa in a position that implied a near equality of status, while Nilgiria occupied a small corner office on the first floor, and Valentine Gunasekera and his staff were relegated to a cramped room in part of the middle pavilion.'[26] When the courtyard complex changed hands again, it should not be a surprise that the robust *parti* of this house has made its new lease of life a rather natural one: entrepreneur Udayshanth Fernando rented this building from Bawa to turn it into a prosperous gallery café called 'Paradise Road' (though Bawa always liked to refer to it as 'Paradise Lost'). Fernando even put up a dining pavilion in the rear courtyard, but along the axis, not across it, as per Bawa's instruction, which, in a clever way, only makes a split of the final courtyard. The original longitudinal sequence of courts, as a result, is even strengthened. Differently put, the *parti* remains the same one.

It is the role of the hidden passageway mentioned above, tucked away in the labyrinth of courts and rooms, that tells of the true Bawa – the modern man, who was camouflaged behind the gregarious pleasure gardens and interconnected rooms. His flamboyancy and eccentricity, overt and showy partly because of his natural attributes (being exceedingly tall and handsome), and his accessories (his lifelong love affair with vintage Rolls-Royce cars), only served to suggest that there was a relentless modern soul behind these masks that was forever searching for the 'eternal House of God' beyond earthly and circumstantial existence. The pleasure, somehow, was to be concealed. Bawa's own house, 33rd Lane in Colombo (1960–1998), became a maze of interconnected rooms with a chequerboard of open tropical garden courts and light wells inserted among them. Its spatial narrative, which Bawa took many years of remodelling and tweaking, is that of pleasurable incidents and surprises in both encountering and concealing. Bawa had been to Mexico, but it is unknown whether he had seen the Mexican architect, Luis Barragán's own house in Mexico City. The two houses share one thing in common: the need for a corridor is, on the surface, eliminated. There are nooks and corners in both houses, though they serve different purposes – places of solitude for Barragán, and in Bawa's house, long and languid conversations accompanied by his obsessive bricolage of elements from old houses and eclectic furniture.

The imagined pleasure behind the high walls in a Chinese house may have served as a driving force for Bawa, but his Colombo courtyard houses also happened to work as radical planning solutions to the progression of urban densification. The courtyard pattern was not vernacular to Colombo. The opposite was in fact true: Colombo was a colonial town of large freestanding bungalows and leafy avenues. The independence of the country and the emergence of the new middle class had meant that more people wanted to stay within close proximity to the city centre where amenities and services had concentrated. High land value and the inevitable reduction of the average plot size demanded a new pattern. Bawa led the way: his own maze-like courtyard house was a result of stitching together freestanding bungalows and placing new buildings on the boundaries so that the house became introvertive with internal voids. An area of 750 square metres was once considered a small residential site, but in the late 1960s a 250 square metre site was quite acceptable.

Bawa's houses proved that one could even build a comfortable courtyard house within the plot size of 200 square metres. That Bawa was seen as a traditionalist shows that his introduction of the courtyard pattern into the Colombo urban fabric – a radical planning reform – had been quietly realized without people consciously knowing it. This however does not make him an avant-garde architect for he did not invent an unprecedented housing pattern, nor was he interested in creating a unique form for the sake of newness. The room opening to the sky – the cosmic underpinning of courtyard, may have, without himself knowing it, saved Bawa from becoming a self-obsessive architect. The languid architect saw no problem in having his sensuality exposed under the heaven's arch, so long as permeability, a potent architectural instrument of pleasure, was neatly contained within the walled enclosure. Better still, there was a secret corridor to guard his unbent right to be a modern, private being. The voids in the works of Mies and Utzon may be a brief brush of modernity with the courtyard, or even barking up the wrong tree. Bawa's courtyard, it seems, is the living proof that the primordial meaning of the pre-modern courtyard, be it a Roman *domus* or a Beijing quadrangle, demands a new lease of life in the modern world.

# Epilogue: The Four
# or the Five

The Chinese courtyard, regardless of its regional variations that we have surveyed thus far, was consistently centred on the pairing of hall and court. What was the core of the Chinese courtyard – the hall building or the actual void of the central court? The answer to this question may help to elucidate the meaning of the Chinese universe, which, to the disbelief of the Chinese, many not be universally applicable. Joseph Rykwert, in an intriguing essay titled 'The Four and the Five', has outlined the difference that lies between Western thinking and that of the Chinese.[1] In a nutshell, Quadripartition, originating from the antiquity of the Mediterranean survey method, was used to divide the world into a four-square grid with the cross axes of south to north and east to west being cardinal orientations. The Romans learned this method from the Etruscans; the Greeks, too, used the same method. Both can be traced back to the Phoenicians of the ancient Near East. The centre of the cross of the four worlds was not occupied, hence a void. Since any ancient survey method inevitably sprung from a divine revelation, the four worlds were meaningful and governed by four seasons and four elements – air, fire, earth and water.

Not only the built world, but also the human body, was sorted and understood by this fourfold division.

The Chinese, however, always had a fivefold division associated with five elements as outlined in Chapter 2 – *Jin* 金 (metal), *mu* 木 (wood), *shui* 水 (water), *huo* 火 (fire) and *tu* 土 (earth). If there was a grid that should be used to lay their buildings and cosmic cities, it was not a four-square but nine-square grid. In the middle is the man – the emperor or the paterfamilias, who ruled over the yellow earth. The rest, like that of the fourfold division in the West, had their designated colours, mythical animals and zodiacal signs. Rykwert therefore concludes that this refined and divine nine-square-grid (where the numbers from 1 to 9 are inserted to magically add up to 15 in any direction) was used to lay out a vast city in the landscape or a building with the centre solidified as built structure. Even the Chinese adaptation of the Buddhist world of the sacred Mount Meru and the Hindu temples into a Chinese version of the pagoda is seen as further proof of this cosmic model.

This assertion seems to give a crystallized understanding of the difference of cosmology and the built worlds to the West and China. There was nothing that could even tenuously be regarded as a building in the centre of a Roman *domus*; the Pantheon, being the centre of the Roman world, is a sheer void. But neither the Chinese hall in a courtyard house, nor the palace hall in the imperial compound, alone constituted the Chinese centre. Confucius could not have conversed with his guest in the elevated hall without his disciples sitting in the lower court to listen to his teaching; the palace hall was only meaningful when the emperor gave his audience to the ministers standing or even kneeling in the vast imperial courtyard. The hall, and the lower court before it, were the architectural manifestation of 'Heaven's agent' (*tianli* 天吏). Mencius (372–289 BCE) would have agreed. Being the most spectacular and staunch preacher of Confucian thought a century or so after the death of the great man, Mencius gave the Mandate of Heaven a more humanist interpretation – that is, the peoples' will. In a more explicit way, Mencius defined Heaven as Nature, and naturally, the ethical cosmic order. This was more or less what Confucius had said. But Mencius went further. Rebellion as such is justified, and only the new dynastic founder who answers to the goodness and satisfaction of the people can be 'Heaven's agent'.[2]

Such was the centre of the Chinese world: the centre was not a void, but it was not the hall standing alone in the middle either, for both the emperor and his subjects, the paterfamilias and the lowly members of his clan, must, from time to time, answer to Heaven. In good times, they might indulge a little more of their earthly life. But when in drought, the emperor must pray to Heaven for rain and a good harvest ahead. The same applied to a quadrangle in Beijing, or a 'skywell' in the Yangtze region, the paterfamilias attended more to the ancestral shrine in the hall, and prayed to Heaven when the son failed the imperial examination or disobeyed the arranged marriage to run for free love … The centre of the Chinese world was, therefore, the combination of the void and the solid shrine that both were under the watchful eye of Heaven. They were predominantly secular though occasionally solemn, but never sacred. To meet in the middle way – that is *zhongyong* 中庸, therefore, is neither a compromise nor mediocrity. Instead it is the supreme propriety, vital and yet composed. Confucius praised it as high morality: pitching in the middle is virtuous because it represents *reason* as demanded by Heaven and Nature, but he regretted that it was not easily found among people.[3] The Chinese nevertheless continued to pursue it for more than two millennia. Despite the physical disappearance of the courtyard in Chinese modern life, this very Chinese locus, material or literary, neither vacuous nor solidified, in its *golden mean*, may not have vanished at all in the mists of time.

# *Notes*

# Prologue

1  It must be said that the notion of 'China' and 'Chineseness' (which will appear later in the book) evolved over time. In general, and also in this book, China refers to a cultural tradition that originated from the Yellow River 'cradle'. A history of 'China' and 'Chineseness', to paraphrase the American geographer and historian Owen Lattimore, can be seen as the expansion of the agricultural society of China to the pastoral society of the steppe. Banpo, one of the earliest sites of what was Chinese in the Yellow River region is distinctively different to Hemudu, the earliest rice as well as mortise-and-tenon site in the Yangtze Delta. Although the evolution of 'China' is not central to the book, through life in the courtyard, in a way this book shows that people and culture of the Yangtze region folded into the story of 'China', and so did the Ba and Shu of Sichuan, among others. Lattimore attributed an 'intensive and irrigated agriculture', and its associated city form as well as administration to the core of this 'Chineseness', which can be used as a useful background at the outset of the book. See Owen Lattimore, *Inner Asian Frontiers of China* (New York: American Geographical Society, 1940).

2  In addition to the brilliant Chinese inventions of gunpowder, the magnetic compass, paper and printing, which, as asserted by Francis Bacon, were catalytic for European modernization, Joseph Needham, through his monumental multi-volume *Science and Civilization in China*, though not without theoretical and philosophical defects, did offer sufficient justification of this claim.

3  On 21 September 1786 when Goethe reached the Villa Rotonda, he remarked: 'The house itself is a habitation rather than a home. The hall and the rooms are beautifully proportioned, but, as a summer residence, they would hardly satisfy the needs of a noble family.' J.W. Goethe, *Italian Journey, 1786–1788*, trans. W.H. Auden and Elizabeth Mayer (London: The Folio Society, 2010), 51.

4  Western visitors to China in the late eighteenth and nineteenth centuries, with either sympathy or bias, commonly complained about the lack of comfort in Chinese houses and in Chinese minds, as both a physical phenomenon and a concept. See the ably assembled summary of this topic by Ronald Knapp in 'In Search of the Elusive Chinese House' in *House Home Family: Living and Being Chinese,* ed. Ronald G. Knapp and Kai Yin Lo (Honolulu: University of Hawai'i Press; New York: China Institute in America, 2005), 63–71.

5  When it comes to the term 'Golden Age', academic conventions differ. Some scholars of Chinese history, for example, regard the Tang dynasty as the Golden Age.

6  See Miriam Gottfried's essay 'Beyond Gifts, More Homes Make Room for Wrapping', *The Wall Street Journal,* 23 December 2010.

7  Jonathan D. Spence, *The Chan's Great Continent: China in Western Minds* (New York and London: W.W. Norton & Company, 1999), xi.

8  Ibid.

9  Lin Yutang, *My Country and My People* (London and Toronto: William Heinemann Ltd, 1936), 10–11.

10  Spence, *The Chan's Great Continent,* xviii.

11  Ibid. xvii.

12  Ibid. 241.

13  Simon Leys (Pierre Ryckmans), *The Hall of Uselessness* (Collingwood: Black Inc., 2011), vii.

14  Ibid. vii–viii.

15  Qian Zhongshu 钱锺书, *Wei cheng* 围城 was first published in 1947 in Shanghai. The English translation, as *Fortress Besieged,* by Nathan K. Mao and Jeanne Kelly, first appeared in 1980; numerous updated editions followed, including a Penguin Classics edition in 2006.

16  Qian Zhongshu 钱锺书, *Guanzhui bian* 管锥编 (Beijing: Zhonghua shuju 中华书局, 1979), 3:875–8; cf. the addenda, 5:72–3 and 201 (Vol. 3: 875–8, Vol. 5, Enlarged Section: 72–3, 201). Qian used the expression 'pathos of distance' in this essay, and asserted that the pre-modern melancholy caused by height and the opportunity of gazing afar is the precursor of similar modern emotions, but he generalized it as being part of European Romanticism without referencing Nietzsche. See the selected translation of *Guanzhui bian* by Ronald Egan in *Limited Views: Essays on Ideas and Letters by Qian Zhongshu* (Cambridge: Harvard University Asia Centre, 1998), 74–82.

17  Such a characteristic of the modern world has led some of the powerful and revered in our society to lament that the biggest challenge facing humanity now is 'a globalization of superficiality'. This term was defined in 2010 by Father Adolfo Nicholas, SJ, the worldwide leader of the Jesuits, to describe the

opinion-flooded digital age where we humans are in danger of gradually losing our critical ability to think and discern the truth.

18  This startling reminder comes from Yi-Fu Tuan, see *Dear Colleague: Common and Uncommon Observations* (Minneapolis and London: University of Minnesota Press, 2002), 134. Also see *Passing Strange and Wonderful* (New York: Island Press, 1993).

19  See Leys, *The Hall of Uselessness*. Leys wrote some of the illuminating essays on this topic, including 'Poetry and Painting: Aspects of Chinese Classical Aesthetics' and 'Ethics and Aesthetics: The Chinese Lesson' in this anthology of his essays.

20  See Qian, *Guanzhui bian*, 2:719–23, cf. the addenda, 5:60 and 190 (Vol. 2: 719–23, Vol. 5, Enlarged Section: 60, 190). I have used the translation rendered by Ronald Egan in *Limited Views: Essays on Ideas and Letters by Qian Zhongshu* (Cambridge: Harvard University Asia Centre, 1998), 29–34.

21  Leslie Martin and Lionel March. 'Speculations' in *Urban Space and Structures*, ed. Leslie Martin and Lionel March (Cambridge: Cambridge University Press, 1972), 38.

22  Leslie Martin, 'The Grid as Generator' in *Urban Space and Structures*, 21–2.

23  Ibid. 22.

24  Reza Aslan, predicated on the anthropologist Stewart Guthrie's theory of the humanization of god (*Faces in the Clouds: A New Theory of Religion* (New York: Oxford University Press, 1995)), has offered a sweeping sketch of this humanization process of god throughout human history. See *God: A Human History* (Bantam Press, 2017). Though Aslan has included the Chinese as part of his all-inclusive narrative (with only his authentic Islam as the exception), I shall show in this book that the Chinese, with vernacular traditions of vulgarized religions aside, went about their life in the high tradition without a humanized god.

25  Aristotle's *On the Heavens* and Ptolemy's *Planetary Hypotheses* belonged to the high tradition. There were also Pliny's *Natural History*, Hesiod's *Works and Days*, and Aratus' *Phenomena* in popular literature. Both Plato and Cicero ended their *Republic* with a cosmic vision. See *The Classical Tradition*, ed. Anthony Grafton, Glenn Most and Salvatore Settis (Cambridge: Harvard University Press, 2010), 89–96.

26  See Joseph Rykwert, *The Idea of a Town* (Cambridge: MIT Press, 1988), 90–1.

# Chapter 1

1  Paraphrased and translated by the author from 'Xuangong er nian – Jinlingong bu jun' 宣公二年 • 晋灵公不君 in *Chunqiu zuozhuan* 春秋左传.

2   For a detailed account of the pile-built dwellings in southern China, see Xing Ruan, *Allegorical Architecture* (Honolulu: University of Hawai'i Press, 2006), 138–66.

3   Zheng Xuan 郑玄: '宫必有碑，所以识日景，引阴阳也；凡碑引物者宗庙则丽牲焉；其材，宫庙以石，窆用木.' See Zheng Xuan 郑玄 [Han]汉, 'Liyi zhushu 礼仪注疏' in *Shisanjing zhushu* 十三经注疏, ed. Li Xueqin 李学勤 (Beijing: Peking University Press 北京大学出版社, 2000), 474.

4   Carbon 14 has been used to verify the date as the Western Zhou. Earlier walled compounds dated in the Shang period, such as the palace foundation no.1, found at Erlitou, Yanshi in Henan province, 3rd stratum, and other palace foundations found at Panlongcheng in Huangpo, Hubei province, prove that courtyards existed long before the Western Zhou, but the early walled enclosures appear rather rudimentary. References of Zhongguo kexueyuan kaogu yanjiusuo erlitou gongzuo dui 中国科学院考古研究所二里头工作队, 'Henan yanshi erlitou zao shang gongdian yizhi fajue baogao,' 河南偃师二里头早商宫殿遗址发掘简报 *Archaeology* 考古, (August 1974), 234, and Du Jinpeng 杜金鹏, 'Panlong cheng gongdian jizhi taolun,' 盘龙城宫殿基址讨论. *Acta Archaeological Sinica* 考古学报, (February 1974), 161–82.

5   Fu Xinian 傅熹年, *Fu Xinian jianzushi lunwenji* 傅熹年建筑史论文集, 33–45.

6   Linguists and historians have carefully sorted the nomenclature of Chinese house components and their symbolic and literary meanings in the Chinese language. For a comprehensive survey, see Xu Jialu 许嘉璐, *Zhongguo gudai yi shi zhu xing* 中国古代衣食住行 (Beijing: Zhonghua shuju 中华书局, 2013), 107–46. The material of the following section is partially drawn from this survey.

7   For an exhaustive account of the building, restoration and rebuilding of Temple of Confucius, see James A. Flath, *Traces of the Sage* (Honolulu: University of Hawai'i Press, 2016). On the slow development of the Confucian school to the state cult, see Michael Nylan and Thomas Wilson, *Lives of Confucius: Civilisation's Greatest Sage through the Ages* (New York: Doubleday, 2010).

8   *Xunzi* 荀子 Dalue 大略 27.3: '天子外屏，诸侯内屏，礼也.' Also see Mengbi Li, 'The "Translation" of Zhaobi in China across Time and Space,' in *Proceedings of the Society of Architectural Historians, Australia and New Zealand*, trans. and ed. Christoph Schnoor (Auckland: SAHANZ and Unitec ePress; and Gold Coast: SAHANZ, 2014), 145–54.

9   Liu Xi 刘熙 [Han]汉, *Shiming* 释名, *Congshu jicheng chubian* 丛书集成初编, ed. Wang Yunwu 王云五 (Shanghai: The Commercial Press 商务印书馆, 1939), 88.

10  何晏集解引郑玄曰 '萧之言肃也；墙谓屏也。君臣相见之礼，至屏而加肃敬焉，是以谓之萧墙'. See He Yan 何晏 [Wei]魏, *Lunyu jijie* 论语集解 (Beijing: Zhonghua shuju 中华书局, 1998), 72.

11  This is not a direct translation but a summary of '臣来朝君... 行至门内屏外，复应思惟，罘罳言复思也'. See Cui Bao 崔豹 [Jin]晋, *Gujin zhu* 古今注, (Beijing: Zhonghua shuju 中华书局, 1998), 6.

12  *The Analects* 'Jishi' 季氏 16.1. I have referenced the translation by Simon Leys, but have made some small modifications to the term *xiao qiang* 萧墙 and the house. See Simon Leys, *The Analects of Confucius: Translation and Notes* (New York and London: W.W. Norton and Company, 1997), 81.

13  This was clearly explained in *Erya shigong* 尔雅 • 释宫: the side halls of the gate are the home school (门侧之堂谓之塾). However, this has not been found in any of the surviving Ming and Qing courtyards perhaps because home schooling had long been replaced by separate schools.

14  *The Analects* 'Weilingong' 卫灵公 15.42. See Leys, *The Analects of Confucius: translation and Notes*, 79. I have replaced 'seat' in Leys translation with 'mat' to reflect the original use of *xi* 席.

15  By *Poems*, Confucius meant the *Book of Odes* (*Shijing* 诗经) here, also translated as the *Classic of Poetry* or *The Book of Poems*. It is a compilation of songs and poems dated between the eleventh and the seventh centuries BCE. It can be seen as a sort of early encyclopaedia of all things, such as animal and plan names.

16  *The Analects* 'Jishi' 季氏 16.

17  *The Analects* 'Yongye' 雍也 6.10, translation. See Leys, *The Analects of Confucius: Translation and Notes*, 25.

18  *The Analects* 'Xianjin' 先进 11.15, ibid. 51.

19  *The Analects* 'Shuer' 述而 7.8, ibid 30. Translation with my modification.

20  This is a fundamental aspect of the Chinese house about which both the scholars of the Chinese house and the general public concur. See *House, Home and Family: Living and Being Chinese*, 13.

21  Kwang-chih Chang, *The Archaeology of Ancient China* (New Haven and London: Yale University of Press, 1963), 62–3. Or reference the original Chinese archaeological report: Zhongguo kexueyuan kaogu yanjiusuo and Shaanxi sheng Xi'an banpo bowuguan 中国科学院考古研究所，陕西省西安半坡博物馆, 'Xi'an banpo-yuanshi shizu gongshe juluo yizhi', 西安半坡-原始氏族公社聚落遗址 in *Zhongguo tianye kaogu baogaoji* 中国田野考古报告集 (Beijing: Wenwu chubanshe 文物出版社, 1967), 9–29.

22  Chang, *The Archaeology of Ancient China*, 80.

23  Ibid. 62–4, 80, 95, 100, 101, 105, 137, 143, 149–61, 171, 183, 185.

24  The commencement of the Western Zhou dynasty is not a conclusive matter. I have used 1099 BCE – the beginning of King Wen's rule – to mark the

starting point of the Zhou era. Some historians tend to use the beginning of King Wu's rule in 1050 BCE as the inauguration of the Western Zhou dynasty. The final conquest of the Shang occurred after King Wen's death; his son King Wu led the army.

# Chapter 2

1   Lillian Lan-ying Tseng, *Picturing Heaven in Early China* (The Harvard University Asia Centre, 2011), 1.

2   Refer to the discussion of this point in Prologue and its note 21.

3   Ibid. 2.

4   Ibid. 3–4.

5   *Shangshu* 尚书 'Zhoushu jushi' 周书 • 君奭.

6   My own translation from *Shangshu* 尚书 'Zhoushu–dagao' 周书 • 大诰: '已！予惟小子，不敢替上帝命。天休于宁王，兴我小邦周，宁王惟卜用，克绥受兹命。今天其相民，矧亦惟卜用？呜呼！天明畏，弼我丕丕基'. See also Edward L. Shaughnessy's translation '*Stop!. I the young son do not dare to disregard the command of the Lord on High. Heaven was beneficent to King Wen, raising up our little country of Zhou, and it was turtle-shell divination that King Wen used, succeeding to receive this mandate. Now Heaven will be helping the people; how much more so should it be turtle-shell divination that I too use. Wuhu! Heaven is brightly awesome – it helps our grand foundation.*' From Michael Loewe and Edward L. Shaughnessy, *The Cambridge History of Ancient China: From the origins of civilization to 221 BC* (Cambridge University Press, 1999), 314.

7   *Shangshu* 尚书 'Zhoushu jushi' 周书 • 君奭.

8   See Frederick W. Mote, *Intellectual Foundations of China* (New York: Knopf, 1989), 14–15. Also Derk Bodde, 'Myths of Ancient China,' in *Mythologies of the Ancient World*, ed. S. N. Kramer (New York: Doubleday Anchor Books, 1961), 367–408.

9   Arthur Danto, *Philosophizing Art* (Berkeley: University of California Press, 1999), 198.

10  Translation from the author. See *The Analects* 'Shuer' 述而 7.17, '加我数年，五十以学《易》，可以无大过矣.' Instead of 'change' in the title, *Book of Changes*, another interpretation is to see *yi* 易 as 'also', hence the meaning of the same sentence is turned into a process of lifelong learning until the age of fifty as the precursor of not making any big mistakes. However, we should not cast any doubt on Confucius' endorsement of the *Book of Changes*. In his biography of Confucius, Sima Qian mentioned Confucius' particular fondness of *Book of Changes*.

11 *The Analects* 'Weizheng' 为政 2.4, '吾十有五，而志于学. 三十而立.
四十而不惑. 五十而知天命. 六十而耳顺. 七十而从心所欲，不逾矩.'
Simon Leys' s translation: 'At fifteen, I set my mind upon learning. At thirty,
I took my stand. At forty, I had no doubt. At fifty, I knew the will of Heaven.
At sixty, my ear was attuned. At seventy, I follow the desires of my heart
without breaking any rule.' See Leys, *The Analects of Confucius: Translation
and Notes*, 6.

12 My paraphrasing of *Tai* hexagram commentary in *Book of Changes*: '彖曰：泰，
小往大来，吉亨. 则是天地交，而万物通也；上下交，而其志同也.' I have
referenced Richard Wilhelm's translation as rendered in English by Cary
Baynes, which too is more an explanation than direct translation. I have
favoured the Wilhelm interpretation, because it forthrightly singles out the
earthly nature of Heaven. This is necessary, for even when it comes to Heaven,
the holy and divine have remained an alien concept to the Chinese. See
Richard Wilhelm and Cary Baynes, *The I Ching*, (Princeton: Princeton
University Press, 1967), 48.

13 Meng Yuanlao 孟元老 [Song]宋, *Dong jing meng hua lu* 东京梦华录 (Beijing:
The Commercial Press 商务印书馆, 1982), 56.

14 *Huainanzi* 淮南子 'Lanming xun' 览冥训 6.6: '凤皇之翔，至德也，……
而燕雀佼之，以为不能与之争于宇宙之间.'

15 *Zhuangzi* 庄子 'Zapian – gengsangchu' 杂篇·庚桑楚: '有实而无乎处者，
宇也；有长而无本剽者，宙也.' *Huainanzi* 淮南子 'Qisuxun' 齐俗训 11.18:
'往古来今谓之宙，四方上下谓之宇.'

16 *Zhuangzi* 庄子 'Zapian – xiangwang' 杂篇·讓王: '余立于宇宙之中，……
日出而作，日入而息，逍遥于天地之间.'

17 *The Analects* 'Zihan' 子罕 9.5, translation by Leys, *The Analects of Confucius:
Translation and Notes*. 39.

18 Ibid. 88.

19 *Shangshu* 尚书 'Ganshi·Hongfan' 甘誓·洪范.

20 *The Analects* 'Yongye' 雍也, 6.

21 N. Brady and R. Weil, *Elements of the Nature and Properties of Soils* (Upper
Saddle River: Prentice Hall, 2000), 89.

22 There have been no definitive versions of 'five crops' throughout Chinese
history. Rice, for example, understandably did not exist in the first instance.

23 Market towns built on major riverbanks, such as those along the Yangtze, did
not follow this cosmic structure.

24 *The Analects* 'Shuer' 述而 7.19: '其为人也，发愤忘食，乐以忘忧，不知老
之将至云尔.' My own translation.

25 Regarding the debate about the origin of bronze technology and chariot
warfare, see Mote, *Intellectual Foundations of China*, 6.

26 See also note 8.

27 The superiority that the Chinese place on the written world warrants more attention, since it is often unquestioned in our age that action and material, which can be seen, are more real than words. For a penetrating discussion of this topic, see Simon Leys, 'The Chinese Attitude towards the Past' in *The Hall of Uselessness* (Collingwood: Black Inc., 2011), 239–58.

28 The Chinese architect Chuin Tung 童寯 (Tong Jun in *pinyin*) in an English essay published in the 1930s discussed briefly the conceptual difference between the Western garden tradition and that of China, with the Japanese garden aligned more with the former. My summary here draws largely from Tong's essay. See Chuin Tung, 'Chinese Gardens: especially in Kiangsu and Chekiang', *Tien Hsia Monthly* 天下月刊 111, No. 3 (October 1936): 220–44.

29 Ibid.

30 Paraphrased by Tong Jun. Ibid.

31 Referring to the discussion in the Prologue.

32 Some architectural historians have heralded a simple triple-*jian* structure Jizhai 姬宅 in Gaoping county, Shanxi province, as the oldest surviving dwelling in China, reputedly built in the early Yuan dynasty (1279–1368), Zhang Guangshan 张广善, 'Gaoping xian Yuan dai minju' 高平县元代民居 in *Wenwu shijie* 文物世界, No. 3 (1993): 29–33.

# Chapter 3

1 Arthur Waley, *The Way and its Power: A Study of the Tao Te Ching and its Place in Chinese Thought*, Vol. 37 (Routledge, 2013), 108. First published in 1934 by Allen and Unwin.

2 See Simon Leys, *The Analects of Confucius*, xvi.

3 *The Analects* 'Zihan' 子罕 9.18: '吾未见好德如好色者也.' 'Weilingong' 卫灵公 15.13: '已矣乎！吾未见好德如好色者也.' I have used Simon Leys' translation here. See ibid. 41.

4 *Dao de jing* 道德经13: 三十辐共一毂, 当其无, 有车之用. 埏埴以为器, 当其无, 有器之用. 凿户牖以为室, 当其无, 有室之用. 故有之以为利, 无之以为用. No English translation does justice to the elegant economy and musical rhyme of the original verse. I have again used Arthur Waley's translation here to keep its wide reach consistent. See Waley, *The Way and its Power*, 122.

5 *The Analects* 'Zilu' 子路 13.4: 樊迟请学稼. 子曰: '吾不如老农.' 请学为圃, 曰: '吾不如老圃.' 樊迟出子曰: '小人哉, 樊须也！'; *The Analects* 'Weizheng' 为政 2.12: '君子不器.' This is my own rendering in English, not a word for word translation.

6   *Zhuangzi* 庄子 'Neipian renshi jian' 内篇・人世间 4.9: '人皆知有用之用，而莫知无用之用也.' I have used the translation rendered by Simon Leys. See Leys, *The Hall of Uselessness*. In this book, this line is also translated by the same author as: Everyone knows the usefulness of what is useful, but few know the usefulness of what is useless.

7   See 'Neipian qiwu lun' 内篇・齐物论 1, 'Neipian renshi jian' 内篇・人世间 4 and 'Neipian da zhongshi' 内篇・大宗师 6 in *Zhuangzi* 庄子, respectively. All these belong to the so-called 'inner chapters' of *Zhuangzi* that have been widely accepted by scholars as the true work of Zhuangzi. That Confucius was caricatured, for example, as a failure in his political career, and, whilst erudite and didactic, also a saint imposter and fame seeker, only appears in the 'outer and miscellaneous chapters' that are reputedly regarded by scholars as the work of Zhuangzi's students and followers.

8   *Dao de jing* 道德经3：不上贤，使民不争；不贵难得之货，使民不为盗；不见可欲，使民不乱是以圣人之治也，虚其心，实其腹，弱其志，强其骨，恒使民无知，无欲也使夫知不敢, 弗为而已，则无不治矣. My own translation.

9   *Shiji* 史记 'Xiaowu benji' 孝武本纪12：公孙卿曰：'仙人可见，而上往常遽，以故不见. 陛下可为观，如缑氏城，置脯枣，神人宜可致. 且仙人好楼居. '於是上令长安则作蜚廉桂观，甘泉则作益延寿观，使卿持节设具而候神人，乃作通天台，置祠具其下，将招来神仙之属. 於是甘泉更置前殿，始广诸宫室. 夏，有芝生殿防内中. 天子为塞河，兴通天台，若有光云，乃下诏曰：'甘泉防生芝九茎，赦天下，毋有复作.' See Sima Qian 司马迁 [Han], *Shiji* 史记, book 2, (Beijing: Zhonghua Shuju 中华书局, 1975), 478.

10  See Lillian Lan-ying Tseng, *Picturing Heaven in Early China* (Cambridge and London: The Harvard University Asia Centre, 2011), 152–62.

11  Refer to note 9 in Prologue.

12  Liu Dunzhen 刘敦桢, *Zhongguo gudai jianzhushi* 中国古代建筑史, 52.

13  Guo Qinghua, *The Mingqi Pottery Buildings of Han Dynasty China 206 BC – AD 220* (Brighton: Sussex Academic Press, 2010), 51. The examples of *mingqi* discussed in the following paragraphs are drawn from the exhaustive collection in Guo's book.

14  See *Zhongguo gudai jianzhushi* 中国古代建筑史, Vol. 1, ed. Liu Xujie 刘叙杰 (Beijing: Zhongguo jianzhu gongye chubanshe 中国建筑工业出版社, 2009), 562.

15  In a few excavated Han house sites, to take the example of one from the Western Han dynasty, found in the western part of Luoyang, there is no sign that a tower ever existed in the walled compound. Fu Xinian 傅熹年, *Chinese Architecture*, ed. Nancy Steinhardt, trans. Alexandra Harrer (New Haven and London: Yale University Press; Beijing: New World Press, 2002), 47.

16 Robert Hughes, *The Shock of the New* (London: Thames & Hudson, 1991), 10.

17 In the House of Fabius Rufus in Pompeii, a suite of rooms with ocean views at the lower level were separated from the ground level where the atrium was located. That someone inscribed the first three words of the second book of Lucretius's philosophical poem *On the Nature of Things*, 'Pleasant it is, when on the wide sea ...' may not be sufficient evidence to prove that ocean views from these suites actually induced happy feelings, as a modern author willingly assumes. See Mary Beard, *Pompeii: The Life of a Roman Town* (London: Profile Books, 2008), 113–15.

18 *Zhuangzi* 庄子 'Zapian yufu' 杂篇 • 渔父 9. 4: '人有畏影恶迹而去之走者, 举足愈数而迹愈多, 走愈疾而影不离身, 自以为尚迟, 疾走不休, 绝力 而死. 不知处阴以休影, 处静以息迹, 愚亦甚矣 !.' My own paraphrasing in English. Since this story is from the 'outer chapters', it is no surprise that Confucius is satirized here as this strawman Confucian, who does not understand the *dao* of life and world. Also refer to note 7.

19 *The Analects* 'Xianwen' 宪问 14. 38: '是知其不可而为之者与 ?.'

20 *The Analects* 'Weizi' 微子 18. 7: '君子之仕也, 行其义也. 道之不行, 已知 之矣.'

21 My own translation of *The Analects* 'Yongye' 雍也 6. 29: 子曰: '中庸之为 德也, 其至矣乎 ! 民鲜久矣.' Much of what Confucius said about moderation is recorded in *The Analects*. One of the four Chinese classics, *Zhongyong* 中庸 (widely translated as *The Doctrine of the Mean*, meaning the middle way, the golden mean, or staying in the middle without losing balance and change), allegedly authored by the grandson of Confucius, Zisi 子思, is an essay devoted to the explanation of this concept, predominantly by the sages, including Confucius himself.

22 *The Analects* 'Zilu' 子路 13.21: 子曰: '不得中行而与之必也狂狷乎 ! 狂者 进取, 狷者有所不为也.'

# Chapter 4

1 For a study of the symbolism of *dougong*, See Jiren Feng, *Chinese Architecture and Metaphor: Song Culture in the Yingzao Fashi Building Manual* (Honolulu: University of Hawai'i Press, 2012).

2 *Xintangshu* 新唐书 'Libai zhuan' 李白传: '子, 谪仙人也.' See Ouyang Xiu 欧阳修 [Song] 宋 et al., *Xintangshu* 新唐书 (Beijing: Zhonghua shuju 中华 书局, 1975), 5763.

3 Lin Yutang, *My Country and My People*, (London and Toronto: William Heinemann Ltd, 1936), 111.

4　See *Zhongguo gudai jianzhushi* 中国古代建筑史, Vol. 2, ed. Fu Xinian 傅熹年 (Beijing: Zhongguo jianzhu gongye chubanshe 中国建筑工业出版社, 2009), 470–71.

5　Bai Juyi 白居易 [Tang]唐, *Baishi changqinji* 白氏长庆集, Vol. 60, 'Chishangpian – bingxu' 池上篇・并序. *Sibu congkanben* 四部丛刊本.

6　See Bai Juyi 白居易 [Tang]唐, 'Cishangpian ・ xu' 池上篇・序.

7　Wolfram Eberhard, *A Dictionary of Chinese Symbols: Hidden Symbols in Chinese Life and Thought* (London and New York: Routledge, 1983), 29.

8　My own translation of *zhongyin* 中隐 by Bai Juyi 白居易, [Tang] 唐. A different translation can be found in Xiaoshan Yang, *Metamorphosis of the Private Sphere, Gardens and Objects in Tang-Song Poetry* (Harvard University Asia Centre, 2003), 38–9.

9　*Zhuangzi* 庄子 'Waipian ・ keyi' 外篇・刻意15. 2: '其生若浮，其死若休.'

10　Chunyeyan congdi taohuayuan xu 春夜宴从弟桃花园序: '而浮生若梦，为欢几何.' See Li Bai 李白 [Tang], *Litaibai quanji* 李太白全集 (Beijing: Zhonghua Book Company 中华书局, 1977), 1292.

11　Xie Lingyun 谢灵运 [Jin]晋: *Shanju fu* 山居赋.

12　See Wang Kangju 王康琚 [Jin]晋: Fanzhao yinshi 反招隐诗: '小隐隐陵薮，大隐隐朝市. 伯夷窜首阳，老聃伏柱史.' The expressions of both court and city hermits also appeared at about the same time between the fourth and the fifth century when the modus operandi of historian Deng Jie 邓粲 was described in the Book of Jin. See Jinshu 晋书 'Dengjie zhuan' 邓粲传: '夫隐之为道，朝亦可隐，市亦可隐. 隐初在我，不在於物.'

13　Dongfang Suo 东方朔 [Han]汉: *Judi ge* 据地歌: '陆沉于俗，避世金马门. 宫殿中可以避世全身，何必深山之中，蒿庐之下？.' See Sima Qian 司马迁 [Han]汉, *Shiji* 史记 'Xiaowen benji' 孝文本纪 10, (Beijing: Zhonghua shuju 中华书局, 1975), 3205.

14　*Yanzi* 晏子 *Chunqiu jishi* 春秋集释: '凌本上方识语云：武帝时有杀上林鹿者，下有司杀之，东方朔在旁曰：是固当死者三：使陛下以鹿杀人，一当死；天下闻陛下重鹿杀人，二当死；匈奴有急，以鹿触之，三当死. 帝默然赦之. 古人讽谏，往往类此.'

15　It should be noted here that the Chinese furniture makers used small segments and tenon joints to make horseshoe chairs and curved armrests. That they never developed the nineteenth-century Thonet technique of using high-temperature steam for wood bending says something about the Chinese attitude towards Nature and things left in the *natural* state.

16　Much scholarly work of edition verification and interpretation of *Yingzao fashi* has been undertaken. Major works include: Liang Sicheng 梁思成, *Yingzao fashi zhushi shang* 营造式注释（上）(Beijing: Zhongguo jianzhu gongye chubanshe 中国建筑工业出版社, 1983); Liang Sicheng 梁思成, *Yingzao fashi zhushi* 营造式注释 in *Liang Sicheng quanji* 梁思成全集

Vol. 7 (Beijing: Zhongguo jianzhu gongye chubanshe 中国建筑工业出版社, 2001) (original edition 1983); Pan Guxi 潘谷西 and He Jianzhong 何建中, *Yingzao fashi jiedu* 营造法式解读 (Nanjing: Dongnan daxue chubanshe 东南大学出版社, 2005); Chen Mingda 陈明达, *Yingzao fashi da muzuo yanjiu* 营造法式大木作研究（Beijing: Wenwu chubanshe 文物出版社, 1981）; Chen Mingda 陈明达, *Yingzao fashi cijie* 营造法式辞解, (Tianjin: Tianjin daxue chubanshe 天津大学出版社, 2010); Guo Daihuan 郭黛姮, *Yingzao fashi xinzhu* 营造法式新注 (Beijing: Zhongguo jianzhu gongye chubanshe 中国建筑工业出版社, 1983); W. Perceval Yetts, 'A Chinese Treatise on Architecture,' *Bulletin of the School of Oriental Studies, London Institution 4*, No. 3 (1927): 473–92, Guo Qinghua, 'Yingzao Fashi: Twelfth-Century Chinese Building Manual,' *Architectural History 41* (1998): 1–13; Else Glahn, 'On the Transmission of the "Ying-Tsao Fa-shih",' *T'oung Pao 61*, No. 4 (1975): 232–65; Else Glahn, 'Chinese Building Standards in the 12th Century,' *Scientific American 244*, No. 5 (1981): 162–73; Li Shiqiao, 'Reconstituting Chinese Building Tradition: The Yingzao Fashi in the Early Twentieth Century,' *Journal of the Society of Architectural Historians 62*, No. 4 (2003): 470–89.

17  Wei Zheng 魏征 [Tang]唐, *Suishu* 隋书 (Beijing: Zhonghua shuju 中华书局, 1982), 1386.

18  Wolfram Eberhard, *A History of China*, 2nd edn. (London: Routledge & Kegan Paul, 1960), 210.

19  Lin Yutang, *The Importance of Living* (Melbourne: Heinemann, 1946), 3–4.

# Chapter 5

1  A few Yuan house archaeological sites found in Beijing, however, show a rather distinctive feature of having a building right on the longitudinal axis in the courtyard. See Figure 2.3. It is unclear whether or not this feature weakened the celestial character of the Chinese courtyard in the Yuan. The Mongols who came with shamanistic beliefs were quick to be converted to Daoists and Buddhists, but they found no particular affinities with Confucianism.

2  Under the influence of the venerated architectural historian Liu Dunzhen and his pioneering work on Chinese housing history, a group of Chinese architects and historians undertook extensive survey and dated a number of surviving Ming houses in the Huizhou region of Anhui province in the late 1950s. The work stopped during the Cultural Revolution, but resumed from the 1980s by the younger generations of academics and students from the Nanjing Institute of Technology (now reverted to its old name of Southeast

University). Although many of the surveyed houses and villages are largely Qing, the Qing house in this region would have only slight stylistic differences from its predecessor in the Ming period.

3   Historical studies and literature of *huishang* have flourished since the 1980s. Major works in Chinese include the exhaustive research in *Huishang yanjiu* 徽商研究, ed. Zhang Haipeng 张海鹏 and Wang Tingyuan 王廷元 (Anhui renmin chubanshe 安徽人民出版社, 1995), and *Ming qin huishang ziliao xuanbian* 明清徽商资料选编, ed. Zhang Haipeng 张海鹏 et al. (Huangshan chubanshe 黄山出版社, 1985). Other notable works include: Bian Li 卞利, *Ming qin huishang shehui yanjiu* 明清徽州社会研究 (Hefei: Anhui daxue chubanshe 安徽大学出版社, 2004); Tang Lixing 唐力行, *Shangren yu wenhua de shuangchong bianzou: Huishang yu zongzu shehui lishi kaocha* 商人与文化的双重变奏--徽商与宗族社会的历史考察 (Wuhan: Huazhong ligong daxue chubanshe 华中理工大学出版社, 1997) and *Ming qing yilai Huizhou quyu shehui jingji yanjiu* 明清以来徽州区域社会经济研究 (Hefei: Anhui daxue chubanshe 安徽大学出版社, 1999).

4   This is a story from a popular late Ming novel *Chuke paian jingqi* 初刻拍案惊奇 by Lin Mengchu 凌濛初. See Vol. 2.

5   Water Henry Medhurst, *A Glance at the Interior of China Obtained During a Journey Through the Silk and Green Tea Districts* (Elibron Classics, 2000). As quoted in Nancy Berliner, *Yin Yu Tang: The Architecture and Daily Life of a Chinese House* (Tuttle Publishing, 2012), 24.

6   See Chapter 1 'Guifang ji le' 闺房记乐 in *Fusheng liu ji* 浮生六记.

7   In a play called *Lian Xiang Ban* 怜香伴, early Qing dramatist Li Yü described the inseparable bond of two young women, so much so that one convinced the other to become the concubine of the former's husband so that they could stay together. See more on Li Yü in Chapter 6 and the gratitude expressed in his poems to his own 'virtuous' wife for her harmonious relationship with his first concubine.

8   A valuable work describing the social and cultural life of Yangzhou in the late eighteenth century is *Yangzhou huafang lu* 扬州画舫录 by Li Dou 李斗 (1749-1817). Though not a scholar-official, Li Dou was versatile and erudite. He used the essay genre (笔记) and took 30 years to complete the work. The anthology of 18 volumes was first printed in 1795. In English, Antonia Finnane's *Speaking of Yangzhou: A Chinese City, 1550-1850* (Harvard University Asia Center, 2004) is an extensive biography of Yangzhou.

9   See 'Wang changjun lun zui xu' 汪长君论最序 in *Tai han ji* 太涵集 Vol. 2: '新安多大贾, 其居盐筴者最豪, 入则击钟, 出则连骑, 暇则召客高会, 侍越女, 拥吴姬, 四座尽欢, 夜以继日, 世所谓芬华盛丽非不足也.'

10  See Xu Chengyao 许承尧, 'Shen Guiyu pin she shiren' 沈归愚评歙诗人 in *Sheshi xiantan* 歙事闲谭 Vol. 20 (Huangshan shushe 黄山书社, 2001).

11  '盐商之财力伟哉！' See Xu Ke 徐珂 [Qing]清, *Qingbai leichao* 清稗
    类钞, Vol. 1 (Beijing: Zhonghua shuju 中华书局, 2010), 207.

12  The English translation by Simon Leys, in *Other People's Thoughts* (Melbourne:
    Black Inc., 2007), 4.

13  Wolfram Eberhard, *A Dictionary of Chinese Symbols: Hidden Symbols
    in Chinese Life and Thought* (London and New York: Routledge, 1983),
    29.

14  '家中都聘有冬烘先生，明言坐馆，暗里捉刀，翻翻诗韵，调调平，
    如唱山歌一般，凑集四句二十八字，使人扬言于众，某能做诗矣，某能
    作文矣.' See 'Yu qilin shangren' 与起林上人 in *Zheng Banqiao wenji* 郑板桥
    文集 (Chengdu: Bashu shushe 巴蜀书社, 2003), 61.

15  Engraved on a stone tablet, Zheng Banqiao's full price list is: '大幅六两，中幅
    四两，小幅二两，书条对联壹两，扇子斗方五钱. 凡送礼物食物，总不如
    白银为妙. 公之所送，未必弟之所好也. 送现银则中心喜乐，书画皆佳.
    礼物既属纠缠，赊欠尤为赖账. 年老神倦，亦不能陪诸君子作无益语言
    也. 画竹多于买竹钱，纸高六尺价三千. 任渠话旧论交接，只当秋风过
    耳边.'

# Chapter 6

1  Matteo Ricci, *China in the Sixteenth Century: The Journals of Matteo Ricci*
   (1580–1610), ed. and trans. Louis Gallagher (New York: Random House,
   1953), 30, as quoted by Jonathan D. Spence, *The Chan's Great Continent: China
   in Western Minds*, 33.

2  Wen Zhenheng 文震亨, *Changwuzhi jiao zhu* 长物志校注, annotated by
   Chen Zhi 陈植 (Hangzhou: Jiangsu kexue jishu chubanshe 江苏科学技术出
   版社). Vol. 1 'Shilu 室庐', Vol. 2 'Huamu 花木', Vol. 3 'Shuishi 水石', Vol. 4
   'Qinyu 禽鱼', Vol. 5 'Shuhua 书画', Vol. 6 'Jita 几榻', Vol. 7 'Qiju 器具', Vol. 8
   'Yishi 衣饰', Vol. 9 'Zhouche 舟车', Vol. 10 'Weizhi 位置', Vol. 11 'Shuguo 蔬果',
   Vol. 12 'Xiangming 香茗'. For a detailed study of this book, see Craig Clunas,
   *Superfluous Things, Material Culture and Social Status in Early Modern China*
   (University of Hawai'i Press, 2004).

3  The book was out of print for centuries, but it was in circulation in Japan. The
   Chinese official and architectural connoisseur Zhu Qiling 朱启钤 referenced
   the Japanese version and reissued the annotated Chinese version in 1932. See
   also the subsequent versions in both Chinese and English: Chen Zhi 陈植,
   *Yuanye zhushi* 园冶注释, first edition (Beijing: Zhongguo jianzhu gongye
   chubanshe 中国建筑工业出版社, 1979); revised edition (Beijing: Zhongguo
   jianzhu gongye chubanshe 中国建筑工业出版社, 1988); Ji Cheng 计成,

*Craft of Gardens* 园冶, trans. Alison Hardie (New Haven and London: Yale University Press, 1988).

4   The years of Li Yü's birth and death are debatable. See Yuan Zhenyu 袁震宇, 'Li Yü shengzu nien kaozheng buju' 李渔生卒年考证补苴, *Fudan Xuebao* 复旦学报 (Social Science Edition), Vol. 1 (1985), 107–9.

5   Although Ji Cheng's *Yuanye* may have remained relatively unknown, Li Yü 李渔, surprisingly, mentioned this book in his *Xianqing ouji* 闲情偶寄, chapter 'Nüqiang 女墙', see Li Yü 李渔, *Xianqing Ouji*, translated and annotated into modern Chinese by Chen Rujiang 陈如江 and Wang Zheng 汪政, (Beijing: Renming wenxue chubanshe 人民文学出版社, 2013), 173. Also see note 14 for the explanation of my own translation of the book's title, and the discussions that follow.

6   The word garden house 園宅 first appeared in the Song dynasty. *Yangyunchang zuang* 杨运长传：运长质木廉正, 治身甚清, 不事园宅, 不受饷遗. See Shen Yue 沈约 [Liang]梁, *Songshu* 宋书 Vol. 94 (Beijing: Zhonghua shuju 中华书局, 1975), 2,318.

7   Wang Shizhen 王世贞[Ming]明, *Youjinling zhuyuanji* 游金陵诸园记：'山居之迹于寂也, 市居之迹于喧也, 惟园居在季孟间耳.'

8   See Frederick W. Mote, 'A Millennium of Chinese Urban History: Form, Time and Space Concepts in Soochow,' *Rice University Studies* 59, No. 4 (1976): 35–65.

9   See Craig Clunas, *Fruitful Sites: Garden Culture in Ming Dynasty China* (Duke University Press, 1996), 67. Clunas has identified 1520 as the year when 'aesthetic horticulture' greatly increased to replace gardens of productivity.

10   County and district level exams were called *yuanshi* (院试), those who passed were called *xiucai* (秀才); provincial level exams were called *xiangshi* (乡试), those who passed were call *juren* (举人); national level exams were called *huishi* (会试), those who passed were called *gongshi* (贡士); imperial court exams were called *dianshi* (殿试), and those who passed were called *jinshi* (进士).

11   In poems titled 'On Taking a Concubine (*naji* 纳姬)' and 'Poems on a Virtuous Wife (*xiannei ling* 贤内令)', Li Yü described this domestic scene of his wife and concubine living happily together. More than that, the two women even collaborated in schemes to increase the chances of bearing a son for Li Yü. See 'Liwen yijia yan shiciji 笠翁一家言诗词集' in *Li Yü quan ji* 李渔全集, Vol. 2. See also Patrick Hanan, *The Invention of Li Yu* (Cambridge: Harvard University Press, 1988), 15. Refer also to note 7 in Chapter 5 regarding the play *Lian Xiang Ban* written by Li Yü.

12   'Nigou yishan bieye wei sui' 拟构伊山别业未遂：拟向先人墟暮边构间茅屋 住苍烟. 门开绿水桥通野, 灶近清流竹引泉. 糊口尚愁无宿粒, 买山那得 有余钱. 此身不作王摩诘, 身后还须葬辋川.

13 See Li Yü 李渔 *Mai shan quan* 卖山券: '买是山木石肢体之铜锱, 则既受之于子矣; 若夫贸精灵易姓名之价值, 尚有俟焉.' I have adopted the translation by Hanan, *The Invention of Li Yü*, 192.

14 *Leisure Marginalia* is my own translation. *Xianqing ouji* 闲情偶寄 has been translated as *A Temporary Lodge for My Leisure Thoughts*; see Nathan Mao and Liu Ts'un-yan, *Li Yü* (Boston: Twayne Publishers, 1977), and also as *Casual Expressions of Idle Feeling*, see Hanan, *The Invention of Li Yü*. They both are accurate and more literal translations. The difference, however, lies in whether or not the original house metaphor 寄 is still rendered in English as such. My preference is to find the equivalent of this metaphor in Western languages; marginalia seems rather fitting for this purpose.

15 See Hanan, *The Invention of Li Yü*, 196.

16 See Dong Han 董含 *San gang shi lü* 三冈识略. I have adopted the translation from Nathan, *Li Yü*, 136. One minor modification to the translation is the change from 'the art of love' to 'the art of lovemaking' to reflect the accurate meaning of 房中术 in the original text, which is quoted in full as follows: '李生渔者性龌龊, 善逢迎. 常挟山妓三四人, 遇贵游子弟便令隔帘度曲, 或使之捧觞行酒, 并纵谈房中术, 诱赚重价. 其行甚秽, 真士林所不齿者. 余曾一遇, 后遂避之.'

17 Also translated in English as *Prayer Mat of Flesh* and *The Before Midnight Scholar*.

18 See note 13.

19 See note 10 in Chapter 2.

20 See Yu Huan 余怀 'Xianqing ouji·xu' 闲情偶寄·序: '不为经国之大业, 而为破道之小言.'

21 Lin Yutang did not provide the reference of this quote. It was his translation of a paragraph from *Xiaochuang youji* 小窗幽记 by the Ming scholar Chen Jiru 陈继儒: '门内有径, 径欲曲; 径转有屏, 屏欲小; 屏进有阶, 阶欲平; 阶畔有花, 花欲鲜; 花外有墙, 墙欲低; 墙内有松, 松欲古; 松底有石, 石欲怪; 石面有亭, 亭欲朴; 亭后有竹, 竹欲疏; 竹尽有室, 室欲幽; 室旁有路, 路欲分; 路合有桥, 桥欲危; 桥边有树, 树欲高; 树阴有草, 草欲青; 草上有渠, 渠欲细; 渠引有泉, 泉欲瀑; 泉去有山, 山欲深; 山下有屋, 屋欲方; 屋角有圃, 圃欲宽; 圃中有鹤, 鹤欲舞; 鹤报有客, 客不俗; 客至有酒, 酒欲不却; 酒行有醉, 醉欲不归.' Reputedly, the original book was titled *Zuigu tang jiansao* 醉古堂剑扫 by the Ming scholar Lu Shaoheng 陆邵珩. Lin must have thought that these lines suited the temperament of Li Yü, hence used it to preface his introduction of Li Yü's art of living. See Yutang Lin, *The Importance of Living* (Melbourne: William Heineman Ltd, 1946, original edition 1937), 288–9.

22 See Clunas, *Superfluous Things*, 95.

23 Tong Jun 童寯, *Jiangnan yuanlin zhi* 江南园林志 (Beijing: Zhongguo jianzhu gongye chubanshe 中国建筑工业出版社, 1984 second edition, original edition 1963), 7.

24 In one of his essays of vast learning on the topic of Chinese poetry and painting, titled 'Zhongguo shi yu zhongguo hua 中国诗与中国画', Qian Zhongshu pointed out that the highest quality of Chinese painting, known as *xu* 虚 (emptiness and intangibility), was never quite regarded by the discerning connoisseurs with the same respect accorded to Chinese poetry for its essence lies in the opposite – *shi* 实 (solidity and objective reality). See Qian Zhongshu 钱锺书, *Qizhui ji* 七缀集, (Beijing: SDX Joint Publishing Company 生活读书新知三联书店, 2002), 1–32.

25 This is the list most ably summarized by Simon Leys. See 'Poetry and Painting: Aspects of Chinese Classical Aesthetics' in *The Hall of Uselessness*, 302. In this remarkable essay, Leys gave some of the taken-for-granted attributes of Chinese poetry and painting a refreshing and illuminating explanation.

26 Ibid. 303.

27 See Mao, *Li Yü*, 15.

28 See chapters 17 and 18, *Honglou meng* 红楼梦.

29 See chapter 16, *Honglou meng* 红楼梦. It is debatable whether or not the three-and-half *li* is the entire perimeter or only two sides of the garden, for the description in the original text is open to interpretation. A *li* however equals to 500 metres.

30 See chapter 38, *Honglou meng* 红楼梦.

31 Li Yü (Liweng) 李渔(笠翁), *Xianqing ouji* 闲情偶寄 – 'Yinzhuan bu 饮馔部 – roushi 肉食 – xie 蟹'.

32 See Chuin Tung (Tong Jun) 童寯, 'Chinese Gardens: especially in Kiangsu and Chekiang', 220–44.

33 See chapter 23, *Honglou meng* 红楼梦.

34 Li Yü (Liweng) 李渔(笠翁), *Xianqing ouji* 闲情偶寄 – 'Zhongzhi bu 种植部 – huamu 花木 – haitang 海棠'.

35 Li Yü (Liweng) 李渔(笠翁), *Xianqing ouji* 闲情偶寄 – 'Zhongzhi bu 种植部 – zhumu 竹木 – zhu 竹'.

36 See chapters 23, *Honglou men g* 红楼梦.

37 Li Yü (Liweng) 李渔(笠翁), *Xianqing ouji* 闲情偶寄 – 'Jushi bu 居室部 – chuanglan 窗栏 – qujing zaijie 取景在借'.

38 Li Yü (Liweng) 李渔(笠翁), *Xianqing ouji* 闲情偶寄 – 'Qiwan bu 器玩部 – zhidu 制度 – chuangzhang 床帐'. I have adopted the translation of Lin Yutang for the quoted paragraph. About 'eating among the flowers', Lin Yutang explained in a footnote that 'a Chinese rich man having a good time with his concubine at night often has food and wine served in bed by attending maidservants.' See Lin, *The Importance of Living*, 291–2.

**39** Charles Benn, *China's Golden Age: Everyday Life in the Tang Dynasty* (Oxford University Press, 2002), 79 and 91.

**40** See chapter 76, *Honglou meng* 红楼梦.

**41** See chapter 3, *Honglou meng* 红楼梦.

**42** Also translated as 'festooned gate' by some scholars. See Ronald Knapp, *Chinese Houses: The Architecture Heritage of a Nation* (Vermont: Tuttle Publishing, 2012), 105.

**43** Ibid 37. I have adopted the translation by David Hawkes. See David Hawkes, *The Story of the Stone* Vol. I (Great Britain: Penguin Group, 1973), 97.

# Chapter 7

**1** The Chinese linguist Wang Li 王力 in *Hanyu shigao* 汉语史稿 (Beijing: Zhonghua shuju 中华书局, 1980) speculated that *hutong* could be the transliteration of Mongolian words since it first appeared in the Yuan dynasty. Other scholars point out the appearance of *hutong* in Chinese literature, and the possible variations of vernacular pronunciation of laneway in Chinese as *hutong*.

**2** Yi-Fu Tuan, *Space and Place* (University of Minnesota Press, 1977), 107.

**3** Email conversation with the author on 9 December 2009.

**4** See for example Liu Lianli 刘莲丽, *Wo xinzhong de siheyuan* 我心中的四合院 (Beijing: Zhongguo renmin daxue chubanshe 中国人民大学出版社, 2013), 3–12.

**5** 'I remember going to China. I remember, vaguely, walking through dusty Chinese squares, yellow walls, big doors. I don't think at the time that one assessed these as walls or doors or colours... but it all gave me a feeling of pleasure, because one enjoyed the whole journey.' Bawa in conversation with Channa Daswatt, 1977 in David Robson and Geoffrey Bawa, *Geoffrey Bawa: The Complete Works* (Thames & Hudson, 2002), 18.

**6** Contrary to the assumed knowledge that the Qing garden, both imperial and private, drew inspiration from those of the Yangtze region, some scholars believe that the emergence of urban gardens in the Yangtze region from the end of fifteenth century was in fact influenced, apart from literature, also by the imperial gardens in Beijing at the time. See Craig Clunas, *Superfluous Things, Material Culture and Social Status in Early Modern China* (University of Hawai'i Press, 2004), 60. In the eighteenth century when the imperial Summer Palace was built in Beijing, the influence of urban gardens from the Yangtze region was evident and on the record.

**7** Jia Jun 贾珺, *Beijing siheyuan* 北京四合院 (Beijing: Tsinghua University Press 清华大学出版社, 2009), 36.

**8**    Aesthetics as a visual concept, or 'the study of beauty' in a literal Chinese translation, did not exist in the Chinese mind. There was no form of Chinese art that could be lazily defined as 'visual art'. See the compelling argument in Simon Leys' essays 'Poetry and Painting: Aspects of Chinese Classical Aesthetics' and 'Ethics and Aesthetics: The Chinese Lesson' in *The Hall of Uselessness*, 114 and 354.

**9**    There is an abridged English translation by Helena Kau, titled rather *The Yellow Storm* (New York: Harcourt, Brace, 1952).

**10**   See the treatment of Mei Lanfang's *siheyuan* in Ronald Knapp's *Chinese Houses: The Architectural Heritage of a Nation* (Vermont: Tuttle Publishing, 2005), 100–7.

**11**   Edmund Leach, *Rethinking Anthropology* (London: Athlone Press, 1961), 2.

**12**   Ibid. 5.

**13**   Lin Yutang, 'A Hymn to Shanghai', in *With Love and Irony* (London and Toronto: William Heinemann Ltd, 1942), 53.

**14**   Ibid. 'Captive Peking', 45–52.

# Chapter 8

**1**    For a detailed account of the entangled acculturation between the Han and the minority groups in southern China, and the architecture and freestanding houses of the Tai linguistic groups in southern China, and the Dong in particular, see Xing Ruan, *Allegorical Architecture* (Honolulu: University of Hawai'i Press, 2006).

**2**    For a discussion of the renewal of ethnicity as desired by the majority population, and the deceiving techniques for survival, though somehow hidden in the psychological substructure, from the minority group, see Ruan, *Allegorical Architecture*, 167–78.

**3**    This English name of *tulou* has been coined by Ronald Knapp in *Chinese Houses: The Architectural Heritage of a Nation* (Vermont: Tuttle Publishing, 2012), 184–91.

**4**    Ruan, *Allegorical Architecture*, 2.

**5**    Most historians believe that *Jingkang bishi qianzheng* 靖康稗史笺证, published in 1164 CE, is a reasonably reliable record of the 'Humiliation of Jingkang', for it includes the observations of the Chinese who witnessed the events as well as those from the Jin side.

**6**    See Zhou Zhenhe 周振鹤, 'Kejia yuanliu yishuo', 客家源流异说, *Xueshu yuekan* 学术月刊 3, (1996): 16–24, 89.

**7**    Pan An 潘安, *Kejia minxi yu kejiajuju jianzhu* 客家民系与客家聚居建筑 (Beijing: Zhongguo jianzhu gongye chubanshe 中国建筑工业出版社, 1998), 115.

**8** Based on the fieldwork observation of the local lore by Knapp, *Chinese Houses*, 189.

**9** Ronald Knapp, *China's Old Dwellings*, (Honolulu: University of Hawai'i Press, 2000), 261.

**10** Ibid. 269.

**11** Jing Zheng, *Interpreting Fujian Tulou: Examining Chinese Vernacular Architecture from the Perspective of Local Craftsmen and Community* (PhD diss., The Chinese University of Hong Kong, 2009), 4.

**12** Jing Zheng, 'Communism in Tulou: A Study on Socio-Politics and Traditional Dwellings', in *Traditional Dwellings and Settlements Working Paper Series* (Berkeley: International Association for the Study of Traditional Environments, 2008).

**13** My paraphrasing. See Guo Songnian 郭松年 [Yuan] 元, *Dali xing ji* 大理行记.

**14** For a detailed study of Bai *zhaobi*, see Mengbi Li, 'The "Translation" of Zhaobi in China across Time and Space', in *Proceedings of the Society of Architectural Historians, Australia and New Zealand*, trans. and ed. Christoph Schnoor (Auckland: SAHANZ and United Press, and Gold Coast, Queensland: SAHANZ, 2014), 145–54.

**15** Though officially regarded by the Chinese government as part of the Naxi, some scholars believe the Mosuo have distinctive cultural traits and should be considered as a separate ethnic group. Linguistically, the Mosuo and the Naxi are closely related and both belong to Sino-Tibetan language group.

**16** '因思变迁之道, 必赖礼乐, 礼乐之兴, 在于文庙.' Requoted from He Jianmei 和建梅, *Naxi zu minjian xunqing wenhua yanjiu* 纳西族民间殉情文化探究 (Master diss., Zhongguo shiyou daxue 中国石油大学, 2015), 20.

# Chapter 9

**1** Wu Jiang 伍江, *Shanghai bainian jianzushi* 上海百年建筑史 *(1840–1949)* (Shanghai: Tongji daxue chubanshe 同济大学出版社, 1997), 9.

**2** Zhang Ailing 张爱玲, 'Tongyan wuji' 童言无忌 in *Liuyan* 流言 (Taipei: Huangguan, 1984), 7. Quoted from Leo Ou-fan Lee, *Shanghai Modern: The Flowering of a New Urban Culture in China 1930–1945* (Harvard University Press, 1999), 270.

**3** Zhang Ailing 张爱玲, 'Daodi shi Shanghai ren' 到底是上海人, in *Liuyan* 流言, 57. Quoted from Lee, *Shanghai Modern*, 269.

**4** Linda Cooke Johnson, *Shanghai: from market town to treaty port, 1074–1858*, (Stanford University Press, 1995), 183. Quoted from Alan Balfour and Zheng Shiling, *Shanghai* (Wiley-Academy, 2002), 51.

**5** Quoted from Wu, *Shanghai bainian jianzushi* 上海百年建筑史 *(1840–1949)*, 23.

**6** Ibid. 13 and endnote 37.

**7** The name was later changed to 洋 (meaning ocean and foreign) 泾浜, a termed coined also to mean broken English.

**8** Wu, *Shanghai bainian jianzushi* 上海百年建筑史 *(1840–1949)*, 13 and 17. Balfour and Zheng, *World City: Shanghai*, 53.

**9** Samuel Y. Liang, 'Where the Courtyard Meets the Street: Spatial Culture of the Li Neighborhoods, Shanghai, 1870–1900', *JSAH 67*, No. 4, (2008), 483.

**10** Ibid. 485.

**11** See Qian Zonghao 钱宗灏 and Liu Chungang 刘存钢， 'The Land Price and Urbanization Features of the Early Period of Shanghai North Bund' 上海北外滩早期地价及城市化特征, *Tongji University Journal* 同济大学学报 (Social Science Section) *28*, No. 6 (2017): 76–82.

**12** Li Yanbo 李彦伯, *Shanghai Lilong jiequ de jiazhi* 上海里弄街区的价值 (Shanghai: Tongji daxue chubanshe 同济大学出版社, 2014), 34.

**13** See Qian and Liu 'The Land Price and Urbanization Features of the Early Period of Shanghai North Bund', 81.

**14** Richard Henry Dana, Jr. *Two Years Before the Mast and other Voyages* (The Library of America, 2005), 709.

**15** Ibid. 649, 662, 666–7, 672–3 and 691.

**16** Ibid. 711.

**17** Ibid. 709.

**18** Xingren Li was demolished in 1980 to give way to a cluster of six-storey free-standing apartment buildings.

**19** The author's great-grandfather, who migrated to Shanghai from the nearby hinterland, established in this period a successful interior fitout business in the French Concession and specialized in installing imported bathroom sanitary wares. The author's grandfather, no doubt influenced by the family trade, attended the French-speaking Université l'Aurore (known as Zhendan University in Chinese) to read civil engineering.

**20** Liang, 'Where the Courtyard Meets the Street', 485–6.

**21** This is quite the contrary to what Samuel Liang has asserted. See ibid. 488. Also see G. William Skinner, 'Introduction: Urban Development in Imperial China', in *The City in Late Imperial China*, ed. G. William Skinner (Stanford, 1977), 23–6; and Shiba Yoshinobu, *Commerce and Society in Sung China, No. 2*, trans. Mark Elvin (Ann Arbor: Centre for Chinese Studies, The University of Michigan, 1970).

**22** Wang, Anyi, *The Song of Everlasting Sorrow: A Novel of Shanghai* (Columbia University Press, 2008), 5.

**23** Ibid. 9.

**24** Ibid. 8.

**25** Zhang Ailin 张爱玲, 'Gongyu shenghuo jiqu' 公寓生活记趣 in *Liuyan* 流言.

**26** See Lee, *Shanghai Modern*.

**27** Li, 39.

**28** Hanchao Lu, *Beyond the Neon Light: Everyday Shanghai in the Early Twentieth Century* (Berkeley: University of California Press, 1999), 169–70.

# Chapter 10

**1** See the exhaustive research of Zhu Tao on the history of the Liang-Chen proposal. Zhu Tao 朱涛, 'Liang-Chen Proposal: A Conclusion and Termination of the Two Histories of China's Capital Planning' '梁陈方案': 两部国都史的总结与终结', *Time+Architecture*, 时代建筑 No. 5 (2013): 130–41.

**2** Wang Jun 王军, *Cheng ji* 城记, (Beijing: SDX Joint Publishing Company 生活读书新知三联书店, 2003), 51–7.

**3** Ibid. 15.

**4** Ibid. 16.

**5** Some new low-density reconstruction of courtyards took place after Juer Hutong, such as the Nanchizi development 2003, which is by nature a conservation project.

**6** See the World Habitat Awards citation: http://www.worldhabitatawards.org/winners-and-finalists/project-details.cfm?lang=00&theProjectID=119

**7** Donia Zhang, 'Juer Hutong New Courtyard Housing in Beijing: a Review from the Residents' Perspective,' *International Journal of Architectural Research 10*, No. 2 (July 2016): 166–91.

**8** Jan Morris, *Among the Cities* (New York: Oxford University Press, 1985), 357.

**9** Jan Morris, 'Australian Distractions', in *Pleasures of A Tangled Life* (London: Barrie & Jenkins, 1989), 146–53.

**10** Jan Morris, *Sydney*, (London: Viking, 1992), 5.

**11** Farnsworth's words documented in Stanley Abercrombie 'Much Ado About Almost Nothing: Rescuing Mies' Farnsworth House, a Clear and Simple Statement of what Architecture can be', *Preservation 52*, No. 5 (September–October 2000): 66.

**12** Mies van der Rohe, interview for the BBC programme (1959), as reported by Peter Carter, *Mies van der Rohe at Work* (London: Phaidon Press, 1999), 181.

The irony, however, is that Mies himself lived in a heavy masonry Spanish colonial-style apartment in Chicago. When asked why he never lived in his famous glass and steel Lake Shore Drive Apartments, the architect replied: 'There is too much glass, not enough wall to hang my Paul Klee's drawings.' See Jean Louis Cohen, *Mies van der Rohe* (Akal Ediciones, 2000), 112.

13  Saint Paul, *2 Corinthians* 4.18 and 5.1.
14  Werner Blaser, *West Meets East – Mies van der Rohe* (Birkhauser, 1996), 6.
15  Ibid. 72–89.
16  Paul Clemence, *Mies van der Rohe's Farnsworth House* (Atglen: Schiffer Publishing, 2006), 21.
17  Wendy Lesser, *You Say to Brick: The Life of Louis Kahn* (New York: Farrar, Straus and Giroux, 2017), 180.
18  See Chenyu Chiu, *Utzon's China* (PhD. diss., University of Melbourne, 2011).
19  Joseph Rykwert, 'Meaning and Building', in *The Necessity of Artifice* (New York: Rizzoli, 1982), 12.
20  Ibid.
21  See John Pardey, *Jørn Utzon Logbook Vol. III: Two Houses on Majorca* (Hellerup, 2004), 17–20.
22  See Utzon, 'Platforms and Plateaus,' *Zodiac*, No. 10 (1962): 113–40.
23  Ibid.
24  Juan Palomar, 'The House of Luis Barragan: Device for an Epiphany', in *Luis Barragán: His House,* ed. Alfonso Alfaro (Mexico City: RM, 2011), 38–42.
25  See note 5 in Chapter 7.
26  David Robson, *Geoffrey Bawa,* (London: Thames & Hudson, 2002), 53–4.

# Epilogue

1  Joseph Rykwert, 'The Four and the Five' in *Chinese Architecture and the Beaux-Arts,* ed. Jeffery Cody, Nancy Steinhardt and Tony Artkin (University of Hawai'i Press, 2011), 361–8.
2  *Mengzi* 孟子 'Gongsunchou shang' 公孙丑上 5: '无敌於天下者, 天吏也.'
3  *The Analects* 'Yongye' 雍也 6.29: '中庸之为德也, 其至矣乎! 民鲜久矣. *Zhongyong* 中庸 3: '中庸其至矣乎, 民鲜能久矣.'

# Index

The letter *f* following an entry indicates a page that includes a figure (illustration).

aesthetics xxxiv–v, 170
against the courtyard (*buting*) 15
agriculture 102, 103–4
alleyway houses (*lilong*) 189, 222
America 228, 230
'An-Shi Rebellion' 197
*Analects, The* (Confucius) 13, 15, 59, 60
ancestors, veneration of 208–10
ancestral halls 108–9, 110*f*, 123, 201, 204*f*
Ancient Greece xxxix–xl
  Icarus myth xli
Ancient Rome xxxii, xxxix–xl, 104, 280
  House of Menander, Pompeii 34*f*
  House of Pansa, Pompeii 35*f*
  Pantheon, the 31, 32*f*
  vertical architecture 70–1
architecture xxxiii–iv, xxxv, 186 *see also* housing
  Ancient Greece xxxix–xl
  Ancient Rome xxxii, xxxix–xl, 70–1
  atriums/skywells/voids 31, 34*f*, 70–1, 104–5*f*, 106–7
  Beijing 249
  building standards 91
  'Compradoric Style' 226
  court forms xxxvii*f*–viii
  decoration 178, 191–2, 236
  English 179–81
  Gothic xxxiii, 46
  immortality 45–6, 63–4
  *li* and *yi* 20
  metaphors 13
  multi-storey xxxii, xxxvii–viii, 72
    *see also* towers
  Nanchan Temple 71, 75
  pavilion forms xxxvii*f*–viii
  Renaissance xl
  towers 63–7, 68–70, 71–2, 74
  urban gridirons xxxvii*f*–viii
  Utzon, Jørn 266–9
arts, the 45, 59–60, 76, 95 *see also* literary world, the
  bamboo 125–6
  Beijing 184–5
  *Dream of the Red Chamber* (Cao Xueqin) 154
  formal structure 143–4
  Huizhou merchants 124, 126
  Leys, Simon 144
  patronage 124–5, 126
  Xin'an School (*Xin'an huapai*) 125–6

astrology 28–9 *see also* divination
astronomy xxxix
atriums 31, 34f, 70–1 *see also* space
austerity 119–20, 121–2, 125–7
autumn, celebration of 33

Bai, the 205–10
Bai Juyi 77–81, 87, 88, 132
balcony buildings 141
Balfour, George 223–4
bamboo 80, 125–6, 150, 151
Banpo houses 21–2f, 25
*banyuan lou* (half-circle house) 203,
    204f
Barragán, Luis 272, 277
Bawa, Geoffrey 168, 272–8
beams (roof) 120–1, 122f
bedchambers 241–2
beds 152–3
Beijing 188, 249, 259, 262 *see also*
    Yuan Dadu
  arts, the 184–5
  city-ring-park proposal 246–7f
  conservation/demolition 248–9,
    250–1, 260
  construction 178
  *da zayuan* 249, 251, 252, 255
  decoration 178, 191–2
  demography 170–1
  design 176–8
  distinctive character 179, 181, 184,
    185
  expansion 245–6, 248
  gardens 169–70, 184
  hierarchy 181
  Japanese occupation 245–6
  Ju'er Hutong 251–7
  lakes (seas) 176–8
  Lao She's courtyard 185
  Liang-Chen scheme 245, 246–7
  Lin Yutang 188–90

  Lu Xun's courtyard 184
  Mei Lanfang's courtyard 185
  modernity 246–8
  new quadrangle 251–7
  quadrangle housing 159–64, 166,
    168–9, 171–3, 181–5, 187–8,
    190–2, 249–51, 258–9
  Residence of Prince Fu 181–2f,
    182f
  Residence of Prince Gong
    182–4
  streets 164–8, 170–4
  taxi drivers 190
  Tiananmen Square 246, 247
  uniformity 179 *see also* patterns
  Xiao Yangjuan *hutong* 170–4
Bess of Hardwick 179–80
Bi residence, Suzhou 141, 142f
Bianjing. *See* Kaifeng
Bianliang 42, 238 *see also* Kaifeng
Blenheim Palace 181
Boniu 15–16
'book courtyards' 47–8
*Book of Changes* (Fu Xi, King Wen,
    Duke of Zhou, Confucius)
    28–9, 31–3
*Book of Poems, The* (*Book of Odes*
    [*Shijing*]) 15, 28
Britain 219, 223–6, 228, 230
Brother Xu legend 198–9
Buddhism 75, 205–6
building standards 91, 94, 266
built world, the 43–9

Cai Wenji 96–7f
calligraphy 144
Can Lis villa, Mallorca 269–70f, 271f
Cao Xueqin 145
  *Dream of the Red Chamber*
    (*Honglou meng*) 144–51,
    153–6, 161, 184

cardinal directions 36–9
Carlisle, 3rd Earl of (Charles Howard) 180
*Carnal Prayer Mat, The (Roupu tuan)* (Li Yü) 136–7
Castle Howard 180–1
Chang, Eileen (Zhang Ailing) 222–3
'Joy of Apartment Living, The' 242
*chaoshou youlang* (running veranda of folded arms) 162–3*f*
Chatsworth House 179
Chen Yun 114–15
Chen Zhanxiang 245, 246
*cheng* (city). *See* cities
Cheng Jinxuan 237
Chengqi Lou 195*f*
China 95, 283 n.1 *see also* Chinese housing *and* Chineseness
art xxxiv–v
bureaucracy 68, 76
Chinese character 192
Communist Party 222
economy 103, 257
ethnic minority groups. *See* ethnic minority groups
interest in xxix–xi
literature xxxiii, 6
People's Republic of 260
philosophy 279–81
unification 53–4
worldview 33–4, 46–7, 279–80
Chinese housing 3–5 *see also* courtyards
in literature 6
prototype 6–7*f*, 10
Western Zhou courtyard house, Fengchu 8*f*–10, 18–19, 46, 159
Chineseness 43, 283 n. 1
ethnic minority groups 193–4
Churchill, Sarah (Duchess of Marlborough) 181

cities (*cheng*) 39–40, 92–4, 95–6, 261–2 *see also* Beijing *and* Shanghai
allure of 236, 242
design 176–7*f*
garden houses 132–4
*lilong* 239
Mongols 101
planning 40–1
streets 164–8, 170–5, 239
walls 24
class. *See* social class
*Classic of Documents (Shu jing)* (Confucius). *See Venerated Documents*
*Classics of Dao and De, The (Dao De Jing)* (Laozi) 56–7, 58
clothing 94, 117
collective living 195, 203–4, 251–7
Colombo 277–8
comfort xxiv–v
commerce 92, 94, 95, 102, 104 *see also* trade
Beijing 157–8
Huizhou 105–6
Shanghai 237
Communist Party 222
compradors 226, 237
concubines (*qie*) 114–15, 117–18
Confucius 43, 59, 265 *see also* Confucianism
as activist 72–4
*Analects, The* 13, 15, 59, 60
Boniu 15–16
*Book of Changes, The/I Ching, The (Yi Jing)* 28–9, 31–3
*Book of Poems, The (Book of Odes [Shijing])* 15, 28
Confucianism 58–9
courtyard house 10–20
Daoism 57–9, 61–2

310 *Index*

employment 11
family 15
government 62
Heaven 33, 35–6
housing analogies 16
*li* and *yi* 19–20, 43
middle way, the 74, 281
regard for 10–11
reputation 291n. 7
*Venerated Documents (Shang shu)/Classic of Documents (Shu jing)* 29–30, 36–9
Zhuangzi 61
Confucianism xl–l, 11, 54–9, 77, 265
Dali 205–6
Daoism 57–9, 61–3
Huizhou merchants 123–4
Li Yü 137–8
Qing dynasty 213
Shanghai 221–2
state 205–6, 213
consumption 131–2, 167–8
corridors 164, 244, 254
country villas 84–6
courtyard lecturing (*tingxun*) 15
courtyards 265 *see also* housing
Bai 207–10
Bai Juyi 78–81, 87
Bawa, Geoffrey 168, 272–8
Beijing 181–5, 249
Beijing quadrangle housing 159–64, 166, 168–9, 171–5, 181–5, 187–8, 190–2, 249–51, 258–9
benefits xxxvif–viii
book 47–8
central ensembles 18–19
Colombo 277–8
composition xxv
construction technique xxix
*da zayuan* 249, 251, 252, 255
domesticity 82

*Dream of the Red Chamber* (Cao Xueqin) 149, 154–5
fortress ramparts 194–5f, 198–203
Hakka, the 194, 199–203
Han 65–9, 71, 74
history xxv–viii
Huizhou 104–13
*hutongs* 168, 249
interchangeability xxviii–ix
interior activities 89–90f
Ju'er Hutong, Beijing 251–7
Kahn, Louis 186
language 15
Lao She 170–5
meanings of 11
Ming 104–5f
Mosuo 212
Naxi 210–11, 214f–15
new quadrangle 251–7
'one bright and two darks' pattern 4–5f, 9, 10, 16, 21, 24–5
*parti* 5–10
as a pattern 185–7, 202
prototype 6–7f, 10
Qing 159
rejection of 250–1
*shiku men*, comparison with 234–5f
Southern Study 159
spanning 169
spatial sequence 18
towers 64–7, 68–9f, 71, 74
urban 96
Utzon, Jørn 267–9, 272
Western Zhou house, Fengchu 8f–10, 18–19, 46, 159
Yuan 101
crab 147–8
*Craft of Gardens (Yuan ye)* (Ji Cheng) 131, 132

creation story 30–1
'crescent moon beam' (*yueliang*)
    120–1, 122*f*
Cui Bao
    *Notes of Things Old and New* 13
culture 95, 158–9, 213 *see also* arts,
    the
    *Dream of the Red Chamber* (Cao
    Xueqin) 154
    Huizhou merchants 124, 126

*da zayuan* (big miscellaneous
    courtyard) 249, 251, 252, 255
Dadu 101, 102, 164, 175–8 *see also*
    Beijing
Dai, the 193
Dali 205–6
Dana, Richard Henry, Jr. 231–2
*danwei* (work unit) 260–1*f*
*dao* 58, 265
Daoism xl–I, 56–62
    Lin Yutang 77
*de* 58
decorum 156
'Deed of Sale for My Hill, A' (Li Yü)
    135
Design 186
divination 28–30
domesticity 82
    scenes of 89–90*f*
*domus* (Roman house) xxxi, xl, 35*f*,
    104 *see also* atriums
Dong, the 193–4, 196
Dong Han 136
*Dong jing meng hua lu* (Meng
    Yuanlao) 92
Dongfang Suo 87–8
*Dream of the Red Chamber* (*Honglou
    meng*) (Cao Xueqin) 144–51,
    153–6, 161, 184
drum towers 72, 73*f*

earth xl–I, 31–3
    composition of 36–9
eaves brackets 120–1
economy, the 103, 257 *see also*
    commerce
Eiffel Tower, Paris 70
*Eight Discourses of the Art of Living*
    (*Junshen bajian*) (Gao Lian)
    131
Eighteen Scenes of a Nomad Flute
    (Liu Shang) 96
elements, the five 36–9
England 164, 179–81
ethnic minority groups 193–4, 197
    Bai, the 205–10
    Dai, the 193
    Dong, the 193–4, 196
    Hakka, the 194–204, 227
    Han, the 207
    Mosuo, the 211–12
    Naxi, the 210–11, 212–15
*Explanation of Names* (Liu Xi) 12

'Failed Plan for Mount Yi Villa' (Li
    Yü) 135
family, the 19–20, 42
    Han gentry 64–5
    Huizhou 110–13
    marriage 110–16, 117–18
Fan Zeng 17, 18
Farnsworth House, Chicago 110,
    111*f*, 263–4
Feast of Hong Gate 16–18
Fengchu courtyard house 8*f*–10,
    18–19, 159
Fernando, Udayshanth 276
five elements, the 36–9
'floating life' 47, 81–2
flowers 152
Form 186
fortress ramparts 194–5*f*, 198–203

'Four and the Five, The' (Rykwert,
        Joseph) 279–80
*Four Generations Under One Roof*
        (*Sishi tongtang*) (Lao She) 170,
        185, 255–6
fragrance 152–3
France 226–7, 229
free love 211–12, 213
freedom 62, 71
'front hall and back room' (*qiantang
        houshi*) layouts 4, 5, 10, 21–2*f,*
        23*f,* 24
Fu Xi 40
Fu Xinian 9, 10
funerals 168
furniture xxiv–v, 14, 65, 90*f*
        beds 152–3
        Ming 119, 120*f,* 121*f*

galleries 162–3*f,* 180
Gao Lian
        *Eight Discourses of the Art of
        Living* (*Junshen bajian*) 131
Gaodi (emperor). *See* Liu Bang
garden houses (*yuanzai*) 124, 129,
        132–4
        Beijing 169–70
        *Dream of the Red Chamber* (Cao
        Xueqin) 144–51
        Li Yü 135–6, 138–9
gardens 44–5, 79–80, 82–4*f,* 86, 140–4
        Beijing 169–70, 184, 247*f*
        *Dream of the Red Chamber* (Cao
        Xueqin) 145–51, 156
        Huizhou 109–10
        Li Yü 139–40
        Lin Yutang 139–40
        matching character 149
        Ming 133
        naming/meaning 146–7
        Palace Banquet (*Qiqiao tu*) 98*f*–9

Pingjiang 141
pleasure 132–3, 190–2, 210
rocks 146
royal visits 118–19
Wang Huan 141
water 176, 210, 211*f*
Yangtze region 133
gates 13, 155, 161, 191
gentry 131–2 *see also* consumption
        Han dynasty 64–9, 71, 74
        Ming dynasty 130–1, 157–8
        Tang dynasty 76
God, humanization of xxxviii
Gongsun Qing 63
good life, the 47
government 62–3
Greece. *See* Ancient Greece
Gu Hongzhong
        Night Revels of Han Xizao (*Han
        Xizai yeyan tu*) 89–90*f*
Gu House, Suzhou xxvii*f*
*guan* (tower; watch) 66
Guan Zhong 122–3
Guo Songnian
        'Travelogue of Dali, The' 205–6

Hakka, the 194–204, 227
hall-like royalty (*tanghuang*) 15
halls (*zhenfang; tang*) 4–5, 13–15, 42,
        201, 280
        ancestral 108–9, 110*f,* 123, 201,
        204*f*
Han, the (ethnicity) 207
Han dynasty 54–60, 74
        gentry 64–9, 71, 74
        *mingqi* pottery houses 67–8*f*
Han Wudi (emperor) 63–4
Han Xizai 89
Han Yuan 115
'hanging flower gate' (*chuihua men*)
        155, 161, 191

Hardwick Hall 179–80
He Shen 182–3
He Yan 12
Heaven (*tian*) xxxiii–iv, xxxviii–xl,
    29–36, 178, 202–3, 281 *see also*
    immortality
  Confucius 33, 35–6
  Heaven's agent 280
  Mencius 281
*Heavenly Questions* (*Tian Wen*) (Qu
    Yuan) 64
Hemudu culture 22–3
hermits 77–91
hierarchies 16, 17–18, 24, 42, 65,
    121–4
  Beijing 181
  clothing 94, 117
  *Dream of the Red Chamber* (Cao
    Xueqin) 153–6
  housing 94, 174, 191
  marriage 113
Hong Xiuquan 227–8
Hongcun housing 105*f*–7
horizontal, the xxxii, xxxiii
House for Dr Bartholomeusz 273–5
House of Menander, Pompeii 34*f*
House of Pansa, Pompeii 35*f*
housing 133 *see also* courtyards *and*
    garden houses
  alleyway houses 189, 222, 238–9,
    242–3, 260
  analogies 16, 33–4
  ancestor commemoration 116
  Ancient Rome xxxii, 35*f*, 104
  Bai 207–10
  Bai Juyi 78–81, 87
  Banpo 21–2*f*, 25
  *banyuan lou* 203, 204*f*
  Beijing quadrangle 159–64, 166,
    168–9, 171–5, 181–5, 187–8,
    190–2, 249–51, 258–9

Chinese. *See* Chinese housing
  as a commodity 240
  corridors 164
  country villas 84–5
  Dai 193
  Dong 22–3*f*, 193–4
  English 4
  ethnic minority groups. *See* ethnic
    minority groups
  fortress ramparts 194–5*f*,
    198–203
  'front hall and back room'
    (*qiantang houshi*) layouts 4, 5,
    10, 21–2*f*, 23*f*, 24
  Hakka 194–5*f*, 199–204
  Han 54, 55*f*, 65–9, 71, 74
  Hemudu 22–3
  hierarchy 94
  Hongcun 105*f*–7
  Huizhou 105*f*–13, 119–21, 126–7
  interior activities 89–90*f*
  Lao She 170–5
  lettings 229–30, 234, 237
  *lilong* 189, 222, 238–9, 242–3,
    260
  Longshan 23–4
  Ming 45, 105*f*–13, 121
  Mosuo 212
  naming buildings/rooms 162–4
  Naxi 210–11, 214*f*–15
  oldest 290 n. 32
  pile-built 193–4
  prehistoric 4
  private ownership 256
  *qiantang houshi* layouts 4, 5, 10,
    21–2*f*, 23*f*, 24
  raised 24
  Shanghai 189, 229, 230–1
  *shiku men* 231, 232*f*–6, 238*f*, 239*f*,
    240, 242–4
  social 251–7

Song 91, 97f–9
stilts 193
terraced 230–1
towers 64–7, 68–9f, 71, 74
*weilong wu* 203
Western-style 244
Houying Fang complex 35f
Howard, Charles (3rd Earl of
    Carlisle) 180
*huanglao xinming* 56
*hudui* (door plugs) 113
Hugo, Victor 46
*huishang* (Huizhou merchants) 105
Huizhou 104–14, 116–26
'Humiliation of Jingkang' 197–8
*hutongs* (streets) 164–8, 170–5, 249
'Hymn to Shanghai, A' (Lin Yutang)
    188–9

*I Ching, The* (*Yi Jing*) (Fu Xi, King
    Wen, Duke of Zhou,
    Confucius). See *Book of
    Changes*
Icarus myth xli
immortality 45–6, 63–4, 67–9, 76
    poetry 78
imperial examination system 68, 76,
    113–14, 297 n. 10
    Huizhou region 123
individualism 56–62
industry 230

Japan 44–5, 175, 245–6
Ji Cheng 131
    *Craft of Gardens* (*Yuan ye*) 131,
        132
Jin dynasty 197–8
*jing* (principles of universe and life)
    28
*ju'an qimei* gesture 82–4
Ju'er Hutong, Beijing 251–7

Kahn, Louis 186, 265
Kaifeng 42, 91–4, 95–6 *see also*
    Bianliang
Kangxi (emperor) 158, 159
Khanbaliq. *See* Yuan Dadu
King's City, the 39–43
Kong Xingxun (tongpan) 213
*kuayuan* (spanning courtyards) 169
Kubla Khan 176

Lady Wenji's Return to the Han
    (*Wenji gui han tu*) 96–7f, 160
land economy xxxvi–viii
land value 230
language 13, 14, 15
    anthropomorphism 162
    architectural metaphors 13
    built world, the 43–4
    Dong 196
    Hakka dialect 196, 198
    housing analogies 16, 33–4
    naming buildings/rooms 162–4
Lao She
    courtyard of 185
    *Four Generations Under One Roof*
        (*Sishi tongtang*) 170–5, 185,
        255–6
Laozi 57, 60, 265
    *Classics of Dao and De, The* (*Dao
        De Jing*) 56–7, 58
    government 62–3
Le Nôtre, André 45
Leach, Edmund 185–6, 187
*Leisure Marginalia* (*Xianqing ouji*) (Li
    Yü) 135, 137–40, 145, 148, 149
Leys, Simon xxx–I, 144
*li* (rite and representation of moral
    principle) 19–20, 43
Li Bai 76–7
Li Dou 295 n. 8
    *Yangzhou huafang lu* 295 n. 8

Li E 124
Li House, Suzhou xxvi*f*
Li Jie
  *Yingzao fashi* 91, 94, 266
Li Yü 131–2, 134–8, 144–5
  beds 152–3
  *Carnal Prayer Mat, The (Roupu tuan)* 136–7
  'Deed of Sale for My Hill, A' 135
  'Failed Plan for Mount Yi Villa' 135
  *Leisure Marginalia (Xianqing ouji)* 135, 137–40, 145, 148, 149
  *Painting Catalogue of Mustard Seed Garden* 135, 144
  picture windows 151–2
Li Yu (emperor) 89
Liang Sicheng 245, 246–7, 248–9
light xxxvi
Lijiang 210, 213
*lilong* (alleyway houses) 189, 222, 238–9, 242–3, 260
Lin Yutang xxx, 77, 139–40, 188–90, 259, 261
  'Hymn to Shanghai, A' 188–9
literary world, the 43–9, 144, 184–5, 231–2 *see also* language
  poetry 76–8, 80–1, 143, 148
Liu Bang (emperor) 16–18, 54–6
Liu Xi
  *Explanation of Names* 12
*Living in the Mountain (Shanju Fu)* (Xie Lingyun) 86
long galleries 180
Longshan Culture 23–4
*longtang* (alleyway) 240–1
Lu Xun 248
  courtyard 184
  'On the Collapse of Leifeng Tower' 248

Ma brothers 24
Ma Yueguan 124
Manchu, the 157–9
Mao Zedong (chairman) 246, 247
Marlborough, Duchess of (Sarah Churchill) 181
marriage 110–16, 117–18, 168, 211–12, 213
matriarchies 211–12
Mayans, the 268, 270–1
Mei Lanfang 185
melancholy xxxiii
Mencius 180–1
*mendang* (stone blades) 113
*mendang hudui* (arranged equal status marriage) 113
Meng Yuanlao
  *Dong jing meng hua lu* 91
merchants 105–6, 110–13, 116–19
  arts, the 124–6
  Shanghai 227, 229
  social class 121–4
metaphysics 56–62
middle way, the (*zhongyong*) xxiii, xli–ii, 74, 281
  Beijing quadrangle 187–8
*Middle Way – Zhongyong, The* (Zi Si) xxiii
middling hermits 77–91
Mies van der Rohe, Ludwig 110, 111*f*, 127, 263–5
migration 196–8
Ming dynasty 45, 102–13, 121–3, 129–31
  fall 157
  furniture 119, 120*f*, 121*f*
  gardens 133
*mingjian* (bright room) 208
*mingqi* pottery houses 67–8*f*, 69*f*
'Minor Exquisite Mountain Residence' 124

minority groups. *See* ethnic minority
  groups
mirror screens (*yingbi*) 11, 160, 190
modernity 245–9, 260
Mogao Caves murals 82, 83*f*
Mongols, the 101–2
Monte Alban, Southern Mexico 272
Morris, Jan 262
  *Sydney* 262
Mosuo, the 211–12
Mount Yi Villa 135
multi-storey architecture xxxii,
  xxxvii–viii
music 79
Mustard Seed Garden 135–6

Nanchan Temple 71, 75
Nanjing 245
Naxi, the 210–11, 212–15
new quadrangle 251–7
New York xxxvii–viii
  Night Revels of Han Xizao (Gu
    Hongzhong) 89–90*f*
  Night Revels of Han Xizao (*Han
    Xizai yeyan tu*) (Gu
    Hongzhong) 89–90*f*
  *Notes of Things Old and New* (Cui
    Bao) 13

'On the Collapse of Leifeng Tower'
  (Lu Xun) 248
'one bright and two darks' courtyard
  pattern 4–5*f*, 9, 10, 16, 21, 24
Opium Wars 219, 223

painting 143–4, 299 n. 24
*Painting Catalogue of Mustard Seed
  Garden* (Li Yü) 135, 144
Palace Banquet (*Qiqiao tu*) 97–100
Palace of Versailles 45
Palladio, Andrea xxiv, 180, 265–6

Pantheon, the 31, 32*f*
pathos of distance xxxiii, 271 see also
  *wang*
patronage 124–5, 126
patterns 185–7, 202
Paul, Saint 264
People's Republic of China 260
perspective 151–2
philosophy 56–62, 130, 279–81
picture windows 151–2
pile-built houses 193–4
Pingjiang 141 *see also* Suzhou
platforms 267–9, 272
'Platforms and Plateaus' (Utzon, Jørn)
  268, 272
pleasure 130–2
  Li Yü 137–8
plumbing xxiv–v
poetry 76–8, 143, 148
  Bai Juyi 80–1
Portrait of a Superior Gentleman
  Scholar, The (*Gaoshi tu*) (Wei
  Xian) 82–4, 85*f*, 86
poverty 94–5
Princes Yi 181
privacy 15–16, 21, 164, 244, 255–6,
  258, 264
property development 229–30, 234,
  237, 240, 257

Qianlong (emperor) 158–9
*qie* (concubine) 114–15, 117–18
Qin dynasty xxv, 534
Qin Shi Huangdi (emperor) 53, 62
Qing dynasty 213, 224, 228–30
Qingming Festival on the River
  (*Qingming shanghe tu*)
  (Zhang Zeduan) 91, 92, 93*f*,
  95–6, 260
Qu Yuan 64
  *Heavenly Questions* (*Tian Wen*) 64

quadrangle housing 159–64, 166, 168–9, 171–3, 181–5, 187–8, 190–2, 249–51, 258–9
Quadripartition 279–80

*Record of Trades* (*Kaogong ji*) 40–1, 175
*Records of the Grand Historian* (*Shiji*) (Sima Qian) 17
reflective screen (*zhaobi*) 12–13, 160–1*f*, 190
refugees 227, 229, 243 *see also* migration
regulations 94
religion 206, 211, 227, 271, 281 *see also* Buddhism *and* Heaven
God, humanization of xxxviii
*ren* (benevolence; being human) 20
Renaissance, the xl
Residence of Prince Fu 181–2*f*, 183*f*
Residence of Prince Gong 182–4
Returning Home (Tao Yuanming) 87
Ricci, Matteo 130
rickshaws 189
*Rites of Zhou, The* 176
ritual (*li*) 15
*Rituals and Etiquettes* 6, 14
Rome. *See* Ancient Rome
rooms (*shi*) 4–5, 15–16, 241–2, 244 *see also* bedchambers
*ru dao hubu* (complementation of Confucianism and Daoism) 57, 265
Rykwert, Joseph 266
'Four and the Five, The' 279–80
Ryoanji temple 44

salt 103, 104, 116–18
merchants 103, 104, 105–6, 116–19

Sassoon family 237
schools 46–7
screens (*ping; xiaoqiang; yingbi; zhaobi*) 12–13, 97, 160–1*f*, 190, 209–10, 214
seating arrangements 16, 17–18
Shang civilization 43
Shanghai 188–9, 219–23, 243
Balfour, George 223–4
British in 223–6
Dana, Richard Henry, Jr. 231–2
*danwei* 260–1*f*
foreign settlements 224–7, 229–30, 237, 243
housing 189, 229, 230–1
industry 230
land value 230
*lilong* 189, 222, 238–9, 242–3, 260
*longtang* 240–1
Opium Wars 219, 223
overcrowding 243–4
real estate 237–8
rebellion 227–9
refugees 227, 229, 243
*shiku men* 231, 232*f*–6, 238*f*, 239*f*, 240, 242–4
*tingzi jian* 241–2
Shen Fu 82, 114–15
*Six Chapters of a Floating Life* 82, 114–15
*shi* (rooms) 4–5, 15–16
Shi Huangdi, Qin (emperor) 53
*shiku men* (stone gate building) 231, 232*f*–6, 238*f*, 239*f*, 240, 242–4
Shizu of Yuan (emperor) 176
shops 157–8
Shrewsbury, Countess of (Elizabeth Talbot) 179–80
Sima Qian 56–7
*Records of the Grand Historian* (*Shiji*) 17

Sino-Japanese War 243
*Six Chapters of a Floating Life* (Shen
    Fu) 82, 114–15
sky, the (*tian*) xxxix, 27, 28, 29, 272
    *see also* Heaven *and* space
skywells (*tianjing*) 106–7, 234, 236
    *see also* space
Small Sword Society 227, 228, 229
social class 94–5, 113, 121–4 *see also*
    hierarchies *and* gentry
social intercourse 255–6, 258–9
Song dynasty 91–5
*Song of Everlasting Sorrow, The*
    (Wang Anyi) 240–1
Southern Study (of Emperor Kangxi)
    159
space xxxii–iii, 18
    atriums 31, 34*f*, 70–1
    freedom of 71
    Laozi 60
    skywells (*tianjing*) 106–7,
        234, 236
    voids 104–5*f*, 263–6
spanning courtyards (*kuayuan*) 169
Spence, Jonathan xxix, xxx
Spring Outing (*Youchun tu*) (Zhan
    Ziqian) 82, 84*f*
stairs 14
starchitects xxxiii–iv
stone tablets 6, 18
streets (*hutong*)164–8, 170–5, 239,
    240
Su Dongpo 125–6
suicide 213
sumptuary laws 94, 121, 122, 123, 178,
    191
superficiality xxxiv
Suzhou 132–3, 141
Sydney 262
    Opera House 266–8*f*
*Sydney* (Morris, Jan) 262

*Taihan ji* (Wang Daokun) 117
Taiping Rebellion 227–8, 229
Tiaping Tianguo dynasty 228, 229
Talbot, Elizabeth (Countess of
    Shrewsbury) 179–80
Talman, William 180
*tang* (hall) 4–5, 13–15, 42 see also
    *mingjan*
Tang dynasty 71–2, 76, 99
Tang Gaozu (emperor) 76
Tao Yuanming 87
    Returning Home 87
taxi drivers 190
Temple of Confucius 10–11
33rd Lane, Colombo 277
thought, unification of 53
*tian* (Heaven; sky, the) xxxiii–iv,
    xxxviii–xl, 29–36, 202–3, 281
    Confucius 33, 35–6
    etymology 27–8
    Heaven's agent 280
    Mencius 281
*tianli* (Heaven's agent) 280
'time recording pearl' story 118
*tingzi jian* (pavilion room) 241–2
Tong Jun 142
towers 63–7, 68–70, 71–2, 74, 248, 271
trade 102, 103, 104, 223 *see also*
    commerce
    Beijing 167–8
    compradors 237
    Huizhou 105–13
'Travelogue of Dali, The' (Guo
    Songnian) 205–6
*Treatise on Superfluous Things*
    (*Changwu zhi*) (Wen
    Zhenheng) 131
trees 82, 83*f*
Tuan, Yi-Fu 166–7
*tulou* (earthen building) 194–5*f*
types 185–6

'Unrest of China under Five Foreign Races, The' 197
urban gridirons xxxvii*f*–viii
USA 228, 230
Utzon, Jørn 266–9
'Platforms and Plateaus' 268, 272

Vanbrugh, John 180–1
*Venerated Documents (Shang shu)* (Confucius) 29–30, 36–9
verandas 162–3*f*
Versailles, Palace of 45
vertical, the xxxii, xxxiii, 19 *see also* towers
vision 44, 45, 270–2
visual life 268, 269, 272
voids 104–5*f*, 263–6, 279 *see also* space

*wang* (gazing from afar; yearning) 66 *see also* pathos of distance
Wang Anyi
*Song of Everlasting Sorrow, The* 240–1
Wang Daokun 117
*Taihan ji* 117
Wang Huan 141
Wang Shizhen 132
Wang Yangming 130
*wanglou* (watchtower) 66–7
watchtowers 66–7, 72
water supply 176, 210, 211*f*
wealth 105, 116–19, 123, 244 *see also* consumption
Li Yü 138
patronage 124–5
weddings 168
Wei Xian
Portrait of a Superior Gentleman Scholar, The (*Gaoshi tu*) 82–4, 85*f*, 86

*weilong wu* (encircling ridge house; encircling dragon house) 203
Wen Zhenheng 130–1
*Treatise on Superfluous Things (Changwu zhi)* 131
Western philosophy 279
women 113–16, 117–18, 211–12, 213, 241–2
writing 43–4, 78, 184–5
Wu Liangyong 251–7
Wu Sangui 157
*wuwei* (doing nothing) 265

Xiang Yu 16–18
*xiaoqiang* (screen) 12–13
Xie Lingyun 86
*Living in the Mountain (Shanju Fu)* 86
Xin'an School (*Xin'an huapai*) 125–6

Yan Hui 61–2
*Yangzhou huafang lu* (Li Dou) 295 n. 8
*yi* (change; decorum and propriety) 19–20, 28, 43
Yin-Shang civilization 24
*Yingzao fashi* (Li Jie) 91, 94, 266
'Yongjia Upheaval' 197
Yongle, (emperor) 129
*You and Me (Women lia)* (Ma Liwen) 258–9
Yuan Dadu 101, 102, 164, 175–8 *see also* Beijing
Yuan dynasty 101–2
*yue* (music; sociality) 20
Yuelu Shuyuan 47–8
Yunxiang, Prince Yi 181
*yuzhou guan* (cosmic view) 33–4

Zai Yuan, Prince Yi 181
Zengchong drum tower 73*f*

Zhan Ziqian
  Spring Outing (*Youchun Tu*)
    82, 84*f*
Zhang Ailing. *See* Chang, Eileen
Zhang Huiyan 6–7, 10, 46
Zhang Zeduan
  Qingming Festival on the River
    (*Qingming shanghe tu*) 91, 92,
    93*f*, 95–6, 260
Zhao Dun assassination story 3, 5
*zhaobi* (reflective screen) 12–13,
    160–1*f*, 190, 209–10, 214
Zhencheng Lou 199–201, 204
*zhenfang* (hall) 162
Zheng, of Qin (king) 53
Zheng Banqiao 126

Zhengde (emperor) 129–30
*zhongyong* (middle way, the). *See*
    middle way, the
Zhou, Duke of 29–30
  Book of Changes, The/I Ching, The
    (*Yi Jing*) 28–9, 31–3
Zhou dynasty 43–4
Zhu Yuanzhang (emperor) 102–3,
    123
Zhu Ziqing 248, 249
Zhuangzi 60–1, 71, 72
  *Zhuangzi* 61–2
*Zhuangzi* (Zhuangzi) 61–2
Zi Si
  *Middle Way – Zhongyong, The*
    xxiii